PENGUIN BOOKS

BETWEEN THE WOODS
AND THE WATER

Patrick Leigh Fermor was born in 1915 of English and Irish descent. After a 'stormy' school career and his year-and-a-half journey on foot to Constantinople, he lived and travelled in the Balkans and the Greek Archipelago. During that time he acquired a deep interest in languages and a love of remote places. He enlisted in the Irish Guards in 1939, joined the 'I' Corps in 1941, became liaison officer in Albania and fought in Greece and Crete to which, during the German occupation, he returned three times, once by parachute. Disguised as a shepherd, he lived for over two years in the mountains, organizing the resistance and, in 1944, the capture and evacuation of the German Commander, General Kreipe. He was awarded the OBE in 1943 and the DSO in 1944 and was made Honorary Citizen of Herakleion, Crete.

Patrick Leigh Fermor has also written *The Traveller's Tree*, about the West Indies, which won the Heinemann Foundation Prize for Literature in 1950 and the Kemsley Prize in 1951, *A Time to Keep Silence*, *The Violins of Saint Jacques*, *Mani*, winner of the Duff Cooper Memorial Prize and a Book Society Choice, and its companion volume, *Roumeli*, and *A Time of Gifts*, winner of the 1978 W. H. Smith and Son Literary Award, described by Jan Morris as 'nothing short of a masterpiece'. The sequel to *A Time of Gifts*, *Between the Woods and the Water*, won the Thomas Cook Travel Book Award for 1986–87 and the Silver PEN Award for 1987.

Patrick Leigh Fermor now lives in Greece in a house he designed and built. He is a visiting member of the Athens Academy.

Patrick Leigh Fermor

BETWEEN THE WOODS
AND THE WATER

On Foot to Constantinople
from The Hook of Holland:
The Middle Danube
to the Iron Gates

Penguin Books

TO BARBARA AND NIKO GHIKA

Penguin Books Ltd, 27 Wrights Lane, London w8 5tz (Publishing and Editorial) *and*
Harmondsworth, Middlesex, England (Distribution and Warehouse)
Viking Penguin Inc., 40 West 23rd Street, New York, New York 10010, USA
Penguin Books Australia Ltd, Ringwood, Victoria, Australia
Penguin Books Canada Ltd, 2801 John Street, Markham, Ontario, Canada l3r 1b4
Penguin Books (NZ) Ltd, 182–190 Wairau Road, Auckland 10, New Zealand

First published in Great Britain by John Murray 1986
First published in the USA by Elisabeth Sifton Books/Viking 1986
Published in Penguin Books 1987

Filmset in Bembo

Printed and bound in Great Britain by
Hazell Watson & Viney Limited,
Member of the BPCC Group,
Aylesbury, Bucks

Völker verrauschen,
Namen verklingen,
Finstre Vergessenheit
Breitet die dunkelnachtenden Schwingen
Über ganzen Geschlechtern aus

Schiller,
from *Die Braut von Messina*

Ours is a great wild country:
If you climb to our castle's top,
I don't see where your eye can stop;
For when you've passed the corn-field country,
Where vine-yards leave off, flocks are packed,
And sheep-range leads to cattle-tract,
And cattle-tract to open-chase,
And open-chase to the very base
Of the mountain, where, at a funeral pace,
Round about, solemn and slow,
One by one, row after row,
Up and up the pine-trees go,
So, like black priests up, and so
Down the other side again
To another greater, wilder country.

Robert Browning,
from *The Flight of the Duchess*

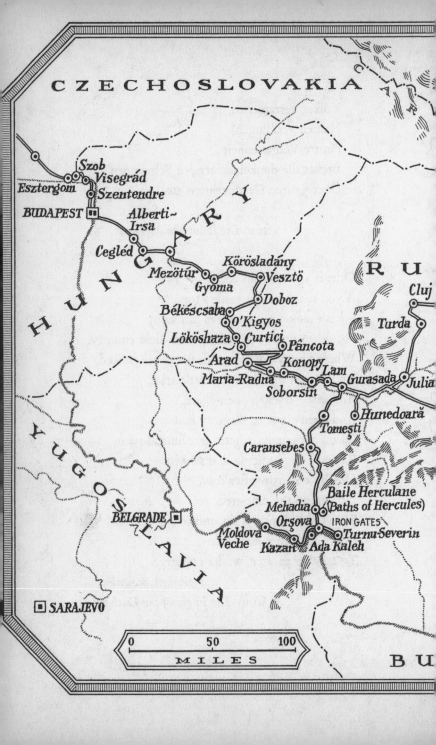

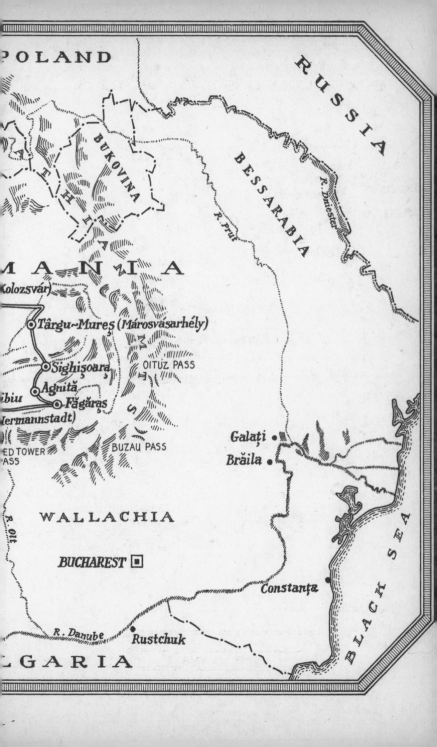

Contents

Introductory Letter
to Xan Fielding

DEAR XAN,

The first part of this narrative, *A Time of Gifts*, ended on a bridge over the Danube between Slovakia and Hungary, and as it must be unlucky to change in midstream, please let me begin the second part with a letter to you, as I did before. Nor will this be the last; there is one more book to come which will carry us to the end of the journey and beyond.

I had set out from Holland in 1934 meaning to mix only with chance acquaintances and fellow-tramps, but almost imperceptibly by the time I got to Hungary and Transylvania I found myself having a much easier time of it than I had expected or planned: ambling along on borrowed horses, drifting from one country-house to another, often staying for weeks or even months under patient and perhaps long-suffering but always hospitable roofs. Many things made this part of the journey quite different from the rest. It was a season of great delight; all seemed immeasurably old and at the same time brand new and totally unknown and, thanks to my dawdling rate of progress and those long sojourns, lasting friendships sprang up.

I suffered occasional pricks of conscience about straying so far from my original intentions, but when I look back now after putting these months together in writing, these twinges vanish. The next decade swept away this remote, country-dwelling world and this brings home to me how lucky I was to catch these long glimpses of it, even to share in it for a while. A subconscious wisdom might almost have been guiding this stretch of the journey and when it came to an end south of the Danube, it struck me, climbing through Balkan passes at my earlier brisk pace, how unusual were the regions I had just traversed: they had begun to take on a glow of retrospective magic which the intervening half-century has enhanced.

The notebook covering this period, lost in Moldavia at the beginning of the War and restored a few years ago by a great stroke of luck, has been a great help, but not the unfailing prop it should have been. When I came to a standstill during those long halts, writing stopped too: as I was keeping a journal of travel, I wrongly thought there was nothing to record. I was often slow to take it up again when I moved on and, even then, jotted notes sometimes took the place of sustained narrative. Fearing some details might have got out of sequence when I started writing the present book, I surrounded these passages with a cloud of provisos and hedged bets. Then the thought that these pages were not a guidebook persuaded me that it didn't matter very much, so I let the story tell itself free of debilitating caveats.

Books about this part of Europe incline to be chiefly, sometimes exclusively, devoted to politics, and this abundance lessens my guilt about how small a part they play in this one, where they only appear when they impinge directly on the journey. I had to give some account of how I thought history had affected life in Transylvania—its aftermath was all about me—but my inconclusive ponderings are offered with well-founded diffidence. Nothing could be less professional or 'inside Europe', and my political torpor at this early stage of life is touched on at some length in *A Time of Gifts* (pp. 108-14). News of grim events kept breaking in from the outside world but something in the mood of these valleys and mountain ranges weakened their impact. They were omens, and sinister ones, but there were three more years to go before these omens pointed unmistakably to the convulsions five years later.

Place names are a minor problem, but a vexing one. For well-known ones I have stuck to the forms longest established by history, and for the lesser, those in force at the time of the journey. Political fashion has altered many; more changed later; Rumanian spelling has been reformed, and earlier shifts of sovereignty have affected the precedence of the three place names that often adorn the smallest hamlet. I have tried to cite the official name first, followed by the others if they are needed. I know there is confusion here and there, but as this is not a guide nobody will be in danger of losing his way. I must apologise for these shortcomings and I hope it will be clear that they have nothing to do with partisanship. A few people's names have been changed when it seemed expedient but very sparingly, and usually of friends who are still actively on the scene from which many of the others have vanished. 'Von' is 'v.' throughout.

The debts a writer owes in a book of this kind are enormous and longstanding and if I fail to thank everyone I should, it is from neither forgetfulness nor ingratitude. I am deeply beholden to my old friend Elemer v. Klobusicky; to the Meran family, then and now; to Alexander Mourouzi and Constantine Soutzo. I would also like to thank Steven Runciman for encouraging words after the first volume, Dimitri Obolensky for wise advice during this one, and David Sylvester, Bruce Chatwin, Niko Vasilakis, Eva Bekássy v. Gescher and, as ever, John Craxton. Also many retrospective thanks to Balaşa Cantacuzène for help in translating *Mioritza*, in Moldavia long ago. My debt to Rudolf Fischer is beyond reckoning. His omniscient range of knowledge and an enthusiasm tempered with astringency have been a constant delight and stimulus during all the writing of this book; his vigilance has saved it from many errors, and I feel that the remaining ones may be precisely those when his advice was not followed.

Many thanks to Stella Gordon for her patient Champollion-Ventris flair for decyphering an illegible hand.

Lastly, devoted thanks for kindness and haven during restless literary displacements to Barbara and Niko Ghika (to whom the book is dedicated) for many weeks among the loggias and swallows of Corfu; to Janetta and Jaime Parladé for high-perched Andalusian asylum at Tramores; to the proprietors of the Stag Parlour near Bakewell for fevered sessions of revision and for the all-but-irresistible suggestion of *Shank's Europe* as an overall title for these books; to Jock and Diana Murray for editorial patience and shelter during the last phase; and lastly, dear Xan, to you and Magouche for diligent spells of cloistered seclusion in the Serrania de Ronda.

Kardamyli, 11 February 1986   P.

I

Bridge Passage

PERHAPS I had made too long a halt on the bridge. The shadows were assembling over the Slovak and Hungarian shores and the Danube, running fast and pale between them, washed the quays of the old town of Esztergom, where a steep hill lifted the basilica into the dusk. Resting on its ring of columns, the great dome and the two Palladian belfries, tolling now with a shorter clang, surveyed the darkening scene for many leagues. All at once the quay and the steep road past the Archbishop's palace were deserted. The frontier post was at the end of the bridge, so I hastened into Hungary: the people that Easter Saturday had gathered at the river's side had climbed to the Cathedral square, where I found them strolling under the trees, conversing in expectant groups. The roofs fell away underneath, then forest and river and fen ran dimly to the last of the sunset.

A friend had written to the Mayor of Esztergom: 'Please be kind to this young man who is going to Constantinople on foot.' Planning to look him up next day, I asked someone about the Mayor's office and before I knew what was happening, and to my confusion, he had led me up to the man himself. He was surrounded by the wonderfully-clad grandees I had been admiring beside the Danube. I tried to explain that I was the tramp he had been warned about and he was politely puzzled; then illumination came, and after a quick and obviously comic conversation with one of the magnificent figures, he committed me to his care and hastened across the square to more serious duties. The charge was accepted with an amused expression; my mentor must have been saddled with me because of his excellent English. His gala costume was dark and splendid; he carried his scimitar slung nonchalantly in the crook of his arm and a rimless monocle flashed in his left eye.

At this very moment, all eyes turned downhill. The clatter of hoofs and a jingle of harness had summoned the Mayor to the Cathedral steps, where a scarlet carpet had been laid. Clergy and candle-bearers were ceremoniously gathered and when the carriage halted a flame-coloured figure uncoiled from within and the Cardinal, Monsignor Serédy, who was also Archbishop of Esztergom and Prince-Primate of Hungary, slowly alighted and offered his ringed hand to the assembly and everyone in turn fell on one knee. His retinue followed him into the great building; then a beadle led the Mayor's party to the front pews which were draped in scarlet. I made as though to slink to a humbler place, but my mentor was firm: "You'll see much better here."

Holy Saturday had filled half the vast cathedral and I could pick out many of the figures who had been on display by the river: the burghers in their best clothes, the booted and black-clad peasants, the intricately-coifed girls in their coloured skirts and their white pleated sleeves panelled with embroidery, the same ones who had been hastening over the bridge with nosegays of lilies and narcissi and kingcups. There were black and white Dominicans, several nuns and a sprinkling of uniforms, and near the great doors a flock of Gypsies in clashing hues leaned whispering and akimbo. It would scarcely have been a surprise to see one of their bears amble in and dip its paw in a baroque holy-water stoup shaped like a giant murex and genuflect.

How unlike the ghostly mood of Tenebrae two nights before! As each taper was plucked from its spike the shadows had advanced a pace until darkness subdued the little Slovak church. Here, light filled the great building, new constellations of wicks floated in all the chapels, the Paschal Candle was alight in the choir and unwinking stars tipped the candles that stood as tall as lances along the high altar. Except for the red front pews, the Cathedral, the clergy, the celebrating priest and his deacons and all their myrmidons were in white. The Archbishop, white and gold now and utterly transformed from his scarlet manifestation as Cardinal, was enthroned under an emblazoned canopy and the members of his little court were perched in tiers up the steps. The one on the lowest was guardian of the heavy crosier and behind him another stood ready to lift the tall white mitre and replace it when the ritual prompted, arranging the lappets each time on the pallium-decked shoulders. In the front of the aisle, meanwhile, the quasi-martial bravery of the serried magnates—the coloured doublets of silk and brocade and fur, the gold and silver chains, the Hessian boots of blue and crimson and turquoise, the gilt spurs, the kalpaks of bearskin with their diamond clasps, and the high plumes of egrets' and eagles' and cranes' feathers—accorded with the ecclesiastical splendour as aptly as the accoutrements in the Burial of Count Orgaz: and it was the black attire—like my new friend's, and the armour of the painted knights in Toledo—that was the most impressive. Those scimitars leaning in the pews, with their gilt and ivory cross-hilts and stagily gemmed scabbards—surely they were heirlooms from the Turkish wars? When their owners rose jingling for the Creed, one of the swords fell on the marble with a clatter. In old battles across the puszta, blades like these sent the Turks' heads spinning at full gallop; the Hungarians' heads too, of course . . .

Soon, after an interval of silence, sheaves of organ-pipes were thundering and fluting their message of risen Divinity. Scores of voices soared from the choir, Alleluiahs were on the wing, the cumulus of incense billowing round the carved acanthus leaves was winding aloft and losing itself in the shadows of the dome and new motions were afoot. Led by a cross, a vanguard of clergy and acolytes bristling with candles was already half-way down the aisle. Next came a canopy with the Sacrament borne in a monstrance; then the Archbishop; the Mayor; the white-bearded and eldest of the magnates, limping and leaning heavily on a malacca cane; then the rest. Urged by a friendly prod, I joined the slow slipstream and soon, as though smoke and sound had wafted us through the doors, we were all outside.

As the enormous moon was only one night after the full, it was almost as bright as day. The procession was down the steps and slowly setting off; but when the waiting band moved in behind us and struck up the opening bars of a slow march, the notes were instantaneously drowned. Wheels creaked overhead, timbers groaned and a many-tongued and nearly delirious clangour of bells came tumbling into the night; and then, between these bronze impacts, another sound, like insistent clapping, made us all look up. An hour or so before, two storks,

16

tired by their journey from Africa, had alighted on a dishevelled nest under one of the belfries and everyone had watched them settle in. Now, alarmed by the din, desperately flapping their wings and with necks outstretched, they were taking off again, scarlet legs trailing. Black feathers opened along the fringes of their enormous white pinions and then steady and unhastening wing-beats lifted them beyond the chestnut leaves and into the sky as we gazed after them. "A fine night they chose for moving in," my neighbour said, as we fell in step.

Not a light showed in the town except for the flames of thousands of candles stuck along the window-sills and twinkling in the hands of the waiting throng. The men were bareheaded, the women in kerchiefs, and the glow from their cupped palms reversed the daytime chiaroscuro, rimming the lines of jaw and nostril, scooping lit crescents under their brows and leaving everything beyond these bright masks drowned in shadow. Silently forested with flames, street followed street and as the front of the procession drew level everyone kneeled, only to rise to their feet again a few seconds after it had moved on. Then we were among glimmering ranks of poplars and every now and then the solemn music broke off. When the chanting paused, the ring of the censer-chains and the sound of the butt of the Archbishop's pastoral staff on the cobbles were joined by the croaking of millions of frogs. Woken by the bells and the music, the storks in the town were floating and crossing overhead and looking down on our little string of lights as it turned uphill into the basilica again. The intensity of the moment, the singing and candle flames and incense, the feeling of spring, the circling birds, the smell of fields, the bells, the chorus from the rushes, thin shadows and the unreality of the moon over the woods and the silver flood—all these things hallowed the night with a spell of great beneficence and power.

When it was all over, everyone emerged once more on the Cathedral steps. The carriage was waiting; and the Archbishop, back in cardinal's robes and the wide ermine mantle that showed he was a temporal as well as an ecclesiastical Prince, climbed slowly in. His gentleman-at-arms, helped by a chaplain with a prominent Adam's apple and pince-nez and a postillion in hussar's uniform, were gathering in his train, yard upon yard, like fishermen with a net, until it filled the carriage with geranium-coloured watered-silk. The chaplain climbed in and sat opposite, then the gentleman-at-arms, sitting upright with black-gloved hands on the hilt of his scimitar. The postillion folded the steps, a small busbied tiger slammed a door painted with arms under a tasselled hat and when both of them had leapt up behind, the similarly fur-hatted coachman gave a twitch to the reins, the ostrich feathers nodded and the four greys moved off. As the equipage swayed down the hill, applause rippled through the gathered crowd, all hats came off and a hand at the window, pastorally ringed over its red glove, fluttered in blessing.

On the moonlit steps everyone was embracing, exchanging Easter greetings and kissing hands and cheeks. The men put on their fur hats and readjusted the slant of their dolmans and, after the hours of Latin, Magyar was bursting out in a cheerful dactylic rush.

"Let's see how those birds are getting on," my mentor said, polishing his monocle with a silk bandana. He sauntered to the edge of the steps, leant on his sword as though it were a shooting-stick and peered up into the night. The two beaks were sticking out of the twigs side by side and we could just make out the re-settled birds fast asleep in the shadows. "Good!" he said. "They're having a nice snooze."

We rejoined the others and he offered his cigarette case round, chose one himself with care and tapped it on the gnarled gold. Three plumes tilted round his lighter flame in a brief pyramid and fell apart. He drew in a deep breath, held it for a few seconds and then, with a long sigh, let the smoke escape slowly in the moonlight. "I've been looking forward to that," he said. "It's my first since Shrove Tuesday."

The evening ended in a dinner party at the Mayor's with *barack* to begin with and floods of wine all through, and then Tokay, and in the end a haze surrounded those gorgeously-clad figures. Afterwards the Mayor apologetically told me that as the house was crowded out, a room had been found for me at a neighbour's. No question of my stumping up! Next morning, soberly dressed in tweed and a polo-necked jersey, my stork-loving friend picked me up in a fierce Bugatti and only the scimitar among his bags on the back seat hinted at last night's splendours. We went to see the pictures in the Archbishop's palace; then he said, why not come in his car? We would be in

Budapest in no time; but I stuck reluctantly to my rule—no lifts except in vile weather—and we made plans to meet in the capital. He scorched off with a wave and after farewells at the Mayor's I collected my things and set off too. I kept wondering if all Hungary could be like this.

*   *   *   *

From the path that climbed along the edge of the forest, backward glances revealed swamps and trees and a waste of tall rushes and the great river loosely dividing and joining again round a chain of islands. I could see the waterfowl rocketing up and circling like showers of motes and stippling the lagoon with innumerable splashes when they settled again. Then high ground put them out of sight. Foothills rose steeply on the other side, lesser hills overlapped each other downstream and the fleece of the treetops gave way to cliffs of limestone and porphyry, and where they converged, the green river ran fast and deep.

A village would appear below and storks stood on one leg among the twigs of old nests on thatch and chimney. There were flurried claps as they took to the air, and when they dropped level with the treetops and crossed the river into Slovakia, sunlight caught the upper sides of their wings; then they tilted and wheeled back into Hungary with hardly a feather moving. Landing with sticks in their beaks, they picked their way along the roofs with black flight-feathers spread like tight-rope-walkers' fingers fumbling for balance. Being mute birds, they improvise an odd courting-song by leaning back and opening and shutting their scarlet bills with a high-speed clatter like flat sticks banging together: a dozen courtships in one of these riverside hamlets sounded like massed castanets. Carried away by sudden transports, they would leap a few yards in the air and land in disarray, sliding precariously on the thatch. Their wonderful procession had stretched across the sky for miles the night before; now they were everywhere, and all the following weeks I could never get used to them; their queerly stirring rattle was the prevalent theme of the journey, and the charm they cast over the ensuing regions lasted until August in the Bulgarian mountains, when I finally watched a host of them dwindling in the distance, heading for Africa.

It was the first of April 1934, and Easter Day: two days after full moon, eleven from the equinox, forty-seven since my nineteenth birthday and a hundred and eleven after I had set out, but less than twenty-four hours since crossing the frontier. The far bank was Slovakia still, but in a mile or two a tributary twisted through the northern hills, and the tiled roofs and belfries of the little tearful-sounding town of Szob marked the meeting place of the two rivers. The frontier wandered northwards up this valley and for the first time both sides of the Danube were Hungary.

For most of this journey the landscape had been under snow; icicle-hung and often veiled in falling flakes, but the last three weeks had changed all this. The snow had shrunk to a few discoloured patches and the ice on the Danube had broken up. When this is solid, the thaw sunders the ice with reports like a succession of thunderclaps. I had been out of earshot downstream when the giant slabs had broken loose, but all at once the water, halted by occasional jams, was crowded with racing fragments. It was no good trying to keep pace: jostling triangles and polygons rushed past, cloudier at the edges each day and colliding with a softer impact until they were as flimsy as wafers; and at last, one morning, they were gone. These were mild portents, it seemed. When the sun reaches full strength, the eternal snows, the glaciers of the Alps and the banked peaks of the Carpathians look unchanged from a distance; but close to, the whole icy heart of Europe might be dissolving. Thousands of rivulets pour downhill, all brooks overflow and the river itself breaks loose and floods the meadows, drowns cattle and flocks, uproots the ricks and the trees and whirls them along until all but the tallest and stoutest bridges are either choked with flotsam or carried away.

Spring had begun as at a starter's pistol. Bird song had broken out in a frenzy, a fever of building had set in, and, overnight, swallows and swifts were skimming everywhere. Martins were setting their old quarters to rights, lizards flickered on the stones, nests multiplied in the reeds, shoals teemed and the frogs, diving underwater at a stranger's approach, soon surfaced again, sounding as though they were reinforced every hour by a thousand new voices; they kept the heronries empty as long as daylight lasted. The herons themselves glided low and waded

20

through the flagleaves with a jerky and purposeful gait, or, vigilantly on one leg like the storks, posed with cunning as plants. Flags crowded the backwaters and thick stems lifted enormous kingcups among the leaves of pink and white water-lilies that folded at sunset.

Between the shore and the reddish-mauve cliffs, aspens and poplars tapered and expanded in a twinkling haze and the willows, sinking watery roots, drooped over fast currents. Tight-lacing forced the yellow flood into a rush of creases and whorls and, after my earlier weeks beside the Danube, I could spot those ruffled hoops turning slowly round and round, telling of drowned commotion amidstream.

The path climbed, and as the hot afternoon passed, it was hard to believe that the nearly mythical country of Hungary lay all around me at last; not that this part of it, the Pilis hills, tallied in the remotest degree with anything I had expected. When the climb had let the Danube drop out of sight, hills and woods swallowed the track and sunbeams slanted through young oak-branches. Everything smelt of bracken and moss, sprays of hazel and beech were opening, and the path, soft with rotten leaves, wound through great lichen-crusted trees with dog-violets and primroses among their roots. When the woods opened for a mile or two, steep meadows ran up on either hand to crests that were dark with hangers, and streams fledged with water-cress ran fast and clear in the valleys. I was crossing one of them on stepping-stones when bleating and a jangle of bells sounded; then barking broke out, and the three demons that rushed down with bared fangs were called to heel by their shepherd. His sheep were up to their bellies in a drift of daisies; the ewes must have lambed about Christmas and some of them were already shorn. I had been in shirt-sleeves for several days, but a heel-length sheepskin cloak was thrown over the shepherd's shoulders; peasants are slow to cast clouts. I shouted, "Jó estét kivánok!"—a quarter of my stock of Hungarian—and the same evening-greeting came back, accompanied by the ceremonious lift of a narrow-brimmed black hat. (Ever since I had come across the Hungarian population in southern Slovakia I had longed for some head-gear for answering these stately salutes.) His flock was a blur of white specks and faraway tinklings by the time I caught sight of a different herd. A troop of still unantlered fallow deer were grazing by the edge of the forest across the valley. The sun setting on the other side of them cast their shadows across the slope to enormous lengths: a footfall across the still acres of air lifted all their heads at the same moment and held them at gaze until I was out of sight.

I had been thinking of sleeping out, and those shorn lambs clinched matters; the wind was so tempered that hardly a leaf moved. My first attempt, two nights before in Slovakia, had ended in brief arrest as a suspected smuggler; but nothing could be safer than these woods high above the hazards of the frontier.

I was casting about for a sheltered spot when a campfire showed in the dusk at the other end of a clearing where rooks were going noisily to bed. A pen of stakes and brushwood had been set up in a bay of the forest under an enormous oak-tree, a swineherd was making it fast with a stake between two twists of withy, and the curly and matted black pigs inside were noisily jostling for space. The hut next door was thatched with reeds and when I joined the two swineherds, both looked up puzzled in the firelight: who was I, and where did I come from? The answers—"Angol" and "Angolország"—didn't mean much to them, but their faces lit at the emergence of a bottle of *barack* which was parting loot from my friends in Esztergom, and a third stool was found.

They were cloaked in rough white woollen stuff as hard as frieze. In lieu of goads or crooks, they nursed tapering shafts of wood polished with long handling and topped with small axe-heads and they were shod in those moccasins I had first seen Slovaks wearing in Bratislava: pale canoes of raw cowhide turning up at the tips and threaded all round with thongs which were then lashed round their padded shanks till half-way up the calf of the leg; inside, meanwhile, snugly swaddled in layers of white felt, their feet were wintering it out till the first cuckoo.

The younger was a wild-looking boy with staring eyes and tousled hair. He knew about ten words of German, learnt from Schwobs in the neighbouring villages (I heard later that these were Swabians who were settled nearby) and he had an infectious, rather mad laugh. His white-headed father spoke nothing but Magyar and his eyes, deep-set in wrinkles, lost all their caution as we worked our way down the bottle.

I could just make out that the deer, betokened by spread fingers for their missing antlers, belonged to a *föherceg* (which later turned out to mean an archduke). Continuing in sign-language, the younger swineherd grunted, scowled fiercely and curled up his forefingers to represent the tusks of the wild boars that lurked in brakes hereabouts; then he twirled them in spirals which could only mean moufflon. The sign-language grew blunter still when he jovially shadowed forth how wild boars broke in and covered tame sows and scattered the pens with miscegenate farrow. I contributed some hard-boiled eggs to their supper of delicious smoked pork: they sprinkled it with paprika and we ate it with black bread and onions and some nearly fossilised cheese.

The swineherds were called Bálint and Géza and their names have stuck because, at this first hearing, they had so strange a ring. The fire-light made them look like contemporaries of Domesday Book and we ought to have been passing a drinking-horn from hand to hand instead of my anachronistic bottle. In defiance of language, by the time it was empty we were all in the grip of helpless laughter. Some kind of primitive exchange had cleared all hurdles and the drink and the boy's infectious spirits must have done the rest. The fire was nearly out and the glade was beginning to change; the moon, which looked scarcely less full than the night before, was climbing behind the branches.

There wasn't much room in their stifling den and when they under-stood I wanted to sleep out they strewed brushwood in the lee of a rick. The old man put his hand on the grass and then laid it on mine with a commiserating look: it was wet with dew. He made gestures of rugging up and I put on everything I possessed, while they dossed down indoors.

When we had said goodnight I lay gazing at the moon. The shadows of the trees lay like cut-out cloth across the clearing. Owls signalled to each other close by and there were sleepy grunts from the sties prompted by dreams, perhaps, or indigestion, and now and then a pig, roused in the small hours by night-starvation, munched in semi-liquid bliss.

*   *   *   *   *

It was still night when we got up, covered with damp as foretold, and while we ate bread and cheese Bálint, the elder, unlatched the sty. The pigs rushed out in a hysterical stampede then settled more temperately to a quiet day's rooting among the acorns and beech-nuts scattered deep under the branches. To put me on the right path Géza led me across the woods, whistling and twirling his long tomahawk and tossing it in the air and catching it as he loped through the bracken; when he left me I went on by myself for two hours by moonlight, and at daybreak I was in the ruins of a huge castle overgrown with trees. The forest dropped steeply for over a thousand feet, and down below, between its leaf-covered mountains, the Danube valley coiled upstream from the east. It turned south beyond the battlements and after a mile twisted westwards, still deep in shadow, and out of sight at last between further green shoulders of forest. The track, following a wall of fortification downhill through slants of beech and hazel, levelled out before a great tower on a knoll; and a final wet scramble brought me down into Visegrád.*

I had been told about this castle.

The Magyars first settled in Central Europe at the end of the ninth century as fierce pagan invaders. Four hundred years later, when they had been respectable for at least three, their country had become a great Christian kingdom and the Arpáds, who ruled over it, by now an ancient dynasty of warrior-kings, legislators, crusaders and saints, were allied to most of the great houses of Christendom; King Béla IV, brother of St. Elizabeth, was the ablest of them. He lived in turbulent times. In recent decades, Jenghiz Khan and his descendants had laid Asia waste from the China Sea to the Ukraine and in the spring of 1241 news of great danger reached Hungary: after burning Kiev, Jenghiz Khan's grandson, Batu, was heading for the eastern passes. Béla tried to prepare defences but the Mongols' onslaught through the Carpathians was so fast that they surprised and routed the sleepy Magyar nobles and then ranged over the Great Plain, emptying and burning the towns all through the summer. Promising the peasants

* If I had come that way a few months later, I would have seen the first fragments of King Matthias's palace dug up. I have seen it since: the magnificent Renaissance ruins give a clear idea of what royal Hungary was like before the Turkish conquest.

their lives if they brought in the harvest, they slaughtered them in the autumn when it was safely threshed; then, crossing the frozen river on Christmas Day, they set about the western regions. A few towns were saved by their walls or by the surrounding fens, but Esztergom was burnt and most of the others were soon in cinders and the inhabitants slain or driven off as slaves.

Suddenly, there was a lull. Messengers had arrived in the Mongol camp with the news that four thousand miles away in Karakorum, Ogodai, the successor of Jenghiz Khan, had died; and all at once, on the marches of Siberia and beyond the Great Wall, in the ruined kingdoms of the Caliphate, among the wreckage of Cracow and Sandomir and the Moravian pine-forests and the smoking Magyar cities, a scattering of savage princes turned their slant-eyed boyish faces towards Chinese Tartary; the race for the succession was about to start; and by the middle of March, they had all vanished. Béla, returning from an island refuge in Dalmatia, found his kingdom in ruins. Death and capture had halved the population and the survivors were cautiously beginning to emerge from the woods. His task resembled the founding of a new kingdom, and the first step was to make it secure against the Mongols. Hence the castle that I was striding through at Visegrád. Up went this tremendous stronghold and many others followed; and the next time the Mongols invaded, they were repulsed.

* * * *

As much German as Magyar was to be heard on the half-awake quay of Visegrád, for the speakers were Géza's Swabians. When the Turks were driven out, thousands of peasant families from South Germany had boarded flat-bottomed boats and set off from the cities of the Upper Danube, chiefly from Ulm; sailing downstream, they landed on the depopulated shore and settled for good. Their language and their costumes on feast days were said to have remained unaltered since the time of Maria Theresa in whose reign they had taken root. There must have been a lot of intermarriage but spotting people with obligingly tow-coloured or raven hair, I thought—and probably wrongly— I could pick out a typical German from a typical Magyar.

When the path along the Danube turned east, the radiance of

morning poured along the valley. Soon the cape of a slender island, plumed with willow trees and patterned with fields of young wheat, divided the river in two. Nets were looped from branch to branch, fishing boats were moored to the trunks of aspens, poplars and willows and pewter-coloured stems lifted a silvery pale-green haze against the darker leaves of the riverside woods. The island followed the river's windings for nearly twenty miles. A trim steamer ruffled the current now and then, and as the day advanced, the sparse traffic of barges multiplied.

But within an hour or two, the river began to conduct itself in a fashion unprecedented since our first snowy meeting at Ulm eleven weeks earlier. (Only eleven weeks! It seemed half a lifetime already!) Indeed, ever since the river had first bubbled out of the underworld in Prince Fürstenberg's park in the Black Forest. For the Danube, after describing two congruent semicircles, was turning due south; and so it would continue, flowing clean across Hungary for a hundred and eighty miles—from the top to the bottom of the atlas page, as it were—until it turned again and streamed eastwards under the battlements of Belgrade. It was an exciting moment.

*   *   *   *

By late afternoon, towards the end of the island which had kept me company all day, I reached Szentendre, a little baroque country town of lanes, cobbled streets, tiled roofs and belfries with onion cupolas. The hills were lower now; vineyards and orchards had replaced the cliffs and the forests and there was a feeling in the air that one was nearing a great city. The townspeople were the descendants of Serbians who had fled from the Turks three centuries ago; they still talked Serbian and worshipped in the Greek Orthodox Cathedral which their ancestors had built. *Griechisch Orientalisch* in German, they are distinct from the Uniats further east—*Griechisch Katholisch*—who, though they cling to the Orthodox rite, acknowledge the Pope. I only learnt about this later but an icon instead of a crucifix on my bedroom wall ought to have put me on the scent.

2

Budapest

WHEN A MID-MORNING SUNBEAM prized one eyelid open a few days later, I couldn't think where I was. An aroma of coffee and croissants was afloat under a vaulted ceiling; furniture gleamed with beeswax and elbow-grease; books ascended in hundreds, and across the arms of a chair embroidered with a blue rampant lion with a forked tail and a scarlet tongue, a dinner jacket was untidily thrown. An evening tie hung from the looking glass, pumps lay in different corners, the crumpled torso of a stiff shirt (still worn with a black tie in those days) gesticulated desperately across the carpet and borrowed links glittered in the cuffs. The sight of all this alien plumage, so unlike the travel-stained heap that normally met my waking eyes, was a sequence of conundrums.

Then, suddenly, illumination came. I was in Budapest.

*   *   *   *

Little remains of the journey from Szentendre: a confused impression of cobbled approaches, the beginnings of tramlines, some steep streets and airy views of the Danube and its bridges and the search for the hill of Buda. The subsequent magnificence was due, at one or two removes, to the Baltic-Russian friends in Munich whose kindness had begun in recent weeks to scatter my rough itinerary with oases like this.

I was back among barons and these ones lived on the steep hill of Buda (the Vár or citadel) which lifted the empty Royal Palace high above the right bank of the river. The Uri utca—die Herrengasse in German—a waving street of jutting windows, tiled roofs and arched doors with coats of arms, ran along the very summit of this castled height. It must have been built soon after 1686, when the city was recaptured from the Turks, and the foundations of many of the houses were tunnelled with sinister Turkish cellars. Perched above the din of the capital, this patrician quarter had something of the hush of a country town, and the houses, inhabited by the same families for generations, were called Palais so-and-so, including the charming one that harboured me. "All rot, of course," my hostess said; she had been brought up largely in England. "We seem to have a passion for grand styles in Hungary. It's a perfectly ordinary town house."

Tibor and Berta were in their mid-forties. Duly forewarned, they had taken me under their wing with a completeness for which Esztergom might have been some preparation; the way Hungarians construed hospitality seemed a recurring miracle. Tibor was a captain in a regiment of Horse-Gunners, and the lowness of his rank, for he had served all through the war, was due to the minute size of the Hungarian army after the Treaty of Trianon. Liked by everyone, amusing, rather caustic, intolerant of nonsense, and usually dressed in a tweed coat and skirt, Berta was tall and handsome with a stripe of grey in her dark hair. Her father, a distinguished Graf—or rather *gróf* in Hungarian—had been governor of Fiume before the war, and as we drove about Budapest in her small car she told me fascinating stories about the lost world of Trieste, Fiume, Pola and the Istrian peninsula. The family, like many another, was fairly hard-up now and some of the house was let; she sat on many committees and was always busy. I was caught up in her activities, accompanying her on shopping expeditions combined with sight-seeing. If she thought they promised interest or amusement, I went with her on calls, and when in a couple of days there was a dance in a house nearby, she got me asked and set about assembling evening things from Tibor's wardrobe and then from neighbours'. When I asked if she were going, she laughed and said, "Catch me! But you'll enjoy it." And so I did.

The ball was all that it should have been and, as she pointed out, it took place in a real palace; on the stairs leading to the ballroom, a friendly touch on the elbow revealed my stork-loving Esztergom ally, who promptly resumed his role of mentor. The ball ended with the band breaking into Gypsy tunes and launching a number of the dancers into the csárdás. One young couple, he with his hands on his partner's hips and hers on his shoulders, threw themselves into it with a marvellously fierce and stamping brio, their hair flinging about like the manes of ponies. When all seemed over, I crammed with them, the stork-fancier, his beautiful partner, a girl I clove to called Annamaria and several others, into a couple of cars and whirled downhill and across the Chain-Bridge to plunge into the scintillating cave of the most glamorous night-club I have ever seen. Did the floor of the Arizona really revolve? It certainly seemed to. Snowy steeds were careering round it at one moment, feathers tossing: someone said he had seen camels there, even elephants . . . A bit later, spangled acrobats were flying through the spot-lit cigarette smoke, joining, somersaulting, spiralling on their own axes, sailing with arms outstretched as timely rings flew to their palms from the temporary surrounding dark; and, finally, poised on the biceps of a sequin-studded titan, they built a human pagoda, skipping nimbly aloft over each others' shoulders until, from the apex somewhere near the ceiling, a slim, frilled figure with a star on her brow was blowing kisses. There was something familiar about this blonde and smiling team . . . suddenly I recognised them: they were my old friends from those sketching forays in Vienna, Conrad's and my indirect benefactors for a dozen *himbeergeist*, the Koschka Brothers!*

There they were, pyramidally extant, glittering in apotheosis! (The friendly impact of their posters—A CSODÁLATOS KOSCHKAK!— kept hitting me in the eye for the rest of my stay.) After this, we drank some more in a house in the Werböczy utca, and when Annamaria showed me the way back to the nearby Uri utca, we were not sure whether it was the moon or dawn that cast our shadows on the cobbles.

So it was no wonder that the reflected eleven o'clock sunlight, when it hit the side of the silver coffee-pot, detonated like silent shell-fire . . . The door flung open and a black Alsatian called Tim bounded in and leapt on the bed. He was followed by his owner, Micky (Miklós), the son of the house, a rather unruly and very entertaining boy of fourteen or fifteen in Tintin plus-fours. "Here," he said, giving me a tumbler of water with one hand and a bottle of Alka Seltzer with the other, "My ma says you'll probably need these."

*　　*　　*　　*

* See *A Time of Gifts*, p. 185.

I had drifted into a noctambulistic set and my stay in Budapest was punctuated by awakenings like this. Life seemed perfect: kind, uncensorious hosts; dashing, resplendent and beautiful new friends against the background of a captivating town; a stimulating new language, strong and startling drinks, food like a delicious bonfire and a prevailing atmosphere of sophistication and high spirits that it would have been impossible to resist even had I wanted. I was excited by the famous delights of the place, especially by certain haunts like Kakuk (the Cuckoo) on the slopes of Buda, where, late at night, half a dozen Gypsies bore down on the guests like smiling crows bent on steeping everything in their peculiar music. Badly played, this can sound like treacle and broken bottles and the tunes may not be authentically Hungarian—Bartók and Kodály are firm about their Gypsy and thus non-Magyar origin—but they deceived Liszt and they enraptured me. In the slow passages, the hammers of the czembalom fluttered and hesitated over the strings and the violins sank to a swooning langour, only to rekindle with an abrupt syncope when the hammers and the bows broke into double time and the czembalist went mad as the leading violinist, with his fingers crowding the strings in a dark tangle, stooped and slashed beside one listener's ear after another and closed in on his instrument like a welterweight in a clinch; passages, one might think, which could only end in ecstasy or a dead faint. Soaring glissandos, cascading pengös: all eyes grew mistier as cork after cork was drawn . . . Who paid for all this? Certainly not me—even a gesture towards helping was jovially brushed aside as though it were not worth the waste of words. (The day after I arrived I had made for the Consulate in the Zoltán utca and picked up a registered envelope with an unprecedented six pounds which had mounted up since Vienna.)

Very many of these people talked English; when an exception cropped up, German was used, sometimes, I think for historical reasons, rather reluctantly; but it was the universal second language. The automatic use of *Du*, even to strangers if they were friends of friends, was very surprising. *Sie*, it seemed, meant relegation to the outer darkness and people had been known to fight with swords about the matter. (The fact that duels were still frequent in Hungary—not mere student encounters, but fierce set-to's with sabres—gave a *Prisoner of Zenda* touch to a fantastic and, no doubt, wildly inaccurate picture which was fast taking shape in my mind.) Their easy ways, like the Austrians', had a stiffening of old-fashioned punctilio. (I liked the kissing of women's hands, but the formal kissing of the hands of men by household staff or by peasants seemed strange. It was the custom all over Eastern Europe and after a while it seemed not servile so much as antiquated, a hoary ritual surviving, like fealty, from feudal times, which, of course, is exactly what it was.) These particular Hungarians cared a lot about dress. Tigers for turnout, they were well-groomed in what used to be thought the English style; but they didn't give a damn about my rough-and-ready outfit. The best I could manage was a tweed coat and some grey canvas trousers, which, with a clean shirt and a blue tie, looked almost presentable; but the footgear let me down—this was always gym or tennis shoes, whichever looked cleaner. But it didn't matter.

After a lifetime of educational croppers and bad school reports, my luck seemed suddenly to have changed. Ever since my halt in Munich, letters with exhortations to kindness from my Baltic-Russian friends there,* and then from the friends they had written to, had been flying eastwards, and they unloosed cornucopias of warm and boundless hospitality when I caught up with them. I was full of gratitude to my benefactors and I loved them, but I don't think I ever actually wondered why I struck so lucky. If their friends had asked them to help, I suppose they couldn't quite wash their hands of me; but the main reason for their hospitality was a general kind feeling towards the young and the broke. The accident of nationality may also have been a help, particularly then: I think Hungarians had a definite soft spot for England. Absorption and enjoyment are catching and my attitude to life resembled a sea-lion's to the flung bloater. They were amused by accounts of the journey: some said they wished they had done the same; and they were impressed that I only took lifts in really bad weather. Nobody else was travelling like this in those days, so the expedition had the value of rarity: it is almost past belief, but only once during the whole journey did I meet another soul who had set out in the same way.

* See *A Time of Gifts*, p. 97.

A couple of months earlier, on the road between Ulm and Augsburg, I had dived out of a snowstorm into a lonely Gasthaus and the only other customer taking refuge there was a strange-looking boy of about my age, dressed in a black corduroy jacket and a scarlet waistcoat with brass buttons, who was banging the snow off an already very battered top-hat with his forearm; back askew on his head, it gave him a look of Sam Weller. He told me, as we threw schnapps down our throats, that he was wearing the traditional costume of a Hamburg chimney-sweep's apprentice. Emblematic of a secret sweeps' guild which stretched all over Europe, it ensured a welcome from his colleagues everywhere; his circular brushes and his slotted bamboo staves were strapped to the bottom of his rucksack, just in case. While he explained that he was heading south to Innsbruck and the Brenner and then down into Italy, he unfolded his map on the table and his finger traced Bolzano, Trento, the Adige, Lake Garda, Verona, Mantua, Modena, Bologna and the Apennine passes leading to Florence; and as he uttered the glorious names, he waved his hand in the air as though Italy lay all about us. "Kommst du nicht mit?"

Why not? It was tempting, and he was an amusing chap. Then I thought of the registered envelope I hoped was waiting in Munich and of all the mysteries of Eastern Europe that I would miss. "Schade!" he said: what a shame. Warmed by another schnapps or two, we helped each other on with our burdens and he set off for the Tyrol and Rome and the land where the lemon-trees bloomed (*Dahin!*) and waved his top-hat as he grew fainter through the snowfall. We both shouted godspeed against the noise of the wind and wondering whether I had done the right thing I plodded on, eyelashes clogged with flakes, towards Bavaria and Constantinople.

*   *   *   *

The house in the Uri utca was full of helpful books. Above all, there were the *Encyclopaedia Britannica* and *Meyers Konversationslexikon*, both of them firm standbys throughout the journey, and I found a wide window-seat to pile them on. There was a book on learning Hungarian and I made a fumbling assault on it, though my vocabulary never got beyond a hundred words or so, most of them nouns.

Coming from a great distance and wholly unrelated to the Teutonic, Latin and Slav languages that fence it in, Hungarian has remained miraculously intact. Everything about the language is different, not only the words themselves, but the way they are formed, the syntax and grammar and above all the cast of mind that brought them into being. I knew that Magyar belonged to the Ugro-Finnic group, part of the great Ural-Altaic family, "Just", one of my new friends told me, "as English belongs to the Indo-European." He followed this up by saying that the language closest to Hungarian was Finnish.

"How close?"

"Oh, very!"

"What, like Italian and Spanish?"

"Well no, not quite as close as that . . ."

"How close then?"

Finally, after a thoughtful pause, he said, "About like English and Persian."

But it seems that one can get one step nearer with the languages of the Ostiaks and the Voguls. Reckoned only in thousands, these small groups of kindly skin-clad folk dwell in the fens and the tundras between the Upper Urals and the Ob river in Western Siberia. They inhabit half-underground huts and birch-bark shelters and, up to their waists in snow, hunt the woods for bears, which, simultaneously gods and quarry, they also worship; and when the ice melts, they fish and set traps and graze their reindeer across the moss, at pains to segregate them from the enormous neighbouring herds of their distant cousins, the Samoyeds. It was no help, at first, to learn that Magyar, whose resonance is fast, incisive and distinct, is an agglutinative language— the word merely conjures up the sound of mumbling through a mouth full of toffee. It means that the words are never inflected as they are in Europe, and that changes of sense are conveyed by a concatenation of syllables stuck on behind the first; all the vowel sounds imitate their leader, and the invariable ictus on the leading syllable sets up a kind of dactylic or anapaestic canter which, to a new ear, gives Magyar a wild and most unfamiliar ring. So, when at the dance I was listening to the vernacular sentences of my monocled and stork-loving Esztergom friend while he poured whisky out of a cut-glass decanter, and then to his marvellous-looking partner—as, with a deft langour, she took a cigarette out of a gold and shagreen case that snapped shut with an emerald, and answered him through the smoke—it was impossible not to wonder among what unconjecturable scenery of marshland and desert and woods, when the Magyar tongue was beginning to shake itself loose from the primitive Ugrian magma, these sounds could first have been uttered.

On a printed page the fierce-looking sentences let slip no hint of their drift. Those tangles of Ss and Zs! Gazing at the peppery strings of diaereses and the tempests of acute accents all swaying one way like wind-blown corn, I wondered if I would ever be able to extort a meaning.

My first effort was discouraging. There was a snug *kávéház*, a coffee-house (if only all Magyar were as easy as this!) less than a minute's walk away in Holy Trinity Square (I could just manage Szent Háromság Tér, Saint Three-ship Place) and I was spending a morning of showery weather there with books and writing things. The coffee-house windows surveyed ancient palaces and the tall restored gothic steeple of the Coronation Church, and just in front, a plinth sprang from the cobbles and lifted a bronze horseman called Andreas Hadik into the raindrops; he was a commander in the Seven Years War who had dodged the armies of Frederick the Great, swooped on Berlin with a cavalcade of hussars, looted the place at lightning speed and galloped away again. At the next table, the only other person in the coffee-house was a frail, white-haired man reading the *Pesti Hirláp*. I couldn't take my eyes off the headline. It ran: *O boldog Angolország!* I knew that the last word meant 'England', and the rest was obvious: it could only mean 'O bulldog England!', 'O English bulldog!' or something of the kind. The photograph below showed the Prince of Wales in a golfing pull-over with a bold lozenge pattern and a tweed cap; but, very puzzlingly, the dog under his arm, which simultaneously stole the picture and turned it into an enigma, was a fox-terrier; they must have muddled the breeds. I couldn't resist asking the reader in German if I had understood the words correctly. He laughed, and answered in English. No, it was nothing to do with dogs; 'boldog' is 'happy'; 'O fortunate England!' was what the caption meant, and the gist of the article was

England's good luck in having so promising a Crown Prince. Hungary was a kingdom too, my neighbour ruefully added, but they only had a regent. The Apostolic crown was empty.

The Apostolic Crown . . . I had heard much about it. Reproduced on buildings, coins, flags, cap-badges and buttons and on the top of all public notices, it was seldom out of sight. Until it should be needed for some future coronation—but whose? and when?—the crown itself was guarded in the Royal Palace. Over the centuries the shrewd marriage policy of the Habsburgs had absorbed most of the neighbouring kingdoms and finally Hungary; and the last sovereigns had been King Karl and Queen Zita, who were also, of course, Austria's last Emperor and Empress. After the loss of both these thrones at the end of the Great War, and the breakdown of their brief and illicit return to Hungary, the lingering hopes of the dynasty had faded; and now the exiled King was dead. In photographs his son Archduke Otto, the present claimant, was usually dressed as a Hungarian magnate; but these pictures were seen more often in his native Austria than here. Nevertheless, the state was constitutionally a kingdom still, under the regency of Admiral Horthy. The beautiful Empress Elizabeth, their last queen but one, who had been assassinated in Switzerland in 1898 by an anarchist, was still their favourite. Framed on desks and tables and grand pianos, there she was, in nineteenth-century coronation robes, reading under a tree, clearing terrific fences in Northamptonshire or Meath or pensively at gaze, stroking her enormous wolfhound, Shadow. She had loved Hungary and the Hungarians, learnt Magyar and rushed to Hungary's defence in all discussions; above all, she flung herself with fearlessness and skill into all their equestrian pursuits. Her love was returned with interest and still declared, thirty-six years after her assassination, with all the ardour of Burke for Marie Antoinette.

Now only the crown was left. It was Hungary's most sacred object. Vicissitudes beset it and unconjecturable journeys and adventures lay ahead. Wrought in battered gold, with its culminating cross askew, it was the actual diadem Pope Sylvester II sent to St. Stephen when he was crowned first King of Hungary in AD 1000. But the later addition of enamel plaques, gold chains and pendant gems give it an unquestionably Byzantine look, fitter for a mosaic sovereign by the Bosphorus or at Ravenna, one would think, than for a canopied monarch of the West. No wonder: the gold-and-enamelled circlet was the gift of a Byzantine emperor to a later sovereign, who promptly clasped it round the Pope's original gift to his ancestor, and the gleaming hybrid is an apt symbol of the early Hungarian kingdom, for blandishments from the East as well as the West had flickered over the great Hungarian Plain with the ambivalence of a mirage.

*　　*　　*　　*

Except for those dank cellars on the Vár, wandering about the steep and exhilarating city unearthed scarce marks of the long sojourn of the Turks: a few Ottoman fragments, the tomb of a dervish on the Hill of Roses, some hammam-cupolas scattered about; later, a mosque here and there in the provinces. There had been two centuries and a half for the Town to recover in; long enough, perhaps, to surround the Turkish interlude with romance and to remind the Magyars that, genealogically speaking, if one goes far enough back into Asian pre-history, the races are distant cousins. But it was hard, during my explorations, to imagine the skyline—the clustering domes, the minarets and the fluttering crescents—which Charles of Lorraine and his reconquering companions must have gazed at when they laid siege to Buda in 1686.

Foreign soldiers flocked to the Hungarian wars, and among them more than one Stuart on the wrong side of the blanket, starting with the sixteen-year-old Duke of Berwick, James II's son with Marlborough's sister Arabella. He astonished the besieging army by his wild valour in the assault on Buda: and two years after it fell, his first cousin St. Albans—Charles II's eighteen-year-old son with Nell Gwyn—fought bravely at the storming of Belgrade. Little is known about them in England, but these faraway campaigns invariably assembled stirring and eccentric figures from the British Isles: every kind of adventurer, Wild Geese, clan chieftains, recusant Catholics, Jacobite exiles and soldiers of fortune trailing the puissant pike rushed to the double-eagle banner, for these wars held all the glamour of the Crusades. Sir Philip Sidney, travelling about Hungary as an ambassador on leave, was in a different category; but otherwise the earliest English arrival I could find was Sir Richard Grenville, fighting on land against Suleiman the Magnificent twenty-five years before the *Revenge*. The next was Thomas Arundell—a great favourite of Elizabeth's in spite of his religion. He won great glory in the Imperial service and at the storming of Esztergom in 1595 he forced the water-tower and captured the enemy's banner with his own hand: a deed which prompted Rudolf II to make him a Count of the Holy Roman Empire. When he got home his joyful flaunting of the title irritated the English nobility; it put his father, Sir Matthew, a mere knight, beside himself; and it infuriated the Queen ('. . . my dogs shall wear no collar but my own . . .'); she sent him to the Fleet prison for a spell. Perhaps it was to stop all this foreign nonsense that James I made him Lord Arundell of Wardour.*

Later, in Rilke's *Weise von Liebe und Tod des Cornets Christoph Rilke*, I came on an evocation of these old Turkish campaigns which suddenly brought all the chronicles to life. The poem commemorates a vague, perhaps imaginary, kinsman of the poet, a young cornet and standard-bearer in a regiment of horse in 1663. Billeted for a night in a Hungarian frontier castle beyond the Raab, he is woken by frenzied neighing and trumpets sounding boot-and-saddle; there is a roar of burning. The enemy have surrounded and set light to the castle. Tearing himself from the arms of the young châtelaine, he is only just in time to seize the smouldering Colour and rush down the stone steps; the flag bursts into a great flame as he charges into the turbaned ranks and he is lost to sight at last under a sixteen-fold flash of scimitars.

*   *   *   *

I explored the Vár—the fortress of Buda, that is—with Micky and Tim, the huge black Alsatian, and began to get the hang of this lofty

* This Holy Roman honour surfaced again generations later when his remarkable and equally courageous descendant, Isabel Arundell, wife of Sir Richard Burton the explorer, cut a dash in Trieste by using her rank as geborene Gräfin—quite in conformity with Austrian custom—when Burton was Consul there. She was running a sort of local RSPCA, and, as the town was Austrian still, it was probably a shrewd move. Her other pursuits were swimming, riding and fencing with her husband. It is a pity she burnt his papers.

quarter and the old houses there, the lanes, the churches and the steep streets; they sank like trenches between silent walls where branches and creepers showered over the coping. On a bus trip a mile or two north to Roman Aquincum, we were joined by a beautiful girl of about fourteen called Harry, part-Croatian and part-Polish as well as Hungarian. Tim bounded about among the sarcophagi and broken walls and the ruined amphitheatre and dug for bones in the Temple of the Unconquered Sun; and in the museum we gazed at one of those disturbing bas-reliefs of Mithras in a Phrygian cap, plunging a dagger into the bull's throat. (The god always wears an expression of unbearable anguish as though the throat were his own; a hound leaps up to drink the blood and, down below, a furtive scorpion wages scrotal war.) A favourite of the legions, he was worshipped all along the frontier and there was hardly a camp between Carlisle and the Black Sea without one of his shrines.

This last gasp of the Alpine range was also the last bastion of Roman Pannonia, for the Empire stopped at the river's bank. The Iberian cavalry stationed here must have peered across with misgiving: beyond the vague settlements of Celts, or Quadi, or Sarmatians, the grim plain ran away to infinity. Gepids, Vandals and finally the Huns replaced them in turn, until Rome itself collapsed and the Dark Ages set in. The Avars came next. *Deserta Avororum!* Their name hung bleakly over the waste for dim unchronicled centuries until Charlemagne scattered them, and, without knowing it, cleared a space for the westernmost settlements of the Bulgars. The new state bombinated briefly in the vacuum, until—*at last!*—the hour struck for the Magyars. After centuries of shadowy Asian wandering, they streamed out of the wings and settled on centre stage forever.

Except for the old quarter along the opposite bank, modern Pest only really came into existence in the last century. It spread insatiably across the plain and I could see great Oxford Streets, like the Andrássy út and the Rákóczi út, slicing their canyons through the boom city; the quiet citadel my side of the water had long ago been outstripped. Precariously linked by boat or, briefly each year, by the ice, Buda and Pest, the names as well as the places, were joined to each other only in the 1840s. One was often told that the tremendous Széchényi chain-bridge was built by two Scotsmen, the Brothers Clark.

Apart from a few old streets and squares, the smart Dunapalota Hotel and the cheerful and pleasure-loving waterfront—especially the Patisserie Gerbaud, a dashing Gunters-like meeting-place by the statue of the poet Vörösmarty—I liked Pest much less than my own side of the town, but I never tired of surveying it from the Fisher Bastion. This vantage point by the Coronation Church commanded steep descending layers plumed all the way down with trees, then a sweep of the Danube, crossed by half a dozen bridges. St. Margaret's Island expanded upstream and the Houses of Parliament loomed from the opposite shore. Built at the turn of the century and aswarm with statues, this frantic and marvellous pile was a tall, steep-roofed gothic nave escorted for a prodigious length by mediaeval pinnacles touched with gilding and adorned by crockets; and it was crowned, at the point where its transepts intersected, by the kind of ribbed and egg-shaped dome that might more predictably have dominated the roofs of a Renaissance town in Tuscany, except that the dome itself was topped by a sharp and bristling gothic spire. Architectural dash could scarcely go further.

Flights of steps, arched and roofed-in like slanting cloisters, zigzagged downhill from this eyrie and I always seemed to be out of breath from toiling up them or rushing down full-tilt and haring across the Széchényi Bridge, late for some appointment in Pest; in one particular case, for luncheon at 7 Joszef tér, just the other side.

My hostess at the Schloss* in lower Austria where I made such a fool of myself on my nineteenth birthday belonged to a Trieste family of Greek origin. She had written to friends and relations in Budapest. One of them was the former Prime Minister, Count Paul Teleki, and he belonged to a famous, rather romantic Transylvanian family. One recent but fairly distant member, exploring Ethiopia, had discovered Lake Rudolf and named it after the ill-fated Archduke; and the volcano at its southern tip was called Mount Teleki (but perhaps no longer). Mine—Count Paul—was a famous geographer too. He had mapped the whole Japanese archipelago and, across the table, he told us stories of travel among the Turks and the Arabs when he was

* Pottenbrunn, near St. Pölten. See *A Time of Gifts*, p. 168.

helping to draw the frontiers of Mesopotamia. He broke off for lively descriptions of Abdul Hamid and Slatin Pasha, that strange Anglo-Austrian for years the prisoner and running-footman of the Mahdi. The Count's alert, pointed face behind horn-rimmed spectacles, lit by a quick, witty and enthusiastic manner, had an almost Chinese look. It is hard to think of anyone kinder. As Chief Scout of Hungary, he took my travel plans to heart, spread maps, indicated passes and routes, traced rivers, suggested alternative approaches and enlivened everything as he did so with anecdotes and asides. He had been Foreign Minister and later Prime Minister for a little less than a year, resigning to return to his geographical work when Horthy sent soldiers to stop the return of King Karl. He asked me back a couple of times and all his family were kind to me in various ways; and when I left, he recommended me to his relations in Transylvania. He even gave me a letter to an old Turkish pasha living on the Asiatic shore of the Bosphorus which suddenly made my journey's end seem something more than an abstraction.*

As Annamaria, the pretty girl I made friends with at the ball, was studying art history, she knew every picture-gallery and museum by heart; thanks to her I haunted them all. It must have been she who pointed out (but where?) a remarkable and untypical wrestling match by Courbet; and she acted as Open Sesame to a private house with a long room which was empty except for half a dozen tremendous El Grecos. I met a lot of people and the tempo of life quickened. One exploratory foray into high life led to the drawing-room of an ex-reigning beauty equally famous for her looks and her exalted rank. Afterwards, when Berta asked what I thought, I said that she was wonderful looking; but wasn't she a shade precious? Berta laughed; "When we were nurses in the War," she said, "Ella insisted on working only in the blind wards, saying 'I have to, you see! In the others they

---

* Count Teleki became Prime Minister again at the approach of war, in the hopes of rescuing something from the tightening toils of Hungary's horrible predicament. Profoundly pro-British at heart, but forced by the imperatives of the situation into the postures he would least willingly have chosen, he committed suicide in Spring 1941 rather than condone Germany's attack on Yugoslavia across Hungarian territory after Hungary had signed a pact of friendship with the Yugoslavs.

all fall in love with me and I mustn't add to those poor boys' sufferings.'"

Every day Tibor used to drive out to some military stables beyond Pest to exercise a favourite charger. One morning he asked me if I would like to come: he had got hold of another horse, so we trotted and cantered round the track and went over a few easy jumps; then we headed for a paddock where I watched him put his horse through the most arcane and mysterious paces in a silence as rapt and with a skill almost as perfect as those experts in the Spanish Riding School in Vienna. I think the outing was a mild vetting and I must have scraped through, for on the way back he said they might be able to fix up a mount for some of my eastward journey, which would pass the estate of a friend who had plenty of horses—perhaps she would lend me one for two or three days. "It's the right way to see the plain." I was so excited by the prospect I hardly dared to speak.

*   *   *   *

Trivial things light fuses in the memory. A flower-woman on the Danube Quay was always calling "Virágot! Szép virágot!"—"Flowers, lovely flowers!" (the plural of *virág*, a flower)—whenever I passed her. Two years later, reading *Ulysses* for the first time, I came on the words 'Nagyságos uram Lipóti Virág', which is Magyar, more or less, for 'Leopold Bloom Esq.' In the book, Bloom was a Jewish immigrant from Hungary; *Virág* is a typical Magyarisation of *Blum*; and the spelling must have changed to 'Bloom' when the author placed his family in Dublin. I feel sure that Joyce, as quick at languages as Borrow, must have picked up some Hungarian when he was teaching at the Berlitz School. Pre-war Trieste was still an Austro-Hungarian city with plenty of Hungarians to instruct him. (A few of them live there still.) He was sometimes thought, but probably wrongly, to have coached Admiral Horthy in English, when the future ruler was last *k. und k.* Commander of the Naval Station at Pola; and at the same time, I have just discovered, he made considerable progress in demotic Greek.* This enthralling port, which I visited for the first time three years ago, keeps cropping up in these pages. Literary ghosts abound

* See his notebooks, published in Manto Aravantinou's *Ta Ellinika tou James Joyce* (Hermes Press, Athens, 1977).

there: not only James Joyce and the Burtons, but also Italo Svevo. Perhaps d'Annunzio's phantom biplane zooms inaudibly overhead on the way to Fiume while the shade of Rilke glides Duino-wards along the Adriatic shore, where they caught a last glimpse of Waring.

It was hard to believe I had only been in Budapest ten days. After a final party, long after midnight, I climbed the steps of Buda with Annamaria and we sat on a wall and gazed down at the bridges looped across the Danube in sparkling necklaces. I asked her yet again to repeat a song which had been running in my head ever since the ball. Some Hungarian music is almost as different to a stranger as the language and nearly as hard. I found the song impossible to get by heart. It tells of a swallow flying low over a field of ripening wheat. She began,

"Érik a, érik a búza kalász"

and went on to the end. But it was no good. The tune escaped yet again, and it is still just out of reach.

3

The Great Hungarian Plain

MALEK, a fine chestnut with a flowing mane and tail, one white sock, a blaze and more than a touch of Arab to his brow, was waiting by a clump of acacias on the Cegléd road. The boy who had ridden him over told Berta he had been newly shod and he would be no trouble except for a short stretch near his stable. We stowed my things in the saddle-bags and tied my rolled greatcoat across the pommel. Berta drove off with Micky and Tim to drop the boy home and I hadn't trotted more than half-an-hour along the same road before they were back. We picnicked under an oak then set off in opposite directions, they for Pest, I for Constantinople, looking back and waving until we were all out of sight.

It was the thirteenth of April. The few clouds in the clear, wide sky were so nearly motionless they might have been anchored to their shadows. The Great Hungarian Plain—the Alföld, in Magyar—is the westernmost steppe in Europe, a last outpost of the Pontic and Caspian wastes. Influenced by pictures of the wilder Hortobágy a hundred miles further east, I was disappointed at first to see ploughland and fields green with young wheat and a taller crop with pointed pale green leaves which turned out to be Indian corn; there were rows of tobacco plants, then orchards and farms set about with trees, and the plain between these tracts of husbandry was dotted with herds. Sheep and swine and troops of cattle grazed across the middle distance, with a village every few miles. The one I had been warned about was Alberti-Irsa;* this was the difficult stretch. Malek tried to turn down a track

* I can only find Irsa on my modern map, but names sometimes change, and this particular square of my old one, frayed and torn by too frequent folding and unfolding, dropped out long ago. But it is 'Alberti-Irsa' in my rough diary notes, so I shall stick to that and risk it.

which led to a gateway and outbuildings and barns, with a glimpse beyond them of a château half-hidden among trees, where his own stable beckoned. When I insisted on going straight on, there were aggrieved backward glances; I knew other horses were at grass there but his passionate whinny went unanswered—perhaps the groom had led them out of earshot—and after a brief tug of wills we were clip-clopping along as briskly as before.

Carts drawn by horses and oxen easily outnumbered the motor-cars. Gypsies were on the move in long, jolting waggons that made all their gear clatter. Branching off the road to the left, I followed lesser tracks where the farmsteads and cottages soon began to scatter the country more thinly. A few, thatched with reed and maize-trash and fenced about with woven sticks, had a dishevelled look, but most were clean and trim with thick walls newly whitewashed, for Easter perhaps, and painted all round with coloured dados. A handily planted tree like a prehistoric dresser had pots and pans stuck on its lopped branches and a family of white hens and a speckled cock roosted in another. Shallow platforms lifted the houses above the plain and women busy with household tasks sat there and gossiped. On one of them a length of cloth, with a red and white pattern suddenly dividing in two, stretched over a long loom and a kerchiefed crone sent a shuttle flying through the taut warps; shifting them through each other with a clack of the treadle, she beat the new weft home with the comb-like reed, and stopped and looked up at my greeting and answered with "Isten áldjs" (God bless you). Understanding I was a foreigner, she asked "Német?" (German?). My answer "Angol" induced a look of polite vagueness: an Angle meant as little to her as a Magyar might in the middle of Dartmoor. As the other side of the house was noisy with mooing, she shouted through the windows and in a minute a grand-daughter brought a foaming glass of milk: they both smiled as they watched me drink it. I sipped it slowly and thought: I'm drinking this glass of milk on a chestnut horse on the Great Hungarian Plain.

By the approach of evening, all trace of the capital and the western hills had vanished. We were in the middle of a limitless space, scattered with woods, and pronged here and there with the solitary and, at first, enigmatic perpendiculars of sweep-wells. These primordial devices (called *shadoofs* in the Egyptian desert) have two posts erected side by side crossed by a bar six feet up—or the branches of a tree lopped until only a fork remains—which is pivot for a cross-beam several yards long. Weights—usually boulders—are lashed to the short end, until the yards of beam beyond the pivot tilt upright; from this lofty tip hangs a pole—or, if necessary, two linked together—from which a bucket hangs. This is sent down the well-shaft by hauling hand over hand while the weighted end of the beam swings aloft: hold is then loosened and the weight sinks, lifting a full bucket to the surface, ready for pouring into a cattle-trough like a dug-out canoe. These lonely uprights give an air of desolation to the plain: they resemble derelict siege-engines by day and the failing light turns them into gibbets or those wheel-topped stakes in pictures by Hieronymus Bosch where vultures wrangle over skeletons spreadeagled in mid-air.

The evening was full of the see-saw creak of their timbers. At one of them, by a ruined farmhouse with a stork's nest in the rafters, two dismounted drovers were toiling; their wide, white linen trousers, worn loose outside black knee-boots, came half-way down the calves of their legs. They had finished watering a large herd of remarkable pale cattle with nearly straight horns of enormous span that filled the air with trampling and lowing and dust. When the drovers had remounted, I waved a greeting. They lifted their black hats with ceremony and wheeled their horses round, then, abetted by rough-coated white dogs, they spurred after the herd, trotting or cantering on the outskirts and whirling long goads to keep strays from wandering. The declining sun outlined all their silhouettes. Haloed in dust and trailing long shadows, they moved westward with a noise of harsh cries, dogs and a jangle of horns and bells. A stork joined its mate in the rafters, probably after swallowing a last frog captured at some quieter oasis and I trotted east towards the darker end of the plain. The clouds had flushed an astounding pink.

But this was not to be compared with the sky behind. The flatness of the Alföld leaves a stage for cloud-events at sunset that are dangerous to describe: levitated armies in deadlock and riderless squadrons descending in slow motion to smouldering and sulphurous lagoons where barbicans gradually collapse and fleets of burning triremes turn dark before sinking. These are black vesper's pageants . . . the least said the better.

*   *   *   *

Whenever he got a chance, Malek broke into a canter, and one of these bursts turned into a long twilight gallop; he may have thought we were far from home and ought to get a move on; and when we had settled to a milder gait, falling dark gave lustre to a thin new moon. A distant string of lights, which I knew must be the town of Cegléd, was behind us to the right, and, here and there as it grew darker, lights of farmsteads showed across the flatness like ships. I had planned to seek shelter at one of them but suddenly there were none, and by the time night had really fallen only a single glow was left. It was hard to tell the distance but the nearer we got the less it resembled a farm, except for the barking of half a dozen dogs that finally rushed forward in a frenzy.

Three camp-fires, spreading spokes of light through the tree-trunks, lit up the canvas of tents and shapes of men and horses. A party of Gypsies had settled for the night by yet another sweep-well, and our arrival caused bewilderment. Except for the fires, there was no glimmer in any direction and I saw, half with excitement and half with a touch of fright, that we would have to spend the night there. I had heard many hair-raising stories about Gypsies recently and I was chiefly scared about Malek. When I dismounted they crowded about him and patted and stroked his neck and his flanks and scanned his points with eyes like shrewd blackberries. Shaggy and unkempt, they were the darkest Gypsies I had ever seen. Some of the men wore loose white Hungarian trousers, the others were in ordinary town clothes and black hats, all in the last stage of decay. Snotty mites and lithe tar-babies wore vests that came to their middles and some had nothing on at all, except one or two insecurely hatted in cast-off trilbies so loose they swivelled as they walked. Beautiful girls, flounced and bedraggled in green and yellow and magenta, stared with effulgent eyes. Beyond the fires there was a munching of unyoked oxen; horses were hobbled under the branches and a couple of mares grazed loose with tall foals beside them. Dogs bickered and snarled and the poultry, loosed from their travelling coop, pecked about the dust. Black and brown tents were stretched over crossed poles and the ramshackle style and the jumbled scattering of household stuff gave no hint of a thousand or two thousand years' practice in pitching camp; except for the reeds and withies and the half-woven baskets on which brown hands were already busy, the whole tribe might have fled half-an-hour ago from a burning slum. I think they were heading for the banks of the Tisza to cut a new stock.

I escaped the hubbub for ten minutes by walking Malek up and down before watering him at the trough, where a man called György helped with the bucket. I had been wondering whether to tether Malek to a tree; there were some oats and a headstall in the saddle-bag, but the halter was far too short for him to graze. Best to hobble him as the Gypsies had done with theirs, but I had no idea how to set about it. György showed me, linking Malek's forelegs with a neat figure of eight. I was anxious about this: Malek couldn't have been used to it; but he behaved with great forbearance. I gave him some of his feed and some hay from the Gypsy, then took the saddle and tack and settled with the rest of them by the fire.

Thank heavens, their informal supper was over! Apart from hedge-hogs, delicious by hearsay, the untoothsomeness and even danger of their usual food were famous. There was a sound of rattling metal: a dog was licking out a cooking-pot by the fire. Seeing my worried look, a girl of ten, who had just begged for a cigarette, hurled an accurate stone at the dog, which scuttled off with a surprised yelp; then, tossing up the vessel so that it caught on a convenient twig, she coiled to the ground again with an indulgent smile as she let the smoke stream lazily from her nostrils. The chief item of Berta's supplies was a salami nearly a yard long, ribboned half-way down with the national colours. I made a good impression by cutting off a third and handing it over; it was the signal for a brief uproar of grabs and curses and blows. Then thirty pairs of eyes, accompanied by a soft chorus of whispers, watched raptly as I ate a sandwich and an apple. I took three fast gigantic gulps out of my wine-bottle before surrendering it. They seemed half-fascinated; also, and I couldn't make out why, half-alarmed by my presence: perhaps all strangers, except as prey, boded ill. We were incommunicado at first; but I had been alerted by what the oldest man had said to György before he helped me give Malek a drink: the mumbled sentence had ended, I thought, with the word *pani*—immediately recognisable, to anyone at all in touch with Anglo-India, as the Hindi for water. When I pointed questioningly at the water-jar and asked what was inside, they said "Víz", using the Magyar word; I cunningly answered, "Nem [not] víz! Pani". There was a sensation! Bewilderment and wonder were written on their firelit features.* When I held up the fingers of my hand and said "Panch!"—the word for five in both Hindi and Romany (*öt*, in Magyar), the wonder grew. I tried the only other words I could remember from *Lavengro*, pointing to my tongue and saying "Lav?"; but drew a blank; *tchib* was their word for it. I drew another blank with "penning dukkerin", Borrow's—or rather Mr. Petulengro's—word for 'fortune-telling'. But I had better luck with the word *petulengro* itself, at least with the first half. The whole word ('horseshoe-master' in Borrow, i.e. blacksmith) caused no reaction, but when I cut it down to *petul*, and pointed to the anvil, a small boy dashed into the dark and came back holding up a horseshoe in triumph.†

As soon as they got the hang of it, each time I pointed at something with a questioning look, back came the Gypsy word. Most of them laughed but one or two looked worried, as though tribal secrets were being revealed. A finger pointing to Heaven, and "Isten?" (the Magyar word for God), at once evoked the cry of "Devel!", which sounds odd at first; until one thinks of *Deva* in Hindi and its probable Sanskrit ancestor. An eager light had come into those swart faces. Lustrous hair, dark eyes, chestnut skin and, among the women, the sinuous walk and brittle flexibility of wrist and ankle—all these encouraged the notion

---

* What makes it all the stranger is that the Hungarian and Rumanian Gypsy word for 'water' is *pai*; the 'n' has evaporated. And yet, that is how I heard it. I wonder if the vanished letter still hovers in the subconscious, like the atavistic and ghostly 's' behind a French circumflex.

† *Petáli* or *pétalo*—but I didn't know it then—is the modern Greek word for a horseshoe and it could have joined the Romany vocabulary during the century or two that the Gypsies must have halted in the Byzantine Empire. The Greek original means 'a leaf' whence both petal and horseshoe, for donkeys in Greece, and all through the Levant, are still shod with a thin leaf-like layer of steel. The modern hollow crescent shape for horses and mules must be a later refinement, for the old term has stuck for all.

that they could have changed hardly at all since they had left Baluchi-stan or Sinde or the banks of the Indus. I had recently read, or been told, two hostile legends connected with their skill as metal-workers: not only had they cast the Golden Calf for the Israelites, but a Gypsy smith is supposed to have forged the nails for the Crucifixion, in punishment for which a similar nail had been hammered into his behind by a turncoat demon.

* * * *

Malek was grazing under the tree where I had left him, a dozen yards from the fire. The hobble seemed secure and comfortable and, with saddle and saddle-bag for pillow, I lay and smoked but couldn't sleep for a long time. When I did, the well-being generated by those hasty swallows of wine and the cheerful session by the fire had worn off. How could I have been so insane as to bring a borrowed horse into such a den of hazards? Later, between waking and sleeping I had nightmare visions of the Gypsies making off with that beautiful Szápáry horse; then (as they were said to do) painting him a different colour before selling him to a cruel stranger; eating him outright, perhaps; or, even worse, getting him secretly turned into salami, the whispered fate of old donkeys, after the hasty despatch of both horse and rider. This last fate was the best solution: should the borrowed horse come to harm, better death than a lifetime of disgrace. When I woke from these dreadful fancies, the new moon had set; but there was Malek, lit by stars under the branches and he was still there when daybreak routed the phantoms of the night. The sun lifted itself out of the wilderness like a blood-red disc and the crowing of the Gypsies' cock ran from one invisible farmyard to another until the whole plain was stirring.

I had brought plenty of sugar-lumps and after gratefully giving Malek a couple I fed him some solider stuff and wandered off to see what was going on. A reversal of last night's shadows striped the plain; smoke was rising and fingers were already threading, plaiting and splicing among the heaped-up reeds. Apart from the dazzling frippery of the girls, I had been disappointed the night before by the tameness of this little company. Not a glimpse of a musical instrument, not a note or a twang; not even a dancing bear. But I was wrong. In the lee of a cart, a huge brown Carpathian beast, his cheek resting on folded paws, lay fast asleep; and even as I watched he began to stir. Sitting up, he yawned long and wide, rubbed his eyes, then dropped his paws in his lap and peered about with bleary goodwill, while his companion, blowing on embers, prepared breakfast for two. I rejoined Malek, and as we both munched, I noticed that our sheltering tree, tall as a medium-sized oak, belonged to a kind I had never seen. The bark was darker, oval leaves the colour of verdigris grew in symmetrical sprays and leathery pods dangled among them like dark runner-beans. It was a carob-tree. (Its blackish pods, with the faint, dull, haunting taste of fossil chocolate, are like teak to chew. A few years later I sometimes used to stem hunger with them on the southern rocks of Crete, unconsciously imitating the Prodigal Son: they are the husks which he and the swine did eat, and they are still fed to pigs. 'Locust-beans' is an alternative name and some rashly think it was these, with wild honey, that kept St. John the Baptist alive in the desert.)

I saddled Malek, and said goodbye. We headed east.

It was time, and perhaps it is again, to see where we were, and to glance at the past of this extraordinary region. Since the centuries of Rome's frontier along the Danube, the logical way from Buda—Strigonium—to the Levant lay due south along the river to its confluence with the Sava, where the huge and crucial fortress of Belgrade was later to spring up: then through the Balkan passes, across the future kingdoms of Serbia and Bulgaria to Adrianople and over Thrace to the Imperial City, or to the Hellespont, where Asia began. This was the overland link between the Kings of Hungary and the Byzantine Emperors; it was the path of Barbarossa and his crusaders on the journey which ended with the Emperor's death in the chill flow of the Calycadnus. But the last crusading army but one—the Hungarians of King Sigismund, with his French, German, Burgundian and Wallachian allies and even, some say, a thousand English—kept on recklessly downstream until Bajazet the Thunderbolt, striking at Nicopolis, utterly destroyed them. (More later of this.) A final Crusade in the next generation was smashed to bits on the Black Sea; then Constantinople itself was lost. The same route in reverse had carried the Turks by fatal stages into the heart of Europe. They had subjugated the Balkans in the late Middle Ages and by Tudor times they were advancing upstream. Suleiman the Magnificent defeated King Louis II,* then he captured and burnt Buda; but in 1529 he laid unsuccessful siege to Vienna, and when the second attempt on Vienna failed at the end of the next century, the Ottoman tide began to turn. Charles of Lorraine, and then Prince Eugene stemmed their advance and harried them downstream along the same watery thoroughfare; and the Austrian army, awfully arrayed, boldly, by battery, besieged Belgrade. The *Stadt und Festung* fell and the time-honoured path became the itinerary for all Western travellers; in particular, for Ambassadors travelling to the Sublime Porte. Strings of carriages with outriders and escorts of musketeers, or ribboned houseboats with many oarsmen wended majestically downstream. (One must imagine Lady Mary Wortley-Montagu during a halt, half-furred and half-flimsy in Turkish dress, reading Pope's *Homer* under a poplar tree.)

Kinglake followed in the next century, but, infuriatingly, his narrative skips Hungary and only begins with the author mimicking the sound and the action of a steam-engine to edify the Pasha of Belgrade; for the coveted citadel was once again Turkish. The railway which eventually linked it to the West and to Constantinople has played a great part in novels of espionage and adventure.

(Years after the present journey, I followed in all these ancient footsteps. If the river before Esztergom had suggested a liquid Champs Elysées, the resemblance on this southward reach is more striking still. A wide ochre flood dwindles across Europe to infinity between symmetrical fringes of willows and poplars with nothing in sight but a heron rising from the flag-leaves or an occasional fisherman's canoe suspended in the haze like a boat in a Chinese painting. I stayed the night in a bargeman's tavern at Mohács in order to see the battlefield where Suleiman had overthrown King Lajos: one of history's most dark and shattering landmarks: a defeat as fatal to Hungary as Kossovo to the Serbs and Constantinople to the Greeks.)

So much for the Danube way to the South, but it was not the one I had taken. Malek and I had abandoned it for the less trodden route

* *Lajos* in Magyar, pronounced Lóyosh, more or less.

across the Great Plain to Transylvania and were trotting south-east steadily further and further from the great river. Later, searching through travellers' tales, I could find only a few who passed this way.

On the fringe of allegory, dimly perceived through legendary mist and the dust of chronicles, these strangers have an outsize quality about them; something of giants and something of ogres, Goyaesque beings towering like a Panic amid the swarms that follow one after the other across this wilderness and vanish. No historical detail can breathe much life into the Gepids, kinsmen of the Goths who had left the Baltic and settled the region in Roman times; and the Lombards only begin to seem real when they move into Italy. Otherwise, all assailants came from the East, with the Huns as their dread vanguard. Radiating from the Great Plain, sacking and enslaving half Europe, they made the whole Roman Empire tremble. Paris was saved by a miracle and they were only halted and headed backwards near the Marne. When Attila died in reckless bridebed after a heavy banquet somewhere close to the Tisza and perhaps not many miles from my present path, the Huns galloped round and round his burial tent in a stampede of lamentation. The state fell to bits, and ploughmen still dream of turning up his hoard of jewels and ingots and gold-plated bows. The shadowy Gepids survived until the Avars scattered them and moved in themselves for nearly three centuries. Like most of these invaders, of Mongol stock and akin to the Turks (they were Turanians all), these hordes of long-plaited savages and their hectoring khans came close to carrying Byzantium by storm. A permanent nuisance to the West, their newly-invented stirrup made them more formidable still: a firm seat in the saddle ousted the bow as the horseman's chief weapon and replaced it with the spear, and then the lance which in its turn led to the heavily armoured knights of the Middle Ages and, in dim barbaric fashion, foreshadowed the tank. When Charlemagne destroyed their enigmatic sevenfold rings of fortification and put an end to them, all Europe heaved a sigh of relief. Meanwhile, spreading like damp, the Slavs had been quietly expanding eastwards and southwards and into the Balkans, giving birth to the insubstantial Kingdom of Great Moravia on the way. Then the state of the newly-arrived Bulgars stretched a north-western wing into the void the Avars had left. (What figure could seem more remote than Swiatopluk, Kral of the brittle Moravian realm? And who could be further from heart's desire than Krum, the early khan of the Bulgars? He and his boyars used to drink out of the skull of the captured Emperor Nicephorus, halved and lined with silver.)

At last the Magyars came. Fen and tundra people originally, they too were akin to earlier and later invaders, but they had strayed away from their Ugro-Finnic relations centuries earlier; they must have rubbed shoulders with the Persians on their wanderings; almost certainly loitered for a Turkic century or two on the Pontic Steppes to the north of the Caspian and the Black Sea, where lay the vast, mysterious and deeply interesting Empire of the Khazars . . . Leaving the Ural river behind them, and then the Volga and the Don and the Dnieper, they reached the delta of the Danube and halted just north of it in Bessarabia. The Byzantine Emperor, fiercely harassed by the Bulgars, persuaded the godsent Magyars to cross to the south of the Danube and attack them. To counter this, Simeon, the Bulgars' leader (soon to be Tzar) called into play the terrible race of the Pechenegs. These, the fiercest, the cruellest and the most perfidious of all the steppe nomads, were already chafing in the halted queue of Asiatic invaders directly behind the Magyars. While the Magyars were busy assaulting the Bulgars, they moved forward and ravaged and then occupied the Magyars' temporarily evacuated Bessarabian stamping ground.

A fateful chain of events was set in motion. Deprived of Bessarabia, the Magyars struck out towards the sunset; some of them went south-west along the Danube, through the Iron Gates, and then sharp right; but the main body headed north-west through the Carpathian passes, and then sharp left until all the tribes were congregated on the Great Plain, which became Hungary at last. They were already organised in a war-like hierarchy; Arpád had been hoisted on a shield by the other chieftains; and his subjects, expert horsemen, javelin-throwers and archers to a man, had saddles and stirrups that enabled them to twist like corkscrews and loose off in all directions at full gallop. The campaign gathered momentum. All rivals were subjugated or swept from the Plain; the whole of Slovakia was taken; Transylvania was occupied; the Great Moravian Kingdom was trampled in pieces and the Slavs of the North and the South were sundered for ever.

No wonder old chroniclers mixed up the Magyars and the Huns! Their origins and conquests and their behaviour in earlier decades were on exactly the same lines. Like them, they became the terror of Europe; they bargained with the Roman Emperor under the walls of Constantinople, rode roughshod through Italy as far as Otranto, crossed the Rhine and ravaged Lorraine and Burgundy until at last, near Augsburg, the Emperor Otto almost annihilated them; they straggled home chastened to their huge captured territory by the Danube. Then everything began to change. In a few more decades, as we have seen, Árpád's descendant, Stephen, was king of a great Christian state; he died a saint; and the frontiers of Hungary, except for expanding later on to take in the kingdom of Croatia and then being fragmented for a century or two by the invading Turks, remained unchanged for nine hundred years. St. Stephen's momentous coronation at Esztergom in AD 1000—like Charlemagne's coronation in St. Peter's on Christmas Day 800—is one of those lucky key-dates which help to give us our bearings in this chaos.

But the Nomad procession had still not dried up. We have seen what happened with the Mongols in 1241, and how King Béla's kingdom was laid in ashes. To re-people the desert, he summoned yet another horde from the steppes, the Cumans;* and the Cumans were even worse than the Pechenegs. Vast numbers settled on the Plain; hoping to tame them, Béla married his son to a Cuman princess but the barbarians' power increased until the country was on the point of relapsing into heathen barbarism; finally the brave and clever dynasty of the Árpáds began to fail. When the last one died in 1301, the Anjous of Naples, their legal heirs, succeeded, and an able line of Angevin kings, culminating in Louis, or Lajos, the Great, resurrected the country; rebuilding began, and for a while generations of house-martins could return to the same eaves each year, and storks to their chimneys, without finding everything in ruins. But offstage, the Turks were already fidgeting in the wings.

*　　*　　*　　*

* They were called 'Kipchaks' beside their Siberian home-river, the Irtish and 'Polovtzi' in South Russia, hence the *danses polovtsiennes* in *Prince Igor*.

When I had unfolded my map under the carob tree, the Tisza river, flowing south-east to join the Danube, uncoiled straight ahead of my path; I was struck by the place-names scattered beyond the east bank: Kúncsorba, Kúnszentmartón, Kúnvegytöke, and so on. The first syllable, it seemed, meant 'Cuman' and the region was still known as Nagykunság or Great Cumania. On my side of the river, a slightly different profusion spread southwards: Kiskúnhalas, Kiskúnfélegyháza, Kiskúndorozsma. 'Kis' means 'little': they belonged to the region of Kiskunság or Little Cumania.

So this was where the Cumans had ended up! And, even closer to my route, lay a still more peculiar paper-chase of place-names. Jászboldogháza, for instance, only a few miles north; and a bit farther afield, Jászladány, Jászapáti, Jászalsószentgyörgy, and many more . . . Here the first syllable recalled a more unexpected and still hoarier race of settlers. In the third century BC, the Jazyges, an Iranian speaking branch of the Sarmatians mentioned by Herodotus, were first observed in Scythian regions near the Sea of Azov, and some of them made their way to the west. They were allies of Mithridates—Ovid speaks of them in his Black Sea exile—and, between the Danube and the Tisza, exactly where their descendants finally settled, the Romans had much trouble with them. We know just what these Jazyges looked like from the column of Marcus Aurelius in the Piazza Colonna. The bas-relief warriors—and their horses, right down to their fetlocks—are sheathed in scale-armour like pangolins. Javelins lost, and shooting backwards in the famous Parthian style, they canter with bent bows up the spiral.

Had they left any other traces in the Plain? Any dim, unexplained custom, twist of feature, scrap of language, or lingering turn of phrase? A few sparse reminders of the Pechenegs and the Cumans still flicker about the Balkans; but this entire nation seems to have vanished like will o' the wisps and only these place-names mark the points of their evaporation. There had been a time when they scattered the hemisphere all the way from the Danube's banks to the fogs of the Oxus and the hushed Chorasmian waste.

*   *   *   *

It was several days before I heard of these wild people, but I can't resist introducing them while we are in their haunts. I learnt, too, that Jászberény, an old town due north, and one of the possible sites for Attila's capital, still contained an old ivory horn carved from a tusk. Although it is really Byzantine work, it was once revered as the oliphant of Lehel, chief of one of the earliest Magyar tribes; his horn is as famous in Hungary as Roland's in the West. I already knew about Charlemagne's conquest of the Avars and I realised rather sadly that these miles on horseback were the last stretch of my itinerary still linked with the great Emperor: he had seemed to preside over the whole of the journey so far. I cursed the ignorance which had allowed me to pass Aachen without knowing it was Aix-la-Chapelle! A fully historical figure, with Alcuin of York and his court of scholars and his dates, wars, sayings and laws intact, including his strange names for the months—'Hornung', 'Ostarmonath' and the rest—he has been touched and then transformed by a cloud of fable. Fireside mutterings, legends, centuries of bards and the lays of minnesingers have set him afloat somewhere between Alexander and King Arthur, where he looms, mural-crowned, enormous, voluminously bearded, overgrown with ivy and mistletoe, announced by eagles and ravens, dogged by wolf-hounds, accompanied by angels and oriflammes and escorted by a host of prelates and monks and paladins; confused with Odin, and, like Adonis, akin to the seasons, he is ushered on his way by earthquakes and eclipses of the sun and the moon and celebrated by falling stars and lightning; horns and harps waft him across the plains; they carry him through canyons and forests and up to steep mountain-tops until his halo is caught up in the seven stars of his Wain.

In AD 802 (I had just learnt) Harun-al-Rashid had sent Charlemagne the gift of an elephant. He was called Abulahaz, Father of the Valiant, and the Emperor kept him in his park at Aachen until he was killed in a battle against the Danes. There is no mention of his route: could it have been the old Danube highway? Or Brindisi and the Appian Way? Venice or Grado, then the Adige and the Brenner—well east of Hannibal's path, this time—and finally the Rhine? *Or could the Caliph have sent him via the Hellespont or the Bosphorus?* He might have; though peril lurked in the Balkans: Krum and his boyars might have

spotted the elephant and eaten him . . . But the Great Plain, still largely
fenland and timber and cleared of Avars eight years before, was
perfect elephant-country. He had probably come from the foothills
of the Himalayas, or perhaps the swamps and *sal*-forests of Azufghur
. . . With no effort at all now, I could see Abulahaz and his mahout
and his grooms and a troop of bedouin lancers treading through the
glades and plains while Slav backwoodsmen and perhaps some stray
surviving Dacian gaped from their rough abodes. He might even have
halted a few miles further along my track, dipped his trunk in the Tisza
and deluged himself with cool jets among the shady reed-beds there.

*　　*　　*　　*

Meanwhile, traversed by the shadows of flat-bottomed clouds,
the level country was variegated still with wheatfields and lines of
poplars and orchards; once a faraway windmill broke the flatness, there
were sweep-wells everywhere and wide expanses of grass for the
pale cattle to graze on. Some of the drovers, leaning on long tomahawk-
like staves among their flocks, still wore cloaks of matted fleece; others,
felt-like homespun with complex yokes of embroidery about the
shoulders. At the entrance to farmsteads and hamlets, geese scuttled
out of their ponds and across the path with a hissing and craning of
necks that always turned into hostile beating of wings as Malek minced
carefully by; if on dry land, they rushed at the ponds and splashed
in. The women were aproned, embroidered, smocked and pleated in
many pretty and unexpected ways and their hair was coifed and
caught up in head-kerchiefs. Many of them had distaffs stuck in bright
sashes of braid. Damping thumb and forefinger with their tongues,
they pulled and twisted strands from the hanks of raw wool that
clouded their distaff-prongs, and with the other hand set them spinning
with twirls of their float-like spindles. These rose and fell like slow-
motion yoyos, gathering thicker and still thicker coils of thread; later
on, stretched on their elongated looms, they went to the weaving of
those dense and unpliant capes. A girl on a stool among the hollyhocks
outside her cottage trod and twirled at a spinning-wheel, a beautifully
carved instrument polished by generations of toil, the only one I
have ever seen in use.

Those long un-desert-like stretches have left a memory of dew and new grass and Malek's hoofs trotting through woods and flowers while the climbing sun showed so clearly through leaves and petals and grass-blades that they seemed alight. The woods flickered with redstarts and wheatears, newly arrived after amazing journeys, their giveaway rumps darting through the tree-trunks among birds with their nests already built, and in the open, crested larks flew up from the grass at our approach and sang as though they were suspended about the sky on threads. There was not a single way in which life could be improved. Malek's alert and good-tempered ears, his tireless and untiring gait and the well-being he radiated, meant that we infected each other's mood, as horse and rider often do.

I had taken too northerly a path in the dark and the unseen town of Cegléd lay to the south-west. We stopped and ate in the shade by the Zagyva river. Later, a change in the cultivation, a sudden increase in the trees and the number of wagtails told of the closeness of another river; and soon, through the willows and the enormous spreading poplars, there it was: the wide Tisza, the second river in Hungary, flowing sedately south between low banks and a flutter of reeds. Some rough boats were beached under the trees and a fisherman near the other bank toiled with a throw-net, gathering it into the boat again and again and casting it over the current in a sequence of momentary clouds.

I had been thinking about the Caliph's elephant as we trotted downstream; then, among the feathery calamus rushes, loomed a vision as unexpected and almost as arresting. Just visible above the surface of a backwater, a wide, black, porous-looking snout emerged, its flaring nostrils weighted with a heavy ring. Sweeping back from a matted clump on the brow grew enormous, crinkled and flattened horns. Dark, liquid eyes gazed with torpid resentment straight into mine. Not far off, another huge and ungainly creature, similarly equipped and plastered with mud, was lazily swishing a tasselled tail. I had passed many ox-carts on the road, but nobody had mentioned water-buffaloes and they were an awe-inspiring surprise. I saw them often after that, especially in Transylvania, wallowing in slime or yoked two and two and drawing heavy loads with unbelievable slowness and ill-will.

Stopping at a bridge that would have taken us on to Törökszent-miklos—the name commemorated the Turks, for a change, and St. Michael as well—we followed the right bank, heading for Szolnok. Soon the carts and the cattle and a pony-trap and a couple of men on horseback coming in the opposite direction hinted that a market-day was ending. Then we were in the dusty outskirts of a town and I soon found the house I was after.

Dr. Imre Hunyor, a rubicund and cheerful man, had been warned of the invasion. We headed at once for a neighbour with a stable and a paddock—the vet, I am almost sure—and put Malek in his kind hands. When we left, two red setters followed us with an eager look. A dachshund joined them. Two sheepdogs arrived. When a whole litter of nearly full-grown puppies came bounding clumsily with an expectant air, the doctor and I halted and exchanged puzzled glances. Meanwhile, two nondescript animals were coming along the lane with alert and friendly mien, and then three more, and they all gazed up as though awaiting a sign. "I wonder", Dr. Hunyor said, "if it could be *that*?" He was pointing at the saddle-bags on my arm. Still too big to fit inside, the salami with its red, white and green girdle had been sticking out under the sun all day and the evening breeze wafted its message over the puszta, until even I, inured as I was by gradual degrees, began to notice something. The dogs were wagging their tails; one or two started to bound in the air with fitful barks. Resigned to loss, I was about to toss the sausage in their midst when the doctor stayed my hand. "Nein, nein!" he said. "Es würde einen Bürgerkrieg lancieren!" It would start a civil war! So I got out my knife, sliced it into fragrant discs and set them spinning. The dogs scattered in delirium and in a moment it was all over.

* * * *

The first volume of this story tells of a thick green manuscript book I bought in Bratislava and used as a notebook and a journal and finally, five years later, at the outbreak of war, left behind by mistake in a friend's country-house in Rumania where I was living.* A few years

* The house was Baleni, in the Moldavian region of Covurlui, not far from the Prut.

ago, after decades of separation, I miraculously got it back, with its green binding a bit frayed and faded, but intact. The pencilled journal in it is a great help, but not the unintermittent stand-by it should be. I started it in Slovakia with a long entry for each day; but in towns, thanks to morning headaches perhaps, it was sometimes neglected: and it didn't always pick up at once when the journey was resumed. The same happened in Budapest and the earlier parts of the ensuing travels. Szolnok, for instance, just has the names of the town and the cheery doctor who put me up: the delicious, boiling hot, scarlet and orange carp soup bursting with paprika we had for dinner is remembered but unrecorded; the rest has gone. Next day mentions 'Baron Schossberger' and 'Pusztatenyö', a small place about a dozen miles to the south-east. Szolnok itself has left only a shadowy recollection. I remember trotting across the Tisza bridge because I halted half-way over to watch a string of rafts coming downstream between great crowds of poplars that grew tall enough along the banks to give the illusion of a pale flickering forest. The rafts disappeared under the bridge, emerged the other side, then dwindled along the current with their burdens of timber, heading for the Danube. Soon after, I reached a low country-house (where kind Dr. Hunyor had already telephoned) and saw Malek put in a loose-box during luncheon. The place belonged to a friend of Tibor v. Thuroczy, brother-in-law of Pips Schey, who had been so kind to me in Slovakia; Baron Schossberger came of a Jewish banking family in Budapest. Tall, brisk and piercing-eyed, he was a passionate farmer and he proudly stroked a newly-arrived threshing-machine as we headed for the house.

Later, as Malek and I tittuped past a sleepy railway-halt called Pusztapo, the scene clears a bit; its name has stuck only because of its oddity. Hamlets like this were hardly more than a row of thatched cottages on either side of the dusty way. Sometimes I would stop and buy some oats; when the word *kocsma* over a door or painted in white on a window-pane indicated a tavern, I would dismount and sit on the bench among the budding hollyhocks over a small glass of a fierce country schnapps called *seprü*, or *cseresznye*, when made of cherries. Sometimes, blinking in the sun and the dust, a waggoner or two might be on the same bench and, though we were incommunicado, I was

60

among friends at once because of the prevalent sympathy for horses: Malek's fine looks won all hearts, and everyone stroked him. "Nagyon szép!" they would murmur, "Very beautiful" or "Az egy szép ló", "He's a fine horse . . ." (Sketchy vocabularies are jotted in the journal here and there: *zab*, oats; *ló*, horse; *lovagolok*, I ride; *lovagolni fogok*, I will ride; *lovagolni fogok holnap Mezötúrra*, I will ride to Mezötúr tomorrow. *Gyönyörü!* excellent or first class, it continues, and *Rettenetes!*, terrible! and so on.) Sitting with the reins loose in my hands under the transparent leaves of the acacias, I felt like a lone cowboy venturing among little-known tribes and the Gypsies and the shepherds with their tomahawk-staves supplied corroborative detail.

When a village fell behind, we were alone once more in a flat and now familiar landscape, half desert and half sown, with its flocks and its herdsmen and its solitary sweep-wells and its cloud-processions along the horizon. In the late afternoon we were picking our way through another enormous herd of cattle with those long straight horns. Soon Gypsy hovels appeared and a straggle of kilns and sheds and thousands of bricks set out to dry and a rambling overgrown churchyard; then solider houses multiplied and we were on the out-skirts of the substantial country-town of Mezötúr.

Smaller than Szolnok, it was a place of some consequence neverthe-less. (Between two coffee-houses in the main street with *kávéház* help-fully inscribed across their fronts, another shop-window full of cosmetics and lotions and pictures of women with lowered lids stroking their soft complexions had a mysterious superscription: *Szépség Szálón*. After a few seconds' delay, like the working of a slow calculating machine, 'Beauty Parlour' came to the surface . . .) Many of the shops had Jewish names, German in origin but spelt in the Hungarian way. Others were simple Hungarian words—Kis, Nagy, Fehér, Fekete— which may have been translations of Klein, Gross, Weiss and Schwarz, changed during Magyarising drives in the past.* A grocer called Csillag—Stern?—set me on the right track for stabling. There were plenty of horses about and many country carts; old and battered four-wheelers with their hoods down waited patiently under the leaves or

---

* My friend R.F. has warned me about jumping to conclusions in this matter. Like many such things in Hungary, these are far more complex than they seem.

trundled about in the dusty evening light. Down a back lane at the stables I fell in with an ex-student called Miklos Lederer. He had just been apprenticed to a chemist; when Malek had been watered and fed, he helped me carry all the tack to a room in the house where he had taken digs. Half Hungarian and half Swabian, he too spoke German. Like everyone else at this time of the day, we strolled about the town, while busy swallows whisked by; there was something indefinably oriental in the atmosphere of the place. (I only discovered later on that south of varying parallels of latitude the *corso*—this universal evening promenade—was a phenomenon that stretched all the way from Portugal to the Great Wall of China.) We shared a paprika chicken in an eating-house and had coffee out of doors. Then noise and music enticed us into a much humbler *vendéglö* full of shepherds and drovers. They were tough, tousled and weather-beaten fellows in knee-boots or raw-hide moccasins lashed on with thongs, and they wore small black hats and smoked queer-looking pipes with lidded metal bowls and six-inch stems of reed or bamboo; the collars of the smarter ones, worn with no tie, were buttoned with apoplectic tightness. The instruments of the Gypsies were a violin, a 'cello, a double-bass, a czembalom and, most improbably, an ornate harp, chipped and gilded and six feet high between the knees of a very dark harpist; his sweeps across the strings added a liquid ripple to the langour and the sudden fury of the tunes. Some of the customers were groggy already: spilt liquor, glassy eyes and benign smiles abounded. Like all country people venturing into towns, new arrivals were shy and awkward at first, but this soon dissolved. One rowdy tableful, riotously calling for wilder music and for stronger wine, was close to collapse. "They will be in tears soon," Miklos said with a smile, and he was right. But they were not tears of sorrow; it was a sort of ecstasy that damped those wrinkled eye-sockets. I learnt about *mulatság* for the first time—the high spirits, that is, the rapture and the melancholy and sometimes the breakage that the stringed instruments of Gypsies, abetted by constant fluid intake, can bring about. I loved this despised music too, and when we got up to go after a couple of hours, felt touched by the same maudlin delectation. A lot of wine had passed our lips.

I wonder how much Cuman and how much Jazygian blood mingled with Hungarian in the veins of all these revellers?

*   *   *   *

Next day the clouds that usually lingered on the skyline looked like closing overhead. A menacing canopy formed and I felt a drop on my neck; Malek quivered and his ears twitched inquisitively and the dark stars that sprang up all round in the dust soon spread and cohered in a wet pockmarked stippling as the rain swept down. It didn't last long. The sun broke through and a rainbow hooped the middle distance. The clouds scattered again, Malek's glistening coat and my shirt were soon dry, and a cool, damp breath of wind and fresh rainy hues transformed the fields and the trees. I wish I had seen the *fata-morgana* which haunts the Great Plain in the summer months; but beyond the thin wet-looking lines that bright sunlight sometimes lays across distant surfaces, there was no sign of it. I had read and heard of the Alföld dust-devils. Maelstroms of dust and straw and dead leaves twirl in the wind and climb to enormous heights and then revolve across the plain at great speed, seeming to mop and mow like rushing phantoms as they go; but autumn is the time for them and I only saw these portents much later, on the Baragan, that desolate expanse of steppe across the river from the Dobrudja in the Danube's penultimate loop.

A wood lay ahead and, all of a sudden, out of the silence a cuckoo began calling. It grew louder as we approached and so clear that the horse's ears twitched again. The strange flat scene, the rainbow and the sudden cuckoo—a sound, like the nightingale, which everyone considers their private property—brought on an abrupt and unexpected onslaught of homesickness. Why was I ranging this beautiful landscape instead of familiar woods and hills in England, a thousand miles west? When we got under the branches, a collusion of tree-trunks stressed and expanded this mood: the place might have been an English spinney. Hazel, elder, dog-roses and cow-parsley grew in a clearing and raindrops lay in the hollows of leaves. There were old man's beard and deadly nightshade and brambles that another couple of months would cover with blackberries; a blackbird, pecking in the dead leaves, flew up and

63

perched among branches aslant with sunbeams. There were two goldfinches, a thrush and a blackcap. Taken unawares, I sat under a tree and ate bread and cheese sprinkled with paprika and then an apple and smoked cigarette after cigarette listening to the cuckoo, the blackbird's song and the thrush's encore while Malek cropped the grass a yard away. The birds were all dominated by the cuckoo; it sounded as though he were perched just overhead, and I could still hear him when the wood was far behind.

Poppies scattered the green crops, the smell of hay, clover and lucerne floated in the air, and tawny-maned horses grazed. I wished the journey would never end. But the next halt, beyond another green line of trees, was the last, and in spite of dawdling over this final equestrian stage, too short a ride. Following a railway line, I was soon crossing a bridge over a fast-flowing river and then riding into Gyoma. The agent of Malek's owner had a friend there to whom I was to surrender him. I thought that the return journey to that leafy, half-glimpsed château near Budapest might be a difficult business; but when I said so, the friend brushed the suggestion aside. Nothing would be easier; he would put Malek in charge of someone going to the capital next day—according to a signpost, it was only 166 kilometres to Budapest—and he would be home in a few hours. I handed him over with a heavy heart.

Dr. vitéz Haviar Gyula was tall, dark and slightly eastern-looking with heavy-lidded eyes, a swooping nose, high narrow temples and a rather sad smile. I wondered if he could have been of Armenian descent: numbers of these, respected for their nimble wits and teased for their prominent noses, were scattered about the country like little gatherings of toucans. But it wasn't an Armenian name, nor yet Hungarian. Rumanian names originating in a profession—equivalent of 'Potter' or 'Tyler'—sometimes ended in -ar, but not here, I think: well-known engravings of Kossuth and Deák hung in his drawing room and apart from the not very fluent German in which we conversed, Magyar was his only language. I had dinner with him and his family in a restaurant in the main street under a new moon and a trellis heavy with lilac (orgona in Magyar; the word has suddenly surfaced in my mind after nearly half a century). The air was motionless after the shower and it was suddenly very hot. The little town was full of evening strollers and many of them halted at our table for a chat; I had a mental glimpse of what towns on the Great Plain must be like in August. Dinner, and then bed appeared as though pre-ordained. Raven-fed like Elijah, I was no longer surprised; but never stopped rejoicing.

I emptied the saddle-bag on a chair next day to re-pack my rucksack and when some sketches dropped out Mrs Haviar gathered them up. They weren't very good but she asked me to do a drawing of her daughter, Erszi, an amazing and pretty little girl of about ten. I had often done sketches in Germany and Austria as a kind of thank-offering to hosts—no one seemed to mind their inexpertness—so I jumped at the suggestion and Erszi ran off excitedly to tidy her hair. When she was still not back after ten minutes, they gave her a shout and she arrived looking extraordinary in a cloche hat of her mother's, long ear-rings and a fox stole; she had covered her face with powder and had turned her lips into a sticky Cupid's bow. Perching on a tuffet, she crooked a bangled wrist on her hip while her other hand flourished a twelve-inch cigarette-holder and tapped off the ash with vampish langour. It was convincing and rather eerie, an advanced case of lamb dressed up as mutton. "Isn't she silly?" her mother said fondly. I'm not sure the sketch did her justice.

Later, back in her ordinary clothes, she and her father and I set off for Malek's quarters. I was armed with some valedictory lumps of sugar and steeled for an Arab's farewell to his steed. We found Malek fooling about with some ponies at the far end of a paddock but when I called him he cantered over with a gratifying flutter of mane and tail and I patted the blaze on his brow and stroked his beautiful arched neck for the last time. I said goodbye and set off. My sitter, still elated by her recent avatar, kept waving and jumping up and down and shouting "Viszontlátásra!" until we were all out of earshot.

*   *   *   *

The Körös kept me company the whole day. The river was banked against flooding and all of it was wooded, so branches dappled the path and the river's edge with shadows all the way. Thistledown fluff from the willow-herb span across the water and diving frogs marked almost every step. Reeds and tall clumps of bullrushes sheltered families of moorhens, and purple dragonflies hovered and settled among the yellow flags. When I sat down for a smoke, an abrupt movement gave away an otter; he looked about, then ran along the root of a willow and slipped in with a plop which stirred the backwater with spreading rings. There was plenty of food for him: fish gleamed in the clear water and, a little further upstream, two boys were busy with long reeds and cork floats. Their catch was strung through the gills inside a hollow tree and we had scarcely exchanged greetings when there was a silver flash and another was whisked leaping out of the current. When I said "Eljen!"—Bravo! I hoped—they offered to give it to me but I felt shy about turning up at my next halt like Tobias. Cattle gathered under the branches and waded knee-deep while flocks, filling every inch of shade in the fields, hid from the noonday as still as fossils.

An abrupt swarm of Gypsies made me look among the tents and the carts in case they were my friends from north of Cegléd, but in vain. Men with bill-hooks carried long sheaves of reeds on their heads that bounced up and down as they walked. Women were thigh-deep in the water, washing and wringing out their rags and their tattered finery, and then festooning them over the undergrowth and branches, while troops of boys, like the ones on the Slovak shore at Easter, scoured the banks for the lairs of their just-edible quarry—voles, weasels, water-rats and so on. They left the serious work to their little sisters, who trotted tirelessly alongside their only prospect of the day, calling out "Bácsi! Bácsi!"—for the masculine prey of small Gypsies are all honorary uncles; and their shrill uncle-uncle cries continued for about a furlong. When the reproachful diminuendo had died away I was alone again with nothing but swallows curvetting through the shadows or the occasional blue-green flash of a kingfisher to ruffle the stillness of leaves and water.

Early in the afternoon, the river branched and I went upstream beside the Sebes (swift) Körös, until a red-shingled steeple told me I had reached the old village of Körösladány.

The look of the Magyar word *kastély*—which is rather perversely pronounced 'koshtay', or very nearly—suggests, like *Schloss*, a fortified and castellated building, but the nearest English equivalent to most of those I saw in Hungary and Transylvania would be a manor house and the term leaps to mind when I try to conjure up the memory, blurred at the edges a little by the intervening decades, of the *kastély* at Körösladány. Single-storeyed like a ranch but with none of the ad hoc feeling the word suggests, it was a long ochre-coloured late eighteenth-century building with convoluted and rounded baroque pediments over great gates, faded tiles and house-martins' nests and louvred shutters hooked back to let in the late afternoon light. Leaving my things under the antlers in the hall, I was led through the open doors of several connecting rooms, meeting my hostess at the middle of a shadowy enfilade. She was charming and good-looking with straight, bobbed fair hair—I think it must have been parted in the middle for it was this, a few years later, that reminded me of her when I met Iris Tree. She wore a white linen dress and espadrilles and had a cigarette-case and a lit cigarette in her hand. "So here's the traveller," she said in a kind, slightly husky voice and took me through a french window to where the rest of her family, except her husband, who was due back from Budapest next day, were assembled round tea things under tall chestnut trees whose pink and white steeples were stickily bursting out. I can see them gathered like a conversation piece by Copley or Vuillard, and can almost catch their reflection in the china and silver. They were Countess Ilona Meran, just described, a son and daughter called Hansi and Marcsi, about thirteen and fourteen, and a much smaller girl called Helli, all three of them very good-looking and nice-mannered and a little grave. There was a friend, perhaps a relation, with horn-rimmed spectacles, called Christine Esterházy, and an Austrian governess. All except the last spoke English; but I can't remember a word that was uttered—only their appearance and the scene under the wide leaves and the charm of the hour. We sat talking until it was lighting-up time, and indoors pools of lamp-light were being kindled with spills along the succession of lavender-smelling rooms. It lit the backs of bindings, pictures, furniture which had reached exactly the right pitch of faded country-house shabbiness, curtains laundered hundreds of times over and music open above the keys of a piano. What music? I can't remember; but suddenly, sailing into my mind after all these years, there is a bowl on the piano full of enormous white and red peonies and a few petals have dropped on the polished floor.

While getting tidy for dinner, and later, before going to bed, I looked at the pictures on the walls of my room. There was a Schloss Glanegg poised on a precipitous rock and many Almásy kinsmen of Countess Ilona and several Wenckheims in furred and scimitared glory; and there was an early nineteenth-century colour print that I was very taken by. It showed a dashing post-Regency buck—I think he was called Zichy—with twirling beard and whiskers, a blue bird's-eye stock and an English scarlet hunting coat. He was one of those tremendous Hungarian centaurs who became famous in the Shires for the intrepid way they rode to hounds. Lounging about the lawn meet at Badminton, or in Ackermann prints of calamities at cut-and-laid fences, hounds in full cry, drawing Ranksborough Gorse, leaping the Whissendine Brook, chasing across green parishes from spire to spire, there they are; and, most notably, in those evening celebrations round laden tables, where bang-up Corinthians in evening pink, jumping to their feet among scattered napkins and wine-coolers and empty bottles, flourish glasses in boisterous unison. The outline-keys in the corner, among the Osbaldestones and the Assheton-Smiths, often bear the names of one or two of these Nimrods from the Great Plain.*

In the library the following day, while lessons went on next door, I found out as much as I could about the Alföld, until it was time to set off for a picnic. A kind of victoria bowled up to the front on twinkling spokes, and everyone piled in. I was very struck by the hat which went with the coachman's black-frogged livery. It was a sort of black felt pork-pie—or could it have been velvet?—with a brim turned up perpendicular and a black ostrich feather across the crown, fixed in a semicircle from front to back while two black ribands ending in fishtails fluttered behind. Was it a legacy of the Turkish spahis or the janissaries; or could it have survived from the early invading Magyars? (Such were the themes I brooded on these days.) There were many

* Esterházy, perhaps or Count Sándor, Pauline Metternich's father; and, later, though he was from Bohemia, the Grand-National-winning Kinsky.

flourished hats and greetings on the way out and when we had driven about half a mile a quavering hail came from the wayside. Countess Ilona stopped the carriage, jumped down, and in a moment was being embraced by an old crone in a head-kerchief, and after cries of recognition and much talk and laughter—some tears, I think, and more embraces—she climbed in again, obviously moved: she kept waving back till we were out of sight. She was the mother of somebody from the village who had migrated to America fifteen years before and grown homesick. She had only been back two days.

We settled on a grassy bank under some willows at a bend in the Körös and feasted there while the horses munched and swished their tails in the shade a little way off. A heron glided through the branches and subsided among the flag-leaves on a midstream shoal. We were on the edge of a large wood. It was full of birds, and in the hushed afternoon hour when talk had languished, three roe deer, with antlers beginning to spring, stole down the river's edge. There was some quiet singing on the way home, prompted by a song from the fields; Austrian and German and English and Hungarian. I was tongue-tied in the last, but they knew *Érik a, érik a búza kalász*, my favourite from Budapest. No song could have been more fitting: we were driving beside a wheat field where swallows dipped and swerved above green ears that would soon be turning, just as the song described. It was the hour of jangling bells and lowing and bleating as flocks and cattle, all fiery in golden dust clouds, converged on the village, and our return to the *kastély* coincided with its owner's arrival. Graf Johann—or Hansi—Meran was very tall with dark hair and moustache and fine aquiline looks that were marked by an expression of great kindness. His children dashed upon him and when he had disentangled himself he greeted the others by kissing first hands then cheeks in that simultaneously polite and affectionate way I had first seen in Upper Austria.

The charms of this place and its inhabitants sound unrelievedly and improbably perfect. I am aware of this, but I can only set it down as it struck me. Also the stay had another dimension, an unexpected one which gave sudden reality to whole fragments of European history of a century earlier and more. Once again, pictures in my room put me on the track. One of these showed Archduke Charles, flag in hand, charging the Napoleonic army through the reeds of Aspern. (His statue opposite Prince Eugene on the Heldenplatz in Vienna shows him at the same moment, on a frenetically rearing steed. How surprised he would have been! He had refused all statues and honours during his lifetime.) I had first become aware of him when I gazed across the Danube at the Marchfeld after leaving Vienna: it was there, a few miles from Wagram, that the battle, the first allied victory over Napoleon, was fiercely fought and won. The next print showed his brother, the subject of that endless song in deep Styrian dialect called the *Erzherzog-Johanns-Lied*: I had first heard it at an inn opposite Pöchlarn and often since. These brothers, two of many, were grandchildren of Maria Theresa, nephews of Marie Antoinette, and sons of Leopold II; and their elder brother, who succeeded as Francis II, was the last Holy Roman Emperor. (Lest Napoleon should attempt to usurp it, he gave up the stupendous honour and became Emperor of Austria, just over a thousand years after the crowning of Charlemagne.)

But Archduke Johann was the most interesting of them. He courageously led an army against Napoleon at the age of eighteen, governed provinces with wisdom and justice and was often called to high office at critical times. Intelligent, determined and steeped in the principles of Rousseau, he was a lifelong opponent of Metternich and his passion for the simplicities of life in the mountains made him a sort of uncrowned king of the Alps from Croatia to Switzerland. In the romantic picture in my room, made about 1830, he was leaning on an alpenstock among forested peaks, a fowling piece on his shoulder, and a broad-brimmed wideawake was thrust back from a thoughtful brow. What a relief to record the qualities of these Habsburg paragons! Courage, wisdom, capacity, imagination and a passion for justice led them in ways deeply at variance with the ill-starred fortunes of their dynasty, and this particular prince put the final touch to his abhorrence of the capital by a morganatic marriage to the daughter of a Styrian postmaster. She and their children were given a title from what was then Meran, in the South Tyrol, now Merano in the Alto Adige.

"Yes," Countess Ilona said when I asked about him, "he was Hansi's great-grandfather, and there", pointing to a picture, "is the charming Anna. She was terrifically pleased when she thought their first child showed signs of a Habsburg lip, poor mite!" (There was not much sign of it in her husband and it seemed entirely to have vanished from their children.) She told me the whole tale with patience and humour, abetted now and then by Count Hansi, who was smoking and reading a paper in a nearby armchair. "I must say," she continued with a laugh, "when there was all that fuss and talk a few years ago about who should be King, I couldn't help thinking"—and here she nodded in the Count's direction—"why not *him*?" Her husband said, "Now, now!" disapprovingly, and after a few seconds, laughed to himself and went on with his paper.

*　　*　　*　　*

I half wished, when I set off, that my plans were leading me in another direction, for a couple of days' march north-east would have brought me to the Hortobágy desert and its herds of wild horses and their fierce and famous herdsmen. (Rather surprisingly these spurred and whip-cracking gauchos were strict Protestants; Debrecen, their steppe capital, had been a Calvinist stronghold since the Reformation.) But I had been swayed by the old maps in the library the day before and there were satisfactory hints of remoteness and desolation in the south-eastern route I was actually taking. A hundred years ago much of this stretch of the Alföld resembled a vast bog relieved by a few oases of higher ground. Hamlets were grudgingly scattered and, unlike the old village of Körösladány, many of these were nineteenth-century settlements which had sprung up when the marsh was drained. The air of desolation was confirmed by those tall and catapult-like sweep-wells rearing their timbers into the emptiness. In the southern parts of the Cuman region celebrated by Petőfi—it is strange how the names of Hungarian poets cropped up the whole time in conversation and books!—heavy rains often marooned the villages on their small hills, until they formed little archipelagoes only to be reached in flat-bottomed boats. But, to redress the balance, there were regions near Szeged which July and August dried up into glittering tracts of soda crystals, and to unwary travellers, already perplexed by mirages and dust-devils, these crystalline acres must have completed the summer's hallucinations. Shallow lakes had been known to dry up completely then fill once more until, after a short evolutionary gap, reeds grew again, fish swam, tadpoles followed and frogs began to croak. It was refreshing to think of the unchanging carp-filled lakes of the south-west and the teeming abundance of the Tisza; and what about the fish those boys had been whisking out of the swift Körös by the armful? When the forlorn woods that lay all about me were no-man's-land still, betyárs infested them: affable highwaymen and brigands who held travellers to ransom, drove away flocks and herds and levied tribute from noblemen islanded in their castles. It was a region of hazards, legends and fierce deeds.

I hadn't far to go. Virtuously shunning the offer of a lift in a pony-trap, I slogged on to Vesztö and reached it in the afternoon. Count Lajos—Louis that is, though he was always referred to by a nickname—was a cousin of my Körösladány friends. (In Central Europe, in those days, if you met one Count, you were likely, if you also came across his kith and kin, to run into a whole team of them. The polymath of the Wachau was very entertaining about this proliferation of prefixes, including his own. "Count and earl are more or less equated," he said, "so if Tennyson's Lady Clara Vere de Vere had been born in this part of the world, she could easily have been the grandmother of a hundred earls, instead of merely their daughter—with a bit of luck, of course. Ten sons, with another ten apiece. There's a hundred for you—instead of only one, as in England.")

I found him strolling in the avenue that led to the house. He must have been about thirty-five. He had a frail look, a slight tremor, and an expression of anguish—not only with me, I was relieved to see—which a rather sorrowful smile lit up. A natural tendency to speak slowly had been accentuated by a bad motor-crash brought about by falling asleep at the wheel. There was something touching and very nice about him, and as I write, I am looking at a couple of sketches in the back of my notebook; not good ones, but a bit of this quality emerges.

German was his only alternative to Magyar. He said, "Come and see my *Trappen*!" I didn't understand the last word, but we strolled to the other side of the house where two enormous birds were standing under the trees. A first glance suggested a mixture of goose and turkey but they were bigger and nobler and heftier than either and, at a closer look, totally different; the larger bird was well over a yard from beak to tail. His neck was pale grey with a maroon collar, his back and his wings a speckled reddish buff and strange weeping whiskers swept backwards from his beak like a slipstream of pale yellow Dundrearies. Their gait was stately; when our advent sent them scuttling, Lajos made me hang back. He approached them and scattered grain and the larger bird allowed his head to be scratched. To Lajos's distress, their wings had been clipped by the farmer who had found them the month before, but when the larger bird opened his, and then spread a fine fan-shaped tail like a turkey's, he looked, for a moment, completely white, but turned dark again as he closed them. They were Great Bustards, rare and wild birds that people wrongly related to the ostrich. They love desolate places like the puszta and Lajos planned to keep them till their feathers had grown enough for them to fly away again. He loved birds and had a way with them, for these two followed him up the steps with a stately pace, then through the drawing-room and the hall to the front door and, when he shut it, we could hear them tapping on it from time to time with their beaks.

At dinner he talked of the spring and autumn migrations of cranes and wild geese. These sometimes travel in a wedge formation, at others beak to tail for miles on end; unlike storks which, as I had seen a couple of weeks ago, move in an endless, loose-knit mob as ragged as nomads in the Dark Ages. I knew he was an excellent shot. He had been talking about woodcock and, when I thought he had finished, he said, very slowly, "Their Latin name is *Scolopax*." A long pause followed; then he said, "*rusticola*", and finally, after an even longer pause, he added another "*rusticola*" as a trance-like afterthought.

His wife was away and during dinner and afterwards, as we sat and chatted by lamplight, the house had a lonely feeling (I suppose that is when the sketches were done; it looks like it by the shading) and when he asked me to stay on for a day or two, I felt it was not just from mere politeness; but I had to get on.

★　　★　　★　　★

Breakfast was brought into a sunny room near his quarters. "I'm not much of an early bird," he said, holding out his cup for some more coffee. He was still in slippers and a smocked old-fashioned nightshirt with the initials W.L.* on the breast under a discreet nine-pointed coronet and I felt sure, as I listened to the almost dreaming pace of his discourse, that a kind heart was beating underneath. Afterwards, people kept coming in and out for orders: some of them kissed hands and the room was soon full of slow gossip and laughter. There was a Molière touch about the mood of the hour, a hint of the *petit lever du roi*; and as he slowly dressed, taking each new bit of apparel from an attentive Jeeves-like figure, he answered his visitors and agents in hasteless and spell-bound tones and finally emerged in a plus-four suit and well polished brogues. He took some maize from a basket in the hall and we went to see the bustards.

"Don't you carry a walking-stick?" Lajos asked in the hall, as I put on my rucksack, about to set off. I said mine was lost. He picked one out of the stand and rather solemnly gave it to me. "Here! A souvenir from Vesztö. My old shepherd used to make them, but he's dead now." It was a very handsome stick, beautifully balanced and intricately carved all over with a pattern of leaves, and embowered in them, a little way down the shaft, were the arms of Hungary: the fesses on the dexter side were the country's rivers, while a triple hillock on the sinister, with a two-barred cross in the middle, symbolised the mountain ranges and the presiding faith, and over them both was the apostolic crown with its lop-sided cross. I was excited by such a present. It was a timely one too: my last one had gone astray a week earlier. Taking Malek's stirrup-leathers up a hole, I had stuck my ash-plant in a bush and, once in the saddle, forgot about it. (Perhaps it's still there. The ferrule had come off so it may have taken root and shot up fifty feet by now.)

I was due that evening, after an easy day's walk, at yet another kinsman of his. "Yes," he said, "there are lots of us, aber wir sind wie die Erdäpfel, der beste Teil unter der Erde"—"We are like potatoes, the best part is underground"—and I couldn't make out whether this was very profound or the reverse. When we said goodbye, I looked back

* Surname and Christian name are reversed in Hungary.

and saw him scattering grain to the huge advancing birds.

★　★　★　★

At one moment the plain looked empty for miles; and at another, soon after, you were among fields and water-meadows, or, as though it had suddenly risen from the puszta, walking across the yard of a moor-farm full of ducks and guinea fowl. (In reality, the opposite sometimes occurred: large buildings had been known to sink five or six feet into the soft soil.) I reached Doboz after dark and got a boisterous welcome from Lajos's cousin László: word of the hazard moving across the south-east Alföld must have got about and thank God I shall never know whether it loomed as a threat or as a bit of a joke. It was treated as the latter by Graf László (or rather, gróf, in Hungary) and the moment we had settled down over drinks, I had to recount the journey to him and his fair-haired grófnö. He was rubicund and dashing and she—as I had been told but had forgotten—was English, indeed from London, "as you can tell," she said cheerfully. She had been on the stage—"not in a very highbrow way, I believe," someone had said—as a dancer or a singer, and though she was no longer a sylph, one could see how pretty she must have been, and how nice she was. Both of them radiated kindness. In Germany and Austria, after I had revealed what I was up to, the first question had invariably been: where were my mother and father? When I had said, "In India and England," a second question always followed, "Und was denkt Ihre Frau Mama davon?"—"What does your Mamma think of it? She must miss you, wandering all over the place like this . . ." and so it was today. I told them all was well and that I wrote to her often.

They showed concern, too, about my crossing the frontier into Rumania. Neither of them had been there, but they were full of foreboding. "It's a terrible place!" they said. "They are all robbers and crooks! You can't trust them. They'll take everything you've got, and"—voices sank collusively here—"whole valleys are riddled with VD, oh do beware!" I could see from their earnest looks that they really meant it and began to experience a touch of misgiving as well as excitement. My days on the Slovakian bank of the Danube, where most of the inhabitants were Hungarians, had given me the first hint of the strength of Hungarian irredentist convictions. The bias against the Slovaks was strong; but, since the loss of Transylvania at the Treaty of Trianon, the very mention of Rumania made them boil over, and I think the amputation was even more angrily and bitterly resented than the loss of Slovakia; far more than the cession of the southern part of pre-war Hungary to Yugoslavia. I shall have to go into this harrowing and insoluble problem later on. This was by no means the first time the subject had cropped up, so I knew how fiercely feelings ran.

Suddenly my hostess ran upstairs and came down holding a neat leather container that looked just too big for a pack of cards. "You *must* take care of yourself, dear," she said. Gróf László nodded gravely. I wondered what it could contain. The thought flitted through my mind, but only for a wild second, that it might be some counter-charm to the insidious medical threat of those valleys. "One comes across all sorts of rum people on tours! This was given me years and years ago by an admirer of mine," she went on. "It's no use to me now so do please take it." When the leather flap came out of its slot, it revealed a minute automatic pistol that could be described as 'a lady's weapon'; the butt was plated with mother-of-pearl and there was a box of rounds of a very small bore. It was the kind of thing women on the stage whisk out of reticules when their honour is at stake. I was rather thrilled and very touched. But their anxiety, which had no foundation as it turned out, was very real.

*   *   *   *

I was halted next day by the Körös. There was no bridge in sight, so I followed a bank teeming with rabbits until an old fisherman, pale as a ghost and dressed all in white, sculled me to the other side. The people in the inn looked different and I pricked my ears at the sound of a Slav language. They were Slovaks who had come here centuries ago, hundreds of miles from their old abode, to settle in the empty region when the Turks were driven out, devout Lutherans of the Augsburg Confession, unlike the Protestants of Debrecen who were Calvinists to a man.

The distance was getting longer than I had reckoned. For once, I sighed for a lift; I didn't want to be late, and just as the wish took shape, a cloud of dust appeared on the path and then a governess-cart with a fleece-capped driver and two nuns. One of the sisters made room with a smile and a clatter of beads. We drove several miles and the town of Békéscsaba hovered far away to the right, with the twin steeples of the Catholic cathedral and the great tea-cosy of the Protestants' green copper dome glimmering beyond the tall maize-stalks. Both had vanished again when they put me down at my turning. The nuns were rather impressed when I told them my destination, and so was I.

László's elder brother Józsi (Joseph), head of that numerous family, and his wife Denise were the only two of all my benefactors on the Great Plain I had met before. It had been at a large, rather grand luncheon at their house on the slopes of Buda and when they had heard I was heading for the south-east, they had asked me to stay. Another brother, Pál, a diplomatist with the urbane and polished air of a Hungarian Norpois, said, "Do go! Józsi's a great swell in those parts. It's a strange house, but we're very fond of it."

Once through the great gates, I was lost for a moment. A forest of huge exotic trees mingled with the oaks and the limes and the chestnuts. Magnolias and tulip trees were on the point of breaking open, the branches of biblical cedars swept in low fans, all of them ringing with the songs of thrushes and blackbirds and positively slumbrous with the cooing of a thousand doves, and the house in the middle, when the trees fell back, looked more extraordinary with every step. It was a vast ochre-coloured pile, built, on the site of an older building perhaps, in the last decades of the nineteenth century. Blois, Amboise and Azay-les-Rideaux (which I only knew from photographs) immediately floated into mind. There were pinnacles, pediments, baroque gables, ogees, lancets, mullions, steep slate roofs, towers with flags flying and flights of covered stairs ending in colonnades of flattened arches.

Great wings formed a courtyard and, from a terrace leading to a ceremonial door, branching and balustraded steps descended in a sweep. As I was crossing this *place d'armes*, several people were coming down the steps, and one of them was Count Józsi. Forewarned by László, he spotted me at once. He waved a greeting and cried, "You are just what we need! Come along!" I followed him and the others across the yard to a shed. "Have you ever played bike-polo?" he asked, catching me by the elbow. I had played a version of it at school with walking sticks and a tennis-ball on the hard tennis-courts; it was thought rather disreputable. But here they had real polo-sticks cut down to the right size and a proper polo ball and the shed was full of battered but sturdy machines. Józsi was my captain, and a famous player of the real game called Bethlen had the rival team; two other guests and two footmen and a groom were the rest of the players. The game was quick, reckless and full of collisions, but there was nothing to match the joy of hitting the ball properly: it made a loud smack and gave one a tempting glimmer of what the real thing might be like. I couldn't make out why all shins weren't barked to the bone; nor why, as one of the goals backed on the house, none of the windows were broken. The other side won but we scored four goals, and when the iron Maltese Cats were back in their stands, we limped back to the steps, where Countess Denise and her sister Cecile and some others had been leaning on the balustrade like ladies gazing down into the lists.

What luck those nuns turning up, I thought a bit later, lapping down whisky and soda out of a heavy glass! Someone took me along a tall passage to my room and I found one of the young polo-playing footmen there, spick and span once more, but looking puzzled as he tried in vain to lay out the stuff from my rucksack in a convincing array. We were reciprocally tongue-tied, but I laughed and so did he: knocking one another off bicycles breaks down barriers. I got into a huge bath.

Countess Denise and Count Józsi were first cousins and earlier generations had been similarly related. "We are more intermarried than the Ptolemies," she told me at dinner. "We all ought to be insane." She and Cecile had dark hair and beautiful features and shared the rather sad expression of the rest of the family; but it likewise dissolved in friendly warmth when they smiled. Her husband's distinguished face, under brushed-back greying hair, had the same characteristic. (In a fit of melancholy when he was very young he had fired a bullet through his breast, just missing his heart.) He looked very handsome in an old claret-coloured smoking jacket. Dürer's family came from the neighbouring town of Gyula, the Countess said; the

Hungarian Ajtós—'doorkeeper'—was translated into the old German Thürer—then into Dürer when the family migrated and set up as gold- and silversmiths in Nuremberg. Afterwards in the drawing room, my footman friend approached Count Józsi carrying an amazing pipe with a cherry-wood stem over a yard long and an amber mouthpiece. The meerschaum bowl at the end was already alight, and, resting this comfortably on the crook of his ankle, the Count was soon embowered in smoke. Seeing that another guest and I were fascinated by it, he called for two more of these calumets and a few minutes later in they came, already glowing; before they were offered, the mouthpieces were dipped in water. The delicious smoke seemed the acme of oriental luxury, for these pipes were the direct and unique descendants of those long chibooks that all Levant travellers describe and all the old prints depict; the Turks of the Ottoman Empire used them as an alternative to the nargileh. (That sinuous affair, the Turkish hookah, still survived all over the Balkans and before summer was out I was puffing away at them, half-pasha and half-caterpillar, in many a Bulgarian khan. But Hungary was the only country in the world where the chibook still lingered. In Turkey itself, as I discovered that winter, it had vanished completely, like the khanjar and the yataghan.)

Ybl, the architect of the castle, had given himself free rein with armorial detail. Heraldic beasts abounded, casques, crowns and mantelling ran riot and the family's emblazoned swords and eagles' wings were echoed on flags and bed-curtains and counterpanes. The spirits of Sir Walter Scott and Dante Gabriel Rossetti seemed to preside over the place and as I had been steeped in both of them from my earliest years, anything to do with castles, sieges, scutcheons, tournaments and crusades still quickened the pulse, so the corroborative detail of the castle was close to heart's desire.

Wheat fields scattered with poppies enclosed the wooded gardens and the castle, and when we got back from a ride through them next morning, my hostess's sister Cecile looked at her watch and cried out, "I'll be late for Budapest!" We accompanied her to a field where a small aeroplane was waiting; she climbed in and waved, the pilot swung the propeller, the grass flattened like hair under a drier and they were gone. Then Szigi, the son of the house, took me up the tower and we looked out over an infinity of crops with shadows of clouds floating serenely across them. He was going to Ampleforth in a few terms, he said: what was it like? I told him I thought it was a very good school and that the monks umpired matches with white coats over their habits, and he seemed satisfied with these scant items. Exploring the library, I was fascinated by a remote shelf full of volumes of early nineteenth-century debates in the Hungarian Diet; not by the contents—humdrum stuff about land-tenure, irrigation, the extension or limitation of the franchise and so on—but because they were all in Latin, and I was amazed to learn that in Parliament until 1839, and even in the county courts, no other language was either spoken or written.

The bicycle polo after tea was even rougher than the day before. One chukka ended in a complete pile-up and as we were extricating ourselves, our hostess called from the balustrade.

A carriage with two horses and a coachman in a feathered and ribboned hat was drawing up at the foot of the steps. Dropping his stick, our host went over to help the single passenger out, and when he had alighted, bowed. This tall, slightly stooping newcomer, with white hair and beard of an Elizabethan or Edwardian cut, a green Alpine hat and a loden cape, was Archduke Joseph. Living on a nearby estate, he belonged to a branch of the Habsburgs which had become Hungarian and during the troubled period after Hungary's defeat and revolution, he had briefly been Palatine of the kingdom—a sort of regent, that is—until the victorious Allies dislodged him. Our hostess had been coming down the stairs as the Archduke was slowly climbing them, calling in a quavering voice, "Kezeit csókólóm kedves Denise grófnö!"—"I kiss your hand, dear Countess Denise";—and when he stooped to do so, she curtseyed, and, diagonally and simultaneously, they both sank about nine inches on the wide steps and recovered again as though in slow motion. When we had been led up steaming and dishevelled and presented, we leaped back into the saddle and pedalled and slashed away till it was too dark to see.

I was lent something more presentable than my canvas trousers and gym shoes for dinner. The Archduke joined in the chibook smoking afterwards and the memory of those aromatic fumes still enclouds the last night and the last house on the Great Plain.

*　*　*　*

Someone had said (though I don't think it was exact) that the Rumanian authorities let no one over the frontier on foot: the actual crossing had to be made by train. So all next day I threaded my way through cornfields in the direction of Lökösháza, the last station before the frontier: an empty region with a few farms and innumerable skylarks, where crops alternated with grazing. A compass forgotten in a rucksack-pocket kept me on a south-easterly course along a loose skein of byways. There were spinneys of aspens and frequent swampy patches and the sound of curlews; goslings and ducklings followed their leaders along village paths. The only traffic was donkey-carts and long, high-slung waggons fitted with hooped canvas. Driven by tow-haired Slovaks, they tooled along briskly behind strong horses with fair manes and tails, harnessed three abreast like troikas. Crimson tassels decorated their harnesses and colts and fillies, tethered on either side, cantered along industriously to keep up. The plain rang with cuckoos.

I fetched up at a hay-rick at the approach of dusk. A wide ledge had been sliced two-thirds of the way up and a ladder conveniently left. I was soon up it, unwrapping the buttered rolls and smoked pork and pears they had given me at O'Kigyos. Then I finished off the wine I had broached at noon. The sudden solitude, and going to bed at the same time as the birds, seemed a bit sad after this week of cheerful evenings; but this was counter-balanced by the fun of sleeping out for the fourth time, and the knowledge that I was near the beginning of a new chapter of the journey. Wrapped in my greatcoat and with my head on my rucksack, I lay and smoked—carefully, because of the combustibility of my sweet-smelling nest—and gave myself up to buoyant thoughts. It was like my first night-out by the Danube: I had the same almost ecstatic feeling that nobody knew where I was, not even a swineherd this time; and, except that I regretted leaving Hungary, all prospects glowed. Not that I had seen the last of the Hungarians, thank Heavens: pre-arranged stopping-places already sprinkled the western marches of Transylvania; but faint worry, coupled with a hint of guilt, hung in the air: I had meant to live like a tramp or a pilgrim or a wandering scholar, sleeping in ditches and ricks and only consorting with birds of the same feather. But recently I had been strolling from castle to castle, sipping Tokay out of cut-glass goblets and smoking pipes a yard long with archdukes instead of halving gaspers with tramps. These deviations could hardly be condemned as climbing: this suggests the dignity of toil, and these unplanned changes of level had come about with the effortlessness of ballooning. The twinges weren't very severe. After all, in Aquitaine and Provence, wandering scholars often hung about châteaux; and, I continued to myself, a compensating swoop of social frogmanship nearly always came to the rescue.

*   *   *   *

Scattered with poppies, the golden-green waves of the cornfields faded. The red sun seemed to tip one end of a pair of scales below the horizon, and simultaneously to lift an orange moon at the other. Only two days off the full, it rose behind a wood, swiftly losing its flush as it floated up, until the wheat loomed out of the twilight like a metallic and prickly sea.

An owl woke in the wood, and a bit later, the sound of rustling brought me back from the brink of sleep. Stalks and wheat-ears swished together and two pale shapes scampered into the open, chased about the stubble, then halted, gazing at each other raptly. They were two hares. Looking much bigger than life-size, motionless and moonstruck, they were sitting bolt-upright with ears pricked.

4

The Marches of Transylvania

WHEN THE EVENING TRAIN from Budapest arrived, I had been hanging about the station platform at Lökösháza since noon and by the time I had climbed in and the red-white-and-green Hungarian flag had disappeared, night had fallen.

This borderland was the most resented frontier in Europe and recent conversations in Hungary had cloaked it with an added shadow of menace. Well, I thought, at least I have nothing to declare . . . I sat up with a jerk in the corner of the empty carriage: what about that automatic pistol? Seeing myself being led to a cell, I dug the little unwanted weapon out of the bottom of my rucksack and undid the flap of the leather case; the smallness, the lightness and the mother-of-pearl-plated stock made it look like a toy. Should I steal away from these bare wooden seats and hide it in the first-class upholstery next door? Or slip it behind the cistern in the lavatory? Or simply chuck it out into No-Man's-Land? In the end I hid it in a thick fold in the bottom corner of my greatcoat, fixed it there with three safety-pins, put the guilty garment on the rack and sat underneath with pounding heart as the train crawled through the moonlight.

In a few miles we reached the border and the blue-yellow-and-red flag of the Rumanian frontier post. Above the desk inside hung a photograph of King Carol in a white-plumed helmet, a steel breast-plate and a white cloak with a cross on the shoulder. Another frame showed Prince Michael, a nice-looking boy in a white jersey with large, soft eyes and thick, neatly brushed hair; he had also been a king during a three years' abdication by his father. It was a relief and rather an anticlimax when the yawning official stamped my passport without a single glance at my stuff. The battered document still shows the date:

Curtici 27 April 1934, the sixth frontier of my journey.

I thought I had been the only passenger, but a party of bearded and spectacled rabbis in long black overcoats and wide hats had climbed out of the end-carriage; they were attended by students with elf-locks corkscrewing down their wax-pale cheeks and the dark-clad gathering on the platform looked as strange under the moon as a confabulation of rooks. Three were dressed differently from the others; they wore soft-legged Russian boots and black caftans and the foxes' brushes coiled round their low-crowned beaver hats exactly matched the beard of one of them: a costume I came across several times later in northern Moldavia and Bukovina; and, later on still, among votaries hastening down the steep lanes of Jerusalem to the Wailing Wall. They were talking Yiddish and I somehow picked up the notion that the ones with the foxes' brushes were Southern Poles from Cracow or Przemysl, perhaps belonging to the zealot sect of the Hasidim; and I think they were all bound for some important meeting in Bucharest. When they got in again, the train went off into the night, the officials vanished and soon I was alone in the ragged streets of Decebal: the place was named after the last king of Dacia before it was conquered by the Romans.

Only dogs were about. Three of them barred the way, snarling and showing their gums and giving tongue through bared teeth, vicious as dingoes in the bright glare of the moon, their shadows crossing and traversing as they retreated down the dust of the main shuttered lane.

* * * *

After the bare frontier date, a mist descends, and the next night's entry in my diary is almost as short: '*27 April, Pankota*—stayed with Imre Engelhardt, owner of the Apollo Cinema'. I have just found it on a map—Pîncota in Rumanian—but the cinema and its owner have slipped away beyond recall. He must have been one of Maria Theresa's settlers from south-west Germany; all of them are loosely styled Swabians.

When the fog lifts, the landscape shows little change from the Great Plain I thought I had left, except for wooded hills in the distance. It was a geometrical interlock of chocolate-coloured ploughland with stripes of barley, wheat, oats, rye and maize with some tobacco and the sudden mustard flare of charlock. Clumps of trees broke it up and every few miles russet and sulphur-coloured belfries rose from shingle roofs. Each village had a rustic baroque church for the Catholics and another for the Uniats, and sometimes, though not so much hereabouts, a third for Calvinists or Lutherans; for though the Counter-Reformation had triumphed in Austria, lively and varied crops survived in Hungary and Transylvania. These churches were outwardly the same, but once indoors, the Stations of the Cross or a roodscreen encrusted with icons or the austerity of the Ten Commandments in Magyar above a Communion table gave their allegiance away at once. There were storks' nests and sweep-wells and flocks and cattle and Gypsies on the move. I began to like buffaloes the more I saw of them; their great liquid eyes, which seemed to lose the resentment I thought I had discerned on the banks of the Tisza, now looked aswim with pathos. But there was an important difference in the people. After the last weeks of blunt Magyar faces, the features were different—or was it merely imagination and recent reading that lent them a more Latin look? I fell in with a party carrying sickles and scythes and slung babies. Their ample white homespun tunics were caught in with belts as wide as girths and sometimes covered in iron studs, and, except for those who were barefoot, they were shod in the familiar canoe-tipped moccasins and rawhide thongs. Their rank sheepskin jackets were put on smooth side out and their hats—bulbous cones of black or white fleece over a foot high—gave them a wild and rakish look. They could all understand my hard-won fragments of Magyar; but I soon felt that the language they spoke to each other would be much easier to learn. A man was *om*, a woman, *femeie*; and *ochi*, *nas*, *mâna* and *foaie* were eyes, nose, hand and leaf. They were a little puzzled at first by my pointing at everything in sight with gestures of enquiry. Dog? Ox? Cow? Horse? *Câine*, *bou*, *vaca*, *cal!* It was marvellous: *homo*, *femina*, *nasus*, *manus*, *folium*, *canis*, *bos*, *vacca* and *caballus* thronged through my brain in a delirious troop. *Câmp* was a field and *fag* a beech-tree ('. . . quatit ungula campum!' . . . 'sub tegmine fagi . . .!'). How odd to find this Latin speech marooned so far from its kindred! The Black Sea hemmed it in to the east and Slavonic to north and south, while the west was barred by the Finno-Ugrian dactyls of the Magyars.

By late afternoon, these linguistic exchanges brought us to the little town of Ineu—'Borosjenö' on my pre-war map—where a market day was ending. The place was full of lowing, bleating and squealing, carts were being loaded, pens broken up and hurdles stacked. Women and girls were busy with long goads keeping troops of poultry together. Kerchiefs of different colours were knotted under their chins and pleated skirts, with embroidered aprons back and front, sprang from girdles woven in patterns of red and yellow. A few of them had scarlet boots to the knee like figures out of the Russian ballet.

* * * *

My goal was a house belonging to a friend called Tibor—I had met him with his namesake in Budapest—who had asked me to stay at an approximate date which was just about now: suddenly, hobnobbing with some farmers under an acacia tree, one foot on the step of a smart trap with a grey pony swishing its tail, here he was: jolly, baronial, rubicund, Jäger-hatted and plumed, an ex-Horse Gunner in the same troop as the other Tibor. His face lit in welcome and two plum brandies appeared on a tray as though by magic, and when they were swallowed we bowled off to the hills, Tibor ceremoniously lifting his green hat in answer to the doffed cones as we went.

* * * *

All through the afternoon the hills had been growing in height and now they rolled into the distance behind a steep and solitary hemisphere clad to the summit with vineyards. We turned into the tall gates at the foot of it and a long sweep of grass brought us to a Palladian façade just as night was falling. Two herons rose as we approached; the shadows were full of the scent of lilac. Beyond the french windows, a coifed and barefoot maid with a spill was lighting lamps down a long room and, with each new pool of light, Biedermeier furniture took shape and chairs and sofas where only a few strands of the original fabric still lingered; there were faded plum-coloured curtains and a grand piano laden with framed photographs and old family albums with brass clasps; antlers branched, a stuffed lynx pricked its ears, ancestors with swords and furred tunics dimly postured. A white stove soared between bookcases, bear-skins spread underfoot: and, as at Kövecsespuszta,* a sideboard carried an array of silver cigarette-cases with the arms and monograms of friends who had bestowed them for standing godfather or being best man at a wedding or second in a duel. There was a polished shellcase from some Silesian battle, a congeries of thimble-sized goblets, a scimitar with a turquoise-encrusted scabbard, folded newspapers—*Az Ujság* and *Pesti Hírlap* sent from Budapest, and the *Wiener Salonblatt*, an Austrian *Tatler* full of pictures of shooting parties, equestrian events and smart balls far away, posted from Vienna. Among the silver frames was a daguerreotype of the Empress Elizabeth —Queen, rather, in this lost province of the former Kingdom— another of the Regent dressed as admiral of a vanished fleet, and a third of Archduke Otto in the pelts and the plumes of a Hungarian magnate. Red, green and blue, the squat volumes of the *Almanach de Gotha* were ready to pounce. A glittering folio volume, sumptuously bound in green leather, almost covered a small table and its name, *Az ember tragediája*, was embossed in gold: *The Tragedy of Man*, by Imre Madács. It is a long nineteenth-century dramatic poem of philosophic and contemplative temper, and no Hungarian house, even the least bookish —like English houses with the vellum-bound Omar Khayyám illustrated by Edmund Dulac—seemed complete without it. Finally, a rack in the corner was filled with long Turkish pipes. This catalogue of detail composes an archetype of which every other country-house I saw in Transylvania seemed to be a variation.

At the other end, beyond the double doors of a room which was half-study and half-gunroom, more antlers proliferated; figures moved in the lamplight and the voices of guests sounded, and I hastened upstairs to wash and get some of the dust off before meeting them. As they all play a part in the following weeks and their houses follow each other like stepping stones I will wait till we reach them rather than introduce them now.

*　　*　　*　　*

Next morning revealed the front of a late eighteenth-century building. Between the wings, four wide-spaced Tuscan columns

* See *A Time of Gifts*, p. 252.

advanced and ascended both floors to form a splendid loggia. White louvred shutters continued the line of windows on either side, each leaf touching its neighbour on the façade when they were open while indoors the light poured across the floors; closed, with their slats ajar when the sun became too hot, they striped the wide polished beams underfoot with bars of light and dark. There was a wheel with a handle which cranked out an enormous slant of white awning and, looking out, one might have been on the deck of a schooner painted by Tissot with tree-tops for waves. Beyond, the vine-clad hemispherical hill of Mokra soared like a volcanic island against snowy heaps of cloud and a pale sky. The smells of lilac, box and lavender drifted in, goldfinches moved about the branches, and now and then house-martins from the nests clustering along the pediment strayed indoors and flew in desperate circles or swept clean through the house and out the other side.

In the middle of this airy expanse I came on Tibor recumbent on a Madame Recamier sofa with a sheet tied round his neck, smoking an after-breakfast cigar while his valet lathered his chin. "Gyula will be ready for you in a minute," he said, sending a perfect smoke ring towards the coffered ceiling; and soon I was lying swathed under Gyula's razor, imitatively wreathed in a fragrant cloud of smoke. Strolling up and down and sitting on the sill against a background of birds, Tibor told me anecdotes of the War and Gypsies and cabaret-girls, spacing out his adventures in Paris, Brussels and Constantinople with amusing and improper stories. As we went downstairs, chins tingling with eau-de-cologne, he wondered what there would be for luncheon; and, across the courtyard below, we caught sight of the cook sitting in the shade outside her kitchen in a whirl of feathers. "Good!" he said. "Margit's plucking a chicken"; and we set off to inspect the fields and the crops in an open carriage behind the coach-man's black ostrich-feather and fluttering ribands. "This is the life," I thought as we bowled along under the leaves.

But the great attraction at Borosjenö was Ria, who presided over everything. 'Housekeeper' is too portentous and misleading a name for that charming and amusing face and the youthful figure that gave the lie to her prematurely grey hair cut in a shingle. She was Polish, the daughter of a music publisher in Cracow whom some misfortune had overtaken. I wondered if there had been a romance between her and Tibor, perhaps. If so, it was over; but they were great friends, and she was hostess in his bachelor household. She spoke beautiful French and Polish, German and Hungarian, with a bit of Rumanian as well. Inspecting my tangled wardrobe as I handed things over to be washed or mended, she asked how many handkerchiefs I had got. All lost except two. "Et quels torchons," she said, holding them up. "Regarde-moi ça! Il faut que je m'occupe de toi!" and she did. She bought a dozen handkerchiefs of homespun linen in the country town of Arad, embroidered my initials on them, tied them neatly with a red ribbon and plonked them in my hands like a packet of sandwiches: "Au moins tu auras de quoi te moucher." She had a delightful voice and we spent hours singing at the picture-laden piano: French and German and a few Polish songs; I could join her in one of these, which I learnt like a parrot; and, all of a sudden as I write, the cheerful tune and the words come back.* She was very amusing and perhaps more sophisticated than Tibor. When she drove to see neighbours in the pony-trap or the carriage, I went too and I was soon abreast of a dozen comic biographies. Everyone loved her, and so did I.

* * * *

The tempo of my journey had slowed up, all sense of time dissolved, and it is only now, half a century too late, that I have sudden retrospective qualms about accepting so much hospitality, and they are not very severe. The industrial revolution had left these regions untouched and the rhythm of life had remained many decades behind the pace of the West—a hundred years, perhaps, when stays in the country were as long and as leisurely as they are in English and Russian novels of the time; and, in this lost province, where the hospitable Hungarians felt cut off from life, visitors from the West were greeted with embraces. I hoped it was so, for the next three months of leisurely sojourns across the marches and the southern parts of Transylvania turned that spring and early summer into a complete exception to the rest of these travels. A blessed and happy spell descended.

* * * *

* 'Pojekai, Hanka, tam u hrustu, tam u hrustu, tam u hrustu . . .' etc.

Transylvania* is nearly three times the size of Wales and to the Hungarians the loss of the province seemed the hardest to bear of all her post-war disasters. Hungary's position in the Dual Monarchy had inextricably involved her in the fortunes of Austria, and then, by chain reaction, of Germany too and finally, in 1918, in the chaos of defeat. But, of the ensuing disasters—the brief Soviet republic of Béla Kun, the conquest by the Rumanians that put an end to it and the White Terror that followed—none seemed so catastrophic as the dismemberment of the country at the Treaty of Trianon. The losses to Czechoslovakia and Yugoslavia were bitter but in comparison simple, the cuts clean and the losses quite literally peripheral. It was the opposite in Transylvania; justice to both sides was and is impossible; and the impossibility resides in the dense mass of Transylvanian Hungarians, isolated two hundred miles east of their fellow-countrymen by a still greater surrounding mass of Rumanians. Short of making this enormous Magyar enclave a detached outpost of Hungary—embedded, as it would have had to have been, in a hostile Rumania like the later experiment of East Pakistan, and perhaps with the same fate—there was no solution. Apart from this, the Rumanians of Transylvania outnumbered the Hungarians by the best part of a million, so *mutatis mutandis*, it would have been equally impossible to frame reasonable frontiers for a victorious Hungary which would have been fair to the Rumanians. Who was to suffer the unavoidable injustice—loss of their Transylvanian kinsmen for Hungary, perpetuation of the status quo for the Rumanians—merely depended on who lost the War. Hungary was involved in the losing side, and the result was inevitable: frontiers were destroyed which, except for the Turkish period, had remained intact for nearly a thousand years and two-thirds of her territory were shared out among the winners; and ever since, the Hungarian flag had remained metaphorically and literally at half mast.

The Hungarians based their claim to Transylvania on historical

* Properly speaking, the region only begins about thirty miles east of the point I had reached. But the narrow tract between this and the post-war Hungarian-Rumanian frontier—the one I had just crossed—seems to have no specific name and, talking loosely, people often wrongly lump it in with Transylvania: it seems a handy name for all the territory which Hungary had lost to Rumania in 1920, and I sometimes find myself following this lax but convenient usage.

priority rather than ethnic preponderance, the Rumanians on both.
The Rumanians claimed descent from a mixture of ancient Dacians
(whose kingdom lay exactly here) with the Romans who conquered
and colonised the country under Trajan, in AD 107; alternatively, they
descended—for theories change—from Dacians who had been Roman-
ised by the occupation which lasted until AD 271, when the over-
whelming flood of the Goths compelled the Emperor Aurelian to
withdraw his troops to the south of the Danube. During the hundred
and sixty-four years between Trajan and Aurelian, a Daco-Roman,
Latin-speaking population, comparable to the Gallo-Romans of Gaul,
had taken shape, and when Aurelian's troops withdrew, they remained
there (rather like, in the West, the Latin-speaking local successors to the
legions when they were recalled to Rome) and bequeathed their
language to their descendants. They attribute a Slavonic element in
Rumanian to the later spread of the Slavs over the whole of Eastern
Europe, a linguistic contribution that could be likened in the West to
the Teutonic elements in the language of northern Gaul when the
Franks crossed the Rhine and spread. The Daco-Romans, then, would
have been the bottom layer of the racial and linguistic make-up of the
country. Invaders swept across it, with their eyes on prizes farther west;
some lingered for a time; but they vanished one by one. Meanwhile,
all through these unchronicled Dark Ages, the Daco-Romans, living as
nomad shepherds—rough nobles, perhaps, with their pastoral liegemen
—grazed their flocks here until the Magyars, turning eastwards again
after their occupation of the Great Hungarian Plain, invaded Transylvania and subjugated them: a subjugation which lasted, according to
this theory of history, until the liberating Treaty of Trianon.

The Hungarian version of history agrees with the Rumanian as far
as Aurelian. According to Hungarians—basing their theory on the only
text which touches on the matter*—the removal of the colonists, and
not only of the troops and the administration, was complete. If a few
Dacians remained, they are presumed to have been dispersed and
obliterated by the Goths and their habitat overlaid by the subsequent
Slav expansion: the only population the Magyars found there in the
ninth century would have been a scattering of Slavs, who were soon

* The late Roman historian Flavius Vopiscus in the Augustan Scriptors.

absorbed; the region was described as 'deserted' by the first chronicler. To fill the void, the Magyars installed their warlike kinsmen, the Szelkers, in the Carpathians (unless they had preceded them) where they still form the bulk of the Hungarian population. Then they summoned the 'Saxons' from the lower Rhine; and it is only after this, in the early thirteenth century (the Hungarians urge), that the Rumanians enter the scene; not as descendants of the Daco-Romans surviving in unbroken incumbency, but as immigrant groups of the famous Vlach population of Macedonia and the Balkans, who spoke a low-Latin language from their long subjection to the Empire. They had wandered north with their flocks, the Hungarians say, perhaps driven there by the Cumans, and perhaps not, and probably in company with the wild Pechenegs. They made their way into southern Transylvania and settled among the Carpathian peaks, where—so this theory continues—they were steadily reinforced by new Vlach arrivals; until finally they outnumbered the Magyars of the region— and the Szeklers, and the Saxons—by an enormous margin.

The speech of the Rumanians and of the Vlachs of the Balkans must spring from the same source. They are too alike for it to be otherwise; few of the Romance languages are so closely related and it is only surprising that the centuries and the distance which separate them have not prised them further apart. Until a hundred and fifty years ago both national groups were loosely called Vlachs, or Wallachs, by the rest of the world (but never by the Rumanians themselves), and this surely points to a common origin. Where? Outside Transylvania, the Hungarians say: they only entered as late immigrants; inside it, the Rumanians insist, only spreading south as later emigrants . . . It is at this point that an inexpert newcomer to the problem begins tentatively to wonder: could the answer not lie somewhere between the two? Vlachs were scattered all over south-east Europe; might there not also have been some in Transylvania when the Magyars invaded, as well as the wandering Slavs?* Similarly, could these putative Vlachs in Tran-

---

* A Hungarian source, the Anonymous Notary of King Béla (1234-70), records a tradition that the invading Hungarians had to overcome the resistance of a certain Gelu, leader of the Vlacho-Slav tribes in central Transylvania, before he could subdue the region.

sylvania not have been part of a wider scattering, and not necessarily the radiating nucleus of the entire race, as the Rumanians uphold? Both parties would answer No: Hungarians insist on a vacuum, Rumanians on a hot-bed. It need hardly be said that controversialists on both sides, quoting or challenging the sources and adducing linguistics, archaeology, geography, place names, religion and a whole supporting array of circumstantial evidence, can explain away all opposing arguments with convincing and long-practised ease.

In the Rumanian view, the Koutzo-Vlachs, the 'Macedo-Rumans' of the Balkans, would be some of the scattered descendants of the inhabitants of two new 'Dacias'—the colonies Aurelian founded for the population he had evacuated to Moesia (modern Serbia and Bulgaria) along the south bank of the Danube. One interesting figure glimmers for a moment among these transplanted Dacians a hundred years after Aurelian's evacuation south of the Danube: the remarkable St. Nicetas of Remesiana (now Bela Palanka, in Serbia) who is the author not only of the *Te Deum*—which was wrongly attributed until early this century to SS. Ambrose and Augustine—but also of a clause in the Apostles' Creed. He was a friend of Paulinus of Nola who wrote an ode to him in sapphics when he visited him in south Italy; this sets him at only one remove from Ausonius and Roman Bordeaux. Then the dark swallows up this twilight beacon.

*   *   *   *

If only we knew what happened at Aurelian's withdrawal! But, apart from Vopiscus's shadowy sentences, we don't; not a thing: the silence and darkness lasted a thousand years. We know that the Roman withdrawal took place in AD 271 (over a century before the Romans left Britain), but after that—apart from Gelu—the earliest mentions of Latin-speaking inhabitants of Transylvania occur in 1222 and 1231, when there is mention of 'the region of the Vlachs' and 'the forest of the Pechenegs and the Vlachs'. They emerge—or re-emerge—from the shadows while the Valois and the Plantagenet dynasties were at their height, only twenty years after the Crusaders had captured Constantinople and a bare six after Magna Carta. It is baffling, and hardly credible, that so little is known about their contemporaries in

Transylvania. Some blame the Mongol invasion the century before for this astounding blank. The Mongols destroyed everything; not only castles and churches and abbeys but, it seems, every single document they may have contained. One longs for news from the buried ruins of some stronghold miraculously untouched since Batu Khan set fire to it, the trove, perhaps, of some Transylvanian forester digging out a fox or a badger and suddenly tumbling through the creepers and the roots into a dry vault full of iron chests abrim with parchments . . .

But, from a different point of view, the advantage of this void to the rival controversialists is enormous. Theories can be evolved in a void, as it were, and the occasional fragments of hard fact—linguistic, geographical, ethnological or religious—need not fit into any jigsaw; indeed, they are unable to do so, because all the other pieces are missing; and within certain loose bounds they can be arranged in whatever pattern suits the speaker best. The interpretations are as different as the work of two palaeontologists, one of whom would reconstruct a dinosaur and the other a mastodon from the same handful of bone-fragments. 'Let us assume' turns in a few pages into 'We may assume', which, in a few more, is 'As we have shown'; and, after a few more pages yet, the shy initial hypothesis has hardened into a brazen established landmark, all the time with not an atom of new evidence being adduced. Advantageous points are coaxed into opulent bloom, awkward ones discreetly pruned into non-being. Obscurity reigns. It is a dim region where *suggestio falsi* and *suppressio veri*, those twin villains of historical conflict, stalk about the shadows with dark-lantern and bow-string.

These ancient ambiguities would be a field for learned conjecture merely, were it not for the bitter rivalries that haunted them in later times and haunt them still. Historic priority, could it be proved, would be vital evidence in a suit of contested ownership; and earlier in this century, before ethnic considerations were the overriding factors they have since become, it was more important still: possession by conquest, backed by historical continuity and stiffened by treaties, was still a valid and respectable consideration. The colonial empires of Great Britain and France flourished unchallenged and Russia was in firm possession, as she still is, of the colossal Asian annexations of the Tsars. In such an atmosphere, all objectivity of research liable to unearth evidence damaging to the researcher's side must seem tainted with treason.

Obviously, I knew very little of all this at the time, but it was impossible not to pick up an inkling; and later, when I stayed for long stretches in 'old' Rumania—*Regat*, or 'the Kingdom', as it was always referred to in Transylvania—I more or less got the hang of the Rumanian approach, but not in very strong doses—it would be hard to think of less chauvinistic people than the family and friends I settled among in Moldavia—and I read all that came my way on both sides. The opposing cases were skilfully and persuasively argued; in each the chains of logic seemed faultless; all objections were faced and demolished; and when I turned from one argument to its rival the same thing would happen, leaving me stranded between the two. I am the only person I know who has feelings of equal warmth for both these embattled claimants and I wish with fervour they could become friends. Would the discovery of those imaginary scrolls in the ruins solve matters? My unsatisfactory position between the two makes me useless to both.

Among the Hungarian landowners in Transylvania there was an added bitterness. Agrarian reforms had expropriated and redistributed the bulk of their estates among the peasants. However just this measure may have been, nobody likes losing land and cries of outrage went up. They could not know it, but these cries were substantially no different from the lamentations one could hear in the country-houses of Rumanian boyars, whose estates had been similarly dismantled. These boyars, what is more, were resentfully convinced that their own Rumanian government gave more favourable treatment to the new and unwilling Hungarian subjects, in order to curry favour with them. On later visits, when I told this to Hungarian Transylvanians, unshakably convinced that they were the special victims of discrimination, they were amazed and disbelieving. They seethed at the inequity of the regime and the venality of the new officials from Regat. Tales of bribery abounded, and their attitude to the new state and to its officials from beyond the Carpathian watershed resembled the distrust and disdain of post-American Civil War plantation owners for the carpetbaggers from the north. Indeed, there were unprepossessing aspects: lack of tact and scruple was backed, perhaps, by promptings of revenge for Hungarian absolutism in the past. The Hungarians over the centuries had handled their alien subjects—and all their own compatriots below a certain rank—with great clumsiness; disdain, oppression, blind feudalism, exclusion from any voice in their counsels, rigorous Magyarisation—no blemish was missing. (In case their iniquities should breed complacency in an English breast, their feelings towards the helot population most compellingly recall the English attitude that Swift satirises in post-Cromwellian Ireland.) Trouble heaped up; it broke out now and then in murderous revolts followed by pitiless retribution. Had a reversal of the positions placed the Hungarians under Rumanian suzerainty for these grim centuries, there is no reason to think that the shifted yoke would have been lighter to bear: Rumanian rulers were as illiberal and oppressive to their own subjects as the Hungarians to theirs. They were fierce times in Eastern Europe; and they still are.*

But there were few traces of all this in everyday life. For better or for worse, landlords and peasants had known each other for many generations, whereas the officials from the Regat were newcomers to both of them; and, on the spot, a certain warmth of feeling had managed to outlive the changes of frontier and ownership and the conflicts of the past. "I remember old Count ——," I heard a Rumanian shepherd say later on, "with all his horses and carriages! It was a fine sight. And look at him now, poor old man!" Comparable feelings often prevailed the other way about and, in my scanty experience, squires who were thunderous over their wine about the iniquities of the state would take care to exempt the locals who had been given their acres. Their ancient feudal relationship may have evaporated but hardy symbols still survived in doffed hats, kissed hands and ceremonious forms of address, and this gave a strange, almost a disembodied feeling of remoteness to this Transylvanian life. Most of the minor landowners had been obliged by circumstances to become Rumanian citizens; but very few of them had ever been to Bucharest. They looked on it as a

* 'All thoughts to rive the heart are here, and all are vain,
  Horror and scorn and hate and fear and indignation . . .'
—the lines would often come to mind.

faraway Babylon of dust and bribery and wickedness and vowed never to set foot there if they could help it, or even cross the former eastern frontier. Pining for the crown of St. Stephen, they had no eyes or ears or heart for anything but their mutilated kingdom to the west.

Finally it remains to be said that hardly a trace of this distress was detectable to a stranger. (In my particular case, the chief thing to survive is the memory of unlimited kindness.) Estates, much reduced, existed still, and at moments it almost seemed as though nothing had changed. Charm and *douceur de vivre* were still afloat among the faded decor indoors, and outside, everything conspired to delight. Islanded in the rustic Rumanian multitude, different in race and religion and with the phantoms of their lost ascendancy still about them, the prevailing atmosphere surrounding these kastély-dwellers conjured up that of the tumbling demesnes of the Anglo-Irish in Waterford or Galway, with all their sadness and their magic. Homesick for the past, seeing nobody but their own congeners on the neighbouring estates and the peasants who worked there, they lived in a backward-looking, a genealogical, almost a Confucian dream and many sentences ended in a sigh.

* * * *

Ria had countless French books and I borrowed them freely. Tibor was no reader but his forerunners must have been, for the library was well stocked, chiefly with works in Hungarian and German. Abandoning hope with Magyar, I longed to plunge deeper in German and began by reading all the rhyming couplets under the marvellous drawings of *Max und Moritz* and *Hans Huckebein* in a large volume of Wilhelm Busch. Elated by this and aiming higher, I moved on to Thomas Mann's *Tod in Venedig* and made a slow start, looking up every other word and seeking Ria's help when I got stuck. But I did manage to finish it in a couple of weeks, and considering that I had only started German five months before, this seemed a big jump forward. I spent the mornings between the library and an outdoor table, poring over Central European history—Hungarian and Transylvanian in particular —in *Meyers Konversationslexikon*; and then moved on to the Béla Kun period in the rather lurid books of Jean and Jérome Tharaud—*La Fin des Habsburgs, Quand Israel est Roi*. These two French brothers, one of whom became an Academician, were great favourites in these parts. Though everyone knew a great deal about the past of Central Europe, their knowledge stopped dead at the crests of the Carpathians. Rumanian history—the history, that is, of Wallachia and Moldavia, the two principalities the other side of the mountains which eventually united under a single prince and then became the Kingdom of Rumania—was beyond their scope; it was invariably dismissed with mention of *die wilde Wallachei*—'wild Wallachia' (a quotation, perhaps: who from?)—as though it lay in the heart of the Mongolian steppe.

Straying from this theme, but not very far, I discovered that the French for 'gelding' was *hongre*—the Hungarians were thought to have introduced the practice into Europe—while the German word is *Wallach*, which suggests a Rumanian origin, each of the countries concerned taking a step further east. My delight in finding that the word 'hussar' was Magyar—*husz*, twenty, conjuring up a squadron twenty-strong—was shortlived, for more recent lexicographers derive it, *via* Serbian, from the Italian *corsaro*, a pirate, feebly substituting a keel for hooves. There had been attempts in the past to derive 'ogre' from 'Hungarian'—or rather from their ancestors the Ugrians; but the word really comes from Orcus, the Roman underworld god. But at least the derivation of 'cravat' from 'Croatia', which had been a vassal-kingdom of Hungary, seemed secure; the word had been implanted into France by the flowing neckwear of Louis XIV's mercenary Croatian cavalry. The word 'coach' is a reminder of the Hungarian town of Kocs, presumably because such a vehicle was first built there.

* * *

These mornings were soon over. Storks presided over them and cuckoos sounded from different woods as long as the light lasted. Three days in a row were singled out by the arrival of birds I had never seen before: the first, with dazzling yellow and black plumage and a short haunting tune, was a golden oriole; next day was marked by the blue-green-yellow flash of bee-eaters; and the third by two hoopoes walking in the grass and spreading and closing their Red Indian head-dresses, then fluttering aloft and chasing each other among the leaves, their wings turning them into little flying zebras until they settled again.

Tibor's sister and some friends arrived from Vienna and there was much festivity and dressing up and picnics and finally a midnight feast on the very summit of the vine-clad hill. A bonfire was lit: a carriage disgorged four Gypsies—a violin, a viola, a czembalom and a double-bass—who assembled under a tree. The amber-coloured wine we drank as we leant on our elbows round the flames was pressed from grapes which had ripened on the very slopes that dropped away all round. The vine-dressers climbed up, forming an outer ring, and when we had run dry they fetched fresh supplies from their cottages, filling all glasses until a cockcrow from an invisible farmyard spread an infectious summons through the dark; other cocks awoke; then the end of the Great Plain glimmered into being underneath us and every-thing except the Gypsies began to grow pale. Their strings and their voices kept us company all the way downhill, then through the gates and along the grass path through the trees. Our footprints showed grey in the dew; and when we reached the pillars along the front of the house, the sound of startled nests and birds waking up and the flapping of a stork from the pediment showed it was too late to go to bed.

These were the daily waking sounds. Soon they were joined every morning by the swish of scythes right up to the house-walls and the voices of the mowers singing to themselves; when one of them broke off for a minute, there was the clang of a whetstone along a blade. The scent of hay filled the house, haymakers peopled the landscape and spread their windrows in stripes of silver across the pale stubble. My room gave on a field where a big rick was going up, the layers ascend-ing and radiating clockwise round the tall centre pole. Women with pitchforks knee-deep in a cart tossed up the hay while the men on the tapering cone fixed it like the whorls on an ammonite. The waggons creaking along the lanes were piled so high that wisps of hay entwined with dead poppies and wild flowers were caught up in all the low branches.

I spent much of the day with Tibor in the fields and walked in the hills for miles, picking up fragments of Rumanian. But I gave up keeping my diary for a while on the principle, I suppose, that these static intervals were irrelevant in a record of travel. I wish I had been less proud: these gaps make it easy to lose count of days and even weeks;

but odd items and a few sketches scattered at the back help me reconstruct them and one of these fixes this particular lapse of time beyond
question. Tibor, as though on a sudden cheerful inspiration, had said
he would drive me to Arad—he remembered he had some things to
do there—and then on to my next halting place, where we were all to
meet later on. After tea a touring-car, only used for journeys out of
carriage range, was brought out to the front with some solemnity.
Tibor was a little mysterious about our trip.

Arad was about the size of Guildford and, unlike the countryside, I
had the impression there of hearing more Magyar than Rumanian in
the streets. There were many Hungarian names over the shops and
many Jewish and a multitude of ordinary German ones that belonged
to Swabian settlers. The place was made famous in Hungarian history
by the Austrian execution of thirteen Hungarian generals at the end of
Kossuth's great rising against Habsburg rule in 1848. (I had just been
reading about it.) There was little time to see much, however; Tibor's
task was a protracted visit to a tall, dark and very pretty girl called
Ilona, a great favourite of his, who lived in a discreet and leafy street
leading down to the river Mureş. She had summoned a friend called
Izabella who was equally pretty in a different way, for my sake, I
think. She had very fair hair and dark blue eyes and spoke no word of
anything but Hungarian, but this didn't matter at all. (I wonder if her
extreme fairness came from a dash of Slovak blood: I had seen similarly
blond descendants of northern settlers in the neighbourhood of my
penultimate Hungarian halt at O'Kigyos: not very far away as the
crow flies.) Anyway, here she is, pressed like a petal in the back pages
of my journal, carefully drawn, with her head leaning on her forearm
and gazing out under arched brows, and, by a stroke of luck, looking
nearly as pretty in the sketch as she did in real life. 'Iza, Arad. May 16,
1934' is pencilled in at the top.

*　　*　　*　　*

Back again north of Arad, the wavy line of hills next morning had
drawn back a few miles and the low, ranch-like manor house of
Tövicsegháza, for which I've searched the map in vain, lay among
cornfields under a clump of elms.

The moment we were shown into the billiard room, Tibor spotted a double-barrelled gun which was propped across the window-sill. He quickly broke it open and two cartridges jumped out of the breech. "Look at that! I ask you!" he said, laughing and putting them on a shelf with a sigh. "Polnische Wirtschaft! There's Polish housekeeping for you!" Jaš, pronounced 'Yash', our host, came in at that moment and said he always kept it loaded and handy for the rooks, "Otherwise they wouldn't leave an ear of the young wheat for miles."

In these circles, it was considered a boorish oversight to withhold from newcomers certain details about anyone they were about to meet. No English circumspection or studied vagueness hampered these utterances, still less the fear of seeming worldly or impressed by the boast of heraldry and the pomp of power. "Jaš?" someone had said. "He comes from an excellent family in southern Poland, eight thousand acres, not far from Cracow. His great-grandfather was Austrian Ambassador to St. Petersburg and their Turk's head crest was granted after capturing three Tatar standards in the Ukraine".

"His wife Clara? From an old, old, old . . . *uralte*"—here the speaker's eyelids would almost close as though in a dream at the thought of such antiquity—"family in the High Tatra mountains. They live in one of the most ancient castles in Hungary—Slovakia now, more's the pity! Counts since the reign of King Mátyás. They carry a double chevron dansetty between three salamanders quartered with five pikes hauriant; arms parlant, you know, after the river that rushes by, and the fish that swim in it." (When armorial fauna were mentioned, for a moment the room or the lawn would seem to fill with fork-tailed lions looking warily backwards with blue claws and fangs; unicorns, mouldywarps, cockatrices, griffins, wyverns, firedrakes and little dragons covered with stripes; hawks and eagles were let loose and the air filled with corbies and martlets and swans with gold chains about their necks in spirals.)

Only after dealing with these essentials were minor points like character, looks or capacity allowed to crop up. In spite of some territorial difficulties, the Hungarians had an undoubted sympathy for the Poles; what a relief to find an exception to the usual East European hatred of neighbours! These feelings were rooted long ago in shared enmity to the Germans, the Turks and the Muscovites and had been signally marked in the late sixteenth century when the Poles elected Stephen Báthory, the Hungarian Prince of Transylvania, to the Polish throne. He routed all their enemies, captured a score of Russian towns and drove Ivan the Terrible out of the Kingdom.

Jaš was slender and fair-haired with a high-bridged nose, hair cut *en brosse*, bright blue eyes behind very thick horn-rimmed spectacles, and an air of vagueness and goodwill. Ideas about archaeology, history, religion and physics seethed in his mind and he was said to be full of expert theories (prone to break down in practice) on economics, rotation of crops, the training of animals, winter fodder, forestry, bee-keeping, sheep dip, and how best to fatten ducks for the spring market. He welcomed eccentric notions and we had not been there five minutes before he asked us what we thought of the idea that the earth might be hollow, with a small sun at the centre and a much larger moon circling it whose shadow was the cause of night and day. Millions of stars about the size of Vienna or Warsaw rotating solar-centrically at different distances and speeds? That morning's post had brought him a tri-lingual pamphlet from the inventor of this theory and his pale eyes were alight behind their lenses. "Die Welt ist eine Hohlkugel!" he read out from the cover; "Le monde est une boule creuse! Ze vorld iss a hollow ball, my dear!" he explained, laying a hand on my forearm; then, turning the pages with emotion, he read out the most telling passages. Tibor, as we said goodbye, gave me the ghost of a wink.

* * * *

Practice may have fallen short of theory in other matters, but Jaš was a phenomenal shot. The gun was soon loaded again and every so often, in mid-sentence and seemingly without aiming, he would fire out of the window and into the air, often single-handed and with hardly a break in his discourse; and a second later, like a heavy parcel, down on the lawn crashed a bird from the enormous rookery that overshadowed the house. I was sorry; all that wheeling and cawing brought homesick thoughts to mind. Haphazard bangs punctuated every hour of daylight.

Clara, the child of those hoary battlements in the High Tatra, had a wild look and her hair was seldom combed. She loved horses and her life revolved round two beautiful black creatures which a dour and one-eyed groom called Antal kept sleek and trim—"unlike me", as she truthfully said, skimming into the saddle. She was as light as a jockey, rode beautifully and sailed over tremendous fences. Jaš had given it up—"no time"—so we went for far-flung rides in the cool of the evening.

During the hot midday hours, iced soda was splashed into the deep golden wine I keep mentioning. This has a barbarous sound, but it was delicious—*Spritzer* they called it in German, and, in Magyar, *hoszú lépés*, 'a long step', one of the many terms for the degrees of dilution. Generically, all these wines were unmistakably from that particular region, yet each one seemed to change with the roof under which it was to be drunk. It was ready for drinking from the moment the vintage had settled from fermentation, and after years in cool cellars, it was beyond praise. At dinner, decanter on decanter was emptied, undiluted now, by the light of candles in tall glass tulip-shaped shields. Jaš liked sitting late after dinner when rash and varied talk ranged far into the small hours. When he lifted a forefinger, we would fall silent and listen to the nightingales for a minute. A restless geometry of fire-flies darted about under the spatulate volume of the chestnut trees, and getting up one night to go to bed, we found emerald-coloured tree-frogs smaller than threepenny-bits clinging to the leaves like miniature green castaways on rafts.

On my last afternoon, Clara and I lay about talking on a bank at the end of the lawn. Indoors, Jaš was playing complicated fugues rather well, breaking off for a few seconds now and then and rushing back to the piano after a bang and a thud, so there was a perturbed circling of rooks above the house. All along the lawn, the chestnut candles had begun to shed their blossom and occasional discs of pink showed among the white petals which scattered the grass. At the end of this vista we could see the two horses, unsaddled a few minutes earlier, rolling in ecstasy before finding their feet again with a snort and a shake, then grazing and idly swishing their tails against the gnats. In the morning, with the bangs of the rook-rifle growing fainter, one of them carried me to my next halt.

* * * *

Ötvenes was the last of this particular concatenation of friends and houses and, like all the others, I had met the inhabitants that first evening at Tibor's. The family were Swabians who had settled here when these territories were regained from the Turks, and the spread of their acres had soon enrolled them into the dominant stratum. Can the preceding centuries of conflict be compared to the long process of the *Reconquista* in Spain, with Ottomans instead of Moors? The earlier campaigns, with the victories of Hunyadi and Báthory and Zrinyi, bear a distinct affinity: but the energies of later Transylvanian heroes were spent in making the Principality, for a time at least, and under Turkish vassaldom, a bastion of Magyar liberties against the Habsburgs. Shrewd connubial skill in marrying the Hungarian royal heiress, and then declaring the crown hereditary instead of elective, had enabled the dynasty to swallow up Hungary; and when the Emperor's armies at last advanced downstream, the Imperialists had come to look on the liberated Hungarians as a conquered race. Hence the foreign settlements and the quantities of non-Hungarian names that suddenly scattered the redeemed lands. Strangers were summoned from abroad; during the last three centuries the Holy Roman Empire and the Kingdom of Hungary became cosmopolitan, and in nothing so much as in the commanders of their armies; but their offspring had been assimilated long ago. As though to illustrate this, two brothers who came over from a nearby estate bore the famous Genoese name of Pallavicini. Were they descended from the margrave who murdered Cardinal Martinuzzi, the saviour of Transylvania, half-Venetian himself? I had just been reading about him, but didn't dare to ask. Another guest, a tall princess, married to an erudite naturalist landowner called Béla Lipthay, from Lovrin in the Banat, was a descendant (not direct, I hope) of Pope Innocent IX of the famous house of Odescalchi, lords of Bracciano.*

Georgina, the daughter of the house, looked like a fair-haired

* According to Sir Walter Scott (or Macaulay quoting him; I've searched both in vain and will probably come on the passage the day after this book is out), Bracciano, by its reedy lake, was the best example of a mediaeval fortress he had ever seen: clustering cylindrical towers soar into the sky of Latium and spread narcissistic machicolated corollas high above their still reflections many fathoms below.

Englishwoman on safari, and she was as good a horsewoman as Clara. Separated from a long-absent Czech husband, she was striving without much hope for an annulment in order to marry an even better horseman than either. He was sun-scorched, lean, delightful and stone deaf. Full of misgivings, her kind-hearted parents, and especially her mother, took the hazards of my journey very seriously. A son of hers had been in Brazil for fifteen years and if I had let her, she would have stuffed the whole of his wardrobe in my rucksack.

I can remember every detail of this house, and of all the others; and the inhabitants, the servants, the dogs and the horses and the scenery are all intact. Perhaps being a stranger in this remote society knocked down some of the customary barriers, for I became an intimate of their lives, and feelings ran deeper and lasted much longer than anything warranted by the swift flight of these weeks in the marches of Transylvania. This particularly joyful sojourn was made even more so by the arrival of Ria for the last few days. We watched the building of an enormous rick and cantered through the woods on a paper-chase; and on my last day we discovered some rockets in a woodshed and sent them all up after dinner.

Every part of Europe I had crossed so far was to be torn and shattered by the war; indeed, except for the last stage before the Turkish frontier, all the countries traversed by this journey were fought over a few years later by two mercilessly destructive powers; and when war broke out, all these friends vanished into sudden darkness. Afterwards the uprooting and destruction were on so tremendous a scale that it was sometimes years after the end of it all that the cloud became less dense and I could pick up a clue here and there and piece together what had happened in the interim. Nearly all of them had been dragged into the conflict in the teeth of their true feelings and disaster overtook them all. But in this charming and cheerful household, the tragedy that smote in the middle of that grim time had nothing to do with conflict: a fire sprang up in the night and the whole family and the combustible manor house that contained it were turned to ashes.

5

Across the Forest

"FRATER PETRE, possumusne kugli ludere post Vesperas?"

"Hodie non possumus, fili," Brother Peter said. "Tarde nimium est. Cras poterimus."

"Quando? Qua hora?"

"Statim post Missam. Expecte me ad egressum ecclesiae."

"Bene, frater, sed nonne ante Missam fieri potest?"

"Velnon. Est contra regulam nostram."

"Eheu!"

Easy to spot the odd man out in this dog-Latin! *Kugli—Kegeln* in German—is Magyar for skittles. Brother Peter was assistant guest-master in the Conventual Franciscan Abbey of Maria Radna, and the cheerful face and tonsured head, the sandals, brown hooded habit and the white cord knotted round his wide waist gave him a convincing look of Friar Tuck; and as we had no common tongue, Latin was forced on us. (My share of the conversation was less glib than it looks. I thought out each sentence in advance, hoping to place a supine in *um*; and I was struck by the use of *velnon*. I couldn't find it in Latin dictionaries later so perhaps it was just the two words, a negative only used in church circles to take the place of the non-existent 'no'; but it sounded single. 'Yes' was *etiam*.) Except for construing at school or spouting verse on the road, I had no more spoken Latin than anyone else, so all this gave an exhilarating illusion of slipping back to the time when Latin was the common tongue of literate Europe: it conjured up the world of the wandering scholars whom I had presumptuously thought of as models before setting out, and lately rather drifted away from.

The way from Ötvenes that morning had run south-east until the wooded hills fell asunder about twenty miles east of Arad, where my path joined the beautiful valley of the Maros; and then, a little way upstream, the bronze cupolas of the Maria Radna caught the afternoon light. The Abbey was founded in 1520, but nobody, at a glance, would have connected this High Baroque pile with the Franciscan Order. Destroyed in the sixteenth century by the army of Mustafa II, it was re-built in its new shape when the Ottomans were routed a hundred years later. Then a wonder-working image of Our Lady made it famous; patronage accumulated, and the church filled with pilgrims and *ex votos*.

Dappled with the shadows of chestnut leaves, a wide staircase climbed between the tall baroque statues of St. Francis of Assisi and St. John Nepomuk. At the top, I fell in with Brother Peter setting up an array of skittles. He was looking for someone to play with, so my arrival was well-timed and we played all through the late afternoon, happily incommunicado except for our occasional cumbrous Latin. It needed some strength to send the heavy balls clashing and scattering among the giant ninepins: we were both in a muck-sweat when the bell for Vespers put an end to play and it was after helping him collect the skittles that the foregoing colloquy took place. Vespers over, he led me to a guest cell and later to the refectory, where about forty monks sat down to supper while one of them read aloud from a pulpit, first in Latin and then in Magyar.* I met him again in the cloisters after Compline and asked him, "Dormitum ibant omnes?"—I had been ready for it!—but he only smiled and put a finger across his lips: it was the first time I had stayed under a monastic roof and the *magnum silentium* had begun.

Next morning, 2nd June, was a Sunday, and he was busy with visitors, so I waited as bidden, fearing he might have to play *non possum*; but he arrived in a flurry of cord and homespun, and when we had finished our game, I tried to leave some money; he waved it aside—I was a stranger, a *viator* and a *pelegrinus*; so I dropped some coins

* The only followers of the Latin Rite in this part of Rumania were the Hungarians and the Swabians. The surrounding population were mostly Uniats, I think: Catholics of the Oriental Rite, that is, whose Orthodox liturgy had been sung in Rumanian since the late seventeenth century, after the Greek period which followed the original Church Slavonic.

through a slot in the church with a face-saving jingle. Helping me on with my rucksack, he said, "May God go with you," in Latin, and then, "Quoniam angelis suis mandavit de te, ut custodiant te in omnibus viis tuis." Impressed by the words, and rather puzzled, I started down the great staircase towards the river; they had been spoken like a quotation and I wondered where they came from.*

* * * *

When the river Danube had fallen behind a month earlier, then the Tisza and finally the Great Hungarian Plain, I had felt I was saying goodbye to famous landmarks. I had never heard of the Maros.†

It is the great river of Transylvania and its tributaries spread like a fan of nerve-ends across the whole western slant of the Carpathians where they rush downhill and cohere in a great stream that wends south-westwards through minor ranges, sweeps past the Abbey, and then rolls on into Hungary. At Szeged it joins the Tisza about seventy miles south of the bridge that Melek and I had clip-clopped across at Szolnok; then the united waters drop deep into Yugoslavia and enter the Danube; soon the Sava, swollen with tribute from Slavonia and the Alps, joins the great river under the walls of Belgrade and then, with all their individualities drowned in the Danubian currents, they advance on the Iron Gates and head for the Black Sea.

Hills enclosed the north bank of this particular reach and the monastery was hardly out of sight before the tapering ruins of the castle of Solymos jutted on a pedestal of rock; it was a stronghold of the great John Hunyadi but much older than he. Then the trees of the foothills began to pile up in waves, with sprays of wild lilac scattered among the branches. The hills on the other shore stood aloof, and between the two ranges the great river lazily unwound. Sometimes it

---

* The problem was solved twenty years later at the Abbey of St. Wandrille in Normandy. It is the eleventh verse of Psalm 91 and, as it is sung every night at Compline, I must have heard it the night before.

† The Rumanian, thus the official name is Mureş (pronounced 'Mooresh'), but as chance willed that I only heard its Magyar form of Maros (pronounced 'Marosh') during this part of the journey, I find it unnatural to put it down differently. From now on there are often two or three names for geographical features, so confusions are bound to occur and I apologise for them in advance.

looped away for a mile or two, then meandered back and the clouds
of willows and aspens that marked its windings were interspersed with
poplars tapering in spindles or expanding like butterfly nets. The
women in the fields wore kerchiefs on their heads under hats of soft
plaited straw as wide as cart-wheels; leaves like broken assegais plumed
the tall maize; an occasional breeze ruffled the wheat; the vines, all
sprayed with sulphate, climbed in tiers. Pale cattle with wide, straight
horns grazed by the score and the fens and water-meadows that lay
about the river were wallows for buffaloes; lustrous as seals, or caked
in dried mud as armour against insects, they were sometimes only to
be spotted in the slime and the swamps by bubbles or an emerging
nostril. Wherever horses and mares with their foals moved loose about
the grass, a few ragged tents were sure to be pitched. Everything in
these reedy windings was inert and hushed under a sleepy spell of
growth and untroubled plenty.

I found a clump of alders full of buttercups, poppies and dandelion-
clocks, ate bread and cheese and gave way to the prevailing lethargy;
then woke up with greenfinches and a cloud of gnats fidgeting in the
twigs overhead. I hadn't far to go. It had been arranged that I should
stay the night at Mr. v. Konopy's. I learnt that I had passed the
kastély a few miles back, so I got a lift on a hay-waggon and the driver
soon pointed out a country house jutting from the wooded hillside.

*   *   *   *

It might have been a rural deanery, and Mr. v. Konopy, with his
mild manner and silvery hair, could easily have been a clergyman;
there was a touch of Evensong about him. His hobby was wheat-
breeding and the two Swedish colleagues staying with him were as
soft-voiced and as quiet as he. Wheat-ears covered the furniture and
one of the Swedes, well versed in the English terminology of his
passion, explained as we strolled from specimen to specimen the
differences between turgid ears and the common bearded kind; then
we surveyed the Polish variety and appraised the spikelets and the
awns, the median florets and the glumes. He had brought Mr. v.
Konopy a German edition of *The Story of San Michele*, which had been
all the rage in England a few years earlier. Two calm days drifted while

he read it aloud. It was all very different from the recent ambience of antlers and hooves and Tibor's memories of champagne out of dancers' slippers.

*　*　*　*

The hills along the north bank grew higher and as the trees multiplied, I had the feeling of plunging inextricably in deep and unknown regions. By mid-afternoon I got to Soborsin,* where a Nádasdy château lay secluded in the woods, and crossed a bridge to the other bank. Although this region south of the river was Transylvanian in feeling, strictly speaking it was the north-easternmost corner of the old Banat of Temesvár, named after its capital—Timişoara in Rumanian—which lies to the west. Lost by Hungary to the advancing Turks in the six-teenth century and largely depopulated, it was reconquered by Prince Eugene and Count Pálffy two centuries later, and resettled. The largest single element of the modern province was Rumanian, as it had been all along my itinerary, but it was said that the newcomers were of such varied origins that a chameleon placed on a coloured population-map of the Banat would explode.†

After an hour or two, I loped exhausted through long shadows to the kastély at Kápolnás. Double flights of steps mounted to a balustraded terrace, where people were sitting out in the cool moment before the sun set; there were glimpses through french windows of lighted rooms beyond. Count Paul Teleki, my kind geographical benefactor in Budapest, had written to the owner, who was his first cousin, and I had telephoned the day before. He was called Count Eugene of the same name—Jenö in Hungarian—and he got up and ambled hospitably across.

"So you managed it?" he said kindly; then, rather surprisingly, "Come and sit ye doon."

He was a tall, spreading, easy-going middle-aged man, with gold-rimmed spectacles and a remarkably intelligent, slightly ugly and very

* Şavarşin.

† A 'Ban', a Persian word first brought to these regions by the Avars, was a military governor and his jurisdiction was a Banat, a term later applied to some frontier provinces of Hungary, Slavonia and Croatia; but the unqualified 'Banat' has always meant this particular region. Rather oddly, a Ban never ruled over it.

amusing face; like his cousin's, it had a remotely Asiatic look. I knew he was a famous entomologist and a great authority on moths, especially those of the Far East, and he was said to keep two insect-hunters permanently busy, one in China, the other in Japan, sending him back a steady flow of specimens. Lepidoptera were on parade in glass cases all over the house. Some of them were large and furry and brightly coloured, some drab or stick-like or transparent and some almost too small to see. Apart from this, he had all the instincts of a polymath: everything aroused his curiosity and sent him climbing unwieldily up the library steps. He delighted in gossip and comic stories, and he had a passion for limericks, the racier the better. He would reminisce for hours: one fascinating anecdote would lead to another; many of them depicted famous or venerable figures in an absurd but always amusing light. He thirsted for similar stories and success was rewarded by overmastering though nearly silent laughter, upheavals of inaudible hilarity that left him carefully wiping his spectacles with his handkerchief as composure returned. He was much travelled and knew the British Isles well; his English was nearly perfect and a nanny from the Highlands had left him with a stock of Scotch sayings uttered with just a hint of inverted commas: asked what he thought of a neighbour, he said, "I hae me doots"; and, toying with some dilemma, "I'll dree my own weird". (Before the war, it would have been hard to exaggerate the sway of British nannies among some Central European children; toes kept count of pigs going to market before fingers learnt to tell beads and Three Blind Mice rushed in much earlier than inklings of the Trinity.) His wife, Countess Catherine —Tinka—was tall, dark-haired, fine looking, very kind and very intelligent, and widely read in quite different fields from his. In one particular, she was literally unique in this marooned Hungarian society: she was Rumanian; but of an unusual kind. A number of Hungarian families in Transylvania had, in fact—however fervently Hungarian they became when they rose in the world—once been of Rumanian stock. The Countess's ancestors were from exactly this mould, except that, though they were Hungarian nobles, they remembered their origins and supported Rumanian aspirations. Magyar may have been their earliest language for generations; but, as MPs, they always expressed heterodox views in the Budapest parliament. Count Jenö, scion of one of the great Hungarian houses of Transylvania, was as deeply rooted in post-war resentment as any backwoods squire, though he was not emphatic in expressing it; while Countess Tinka, when occasion arose, was discreetly eloquent on the opposite side; and when one of them uttered controversial views, the other would later make it privately clear to a guest that they were nonsense. ("What a pity! Jenö's such a clever man, but so biased," and, "Well, I'm afraid Tinka was talking through her hat again . . .") They were extremely fond of each other and far too civilised for public contradiction. There was a nice looking, rather spoilt son called Michael and his Hungarian tutor at the castle, and a moving population of visitors; and one was aware of the Countess's recently invalid mother in one wing of the building. "She's not feeling quite the thing," the Count said.

* * * *

Dense woods shot up steeply behind the house. In front, wavering meadows sank gently towards the Maros but the steep woods were echoed on the northern bank. "It's only early nineteenth-century," the Count said, referring to his house, "and perhaps a bit showy." Rusticated ashlars formed the first storey, pilasters rose to a cornice and fluted Corinthian columns ran the length of a façade adorned with the masks of sibyls and nymphs and satyrs.

The terrace was the Count's afternoon and evening retreat. He would sit and talk in one of the wicker chairs for hours or stroll disquisitively under a grey linen sunshade lined with green. A more ambitious walk led to the stables. A loft there harboured fantails and a brood of tumbler pigeons which soared, hovered, turned back-somersaults, then dropped like stones and recovered in a flurry of snowy plumage that was entrancing to watch. Lilac shaded the homeward path. The peonies were dropping their last petals and the air was full of the scent of lime trees in flower.

But the library, with its thousands of books and its nets and vascula and collector's gear, was his favourite haunt. He led me there after breakfast and I would explore with the step-ladder while he settled down at his table with a sigh of pleasure. Unpacking parcels, covered with strange stamps and posted in the foothills of Fujiyama or at some river-port on the Yangtse, he would begin sorting out the contents with tweezers, inspecting them under a lens or a microscope and accompanying his task with a murmured multilingual commentary. ". . . Jól van . . . gyönyörü! . . . What a beauty. Look at this chap! Ah so *there* you are at last! . . . and here's *Euploea leucostictus* . . . from Java, I bet . . . *Hullo. What's this?* . . . I'll look him up in Hampson . . . or Kirby . . . I dinna ken, I dinna ken . . . or in Breitenbach, perhaps . . ." It was impossible to think of anyone happier. As far as I was concerned, boundless treasures beckoned: rows of encyclopaedias in several languages, the cynical Latin verses of Janus Pannonius, a fifteenth-century Hungaro-Croatian bishop of Pécs, 'the Martial of Hungary'; memoirs and prints of old Transylvanian life, letters-patent, transfers of villeins, parchment title-deeds with bulky red seals; genealogies gleaming with scutcheons tricked or illuminated in faded hues and the marvellous and many-volumed *Geographie Universelle* of Elysée Reclus. A score of temptations lured one to trifle the morning away.

The Count was prone to abstruse prepossessions. At the moment he was much taken by Hugo v. Kutschera's theory about the Ashkenazi Jews of Eastern Europe: could they really spring from the inhabitants of the old Khazar empire, whose rulers abandoned paganism for the Jewish faith in the Dark Ages? He was particularly interested by the evidence of correspondence between Itil—the Khazar capital near the mouth of the Volga, roughly on the site of Astrakhan—and the Hebrew scholars of Cordova: were the letters forgeries? Had King Joseph of the Khazars and the Andalusian Rabbi Hazdai-ibn-Shaprut really been in touch?* Once, following up some research on the runic inscriptions of the Goths, he got led astray and, looking up from a book, asked in a surprised voice what I thought the Huns used to wear. I said I should have guessed the hides of animals with some metal here and there. "So should I," he said, "but we are wrong," and he read

* The memory of Count Jenö's prepossession cropped up at luncheon with Arthur Koestler in an Athens taverna about twenty years ago. Immediately alert, Koestler said it had interested him too, but he didn't know as much about it as he would like. A year or two later *The Thirteenth Tribe* appeared, causing a stir among Jewish historians. Could this taverna conversation have been the impulse that prompted him to take it up again? It is too late to ask him.

out from Ammianus Marcellinus' account of the mission to Attila: "They are clad in linen raiment or in the skins of field mice sewn together."*

His family had always been immersed in travel and science and literature. One branch explored Central Africa and discovered lakes and volcanoes on the Ethiopian border; my Budapest friend had mapped archipelagoes in the Far East; Count Samuel Teleki, a wily Transylvanian chancellor in the eighteenth century gathered 40,000 books together in Márosvásarhély—Târgu Mureș in Rumanian—in a library specially built for them, and gave it to the town: it was crammed with incunabula and *princeps* editions and manuscripts, including one of the earliest of Tacitus. (He must be the same as a namesake who collected and edited the epigrams of Pannonius.) A Count Joseph Teleki, travelling in France with this bibliophile cousin, became a friend and partisan of Rousseau and launched a clever attack on Voltaire, which ran into three editions; and here it was on the shelf: *Essai sur la Foiblesse des Esprits Forts*, Leyden, 1760. My bedroom contained part of the library's overflow: Henty, Ballantyne, *Jock of the Bushveld*, *Owd Bob*, *The Story of the Red Deer*, *Black Beauty*, *The Jungle Books* and the *Just So Stories*. There were any amount of Tauchnitz editions, industriously tunnelled by insects, faded by the last summers of the Habsburg monarchy and redolent of those peaceful times when, apart from the habitual ragged fusillade in the Balkans, scarcely a shot was fired between the battle of Sedan and Sarajevo: Ouida, Mrs. Belloc Lowndes, *The Dolly Dialogues*, *My Friend Prospero*, *The Cardinal's Snuffbox*, *The Indiscretions of Ambrosine*, *Elizabeth and her German Garden*; Maupassant, Gyp, Paul de Kock, Victor Margueritte, early Colette . . . But the most important and revealing trove was half a dozen historical novels by the Hungarian writer Maurus Jókai (1825-1904), translated in Victorian days: *'Midst the Wild Carpathians*, *Slaves of the Padishah*, *An Hungarian Nabob*, *The Nameless Castle*, *The*

---

* Bruce Chatwin, for whom nomads and their history hold fewer and fewer secrets, tells me that this is borne out by finds from 400 BC, dug up in a Turkic *kurgan* (barrow) at Katanda in the Altai kept intact by the permafrost, of a nomad chief clad in a patchwork jerkin of lozenges, 4″ × 3″, dyed orange, blue, yellow and red, skinned off small mammals—jerboas, perhaps, that bound about the steppe.

Poor Plutocrats, Pretty Michael, Halil the Pedlar, Ein Fürstensohn—there were several more. The plots were laid in stirring times: the Kossuth rebellion, the wars against the Turks with the whole of Transylvania going up in flames; soaring castles, yawning chasms, wolves, feuding magnates, janissaries, spahis, pashas with six horsetails, sieges, battle-fields and last stands; stories involving all the great figures of local history: Hunyadi, Zrinyi, Thököly, the Rákóczi dynasty, Bocskays, Bethlens, Báthorys, Bánffys—B's seem to abound among Transylvanian leaders and princes; and Telekis, of course. The plots were a heady mixture of Scott, Harrison Ainsworth and Dumas *père* transposed to the Carpathians and the puszta. It was after dipping into these and asking about them, on the banks of the Maros where the Countess had taken us all to a bathing picnic, that the idea of an historical jaunt cropped up.

It warranted the emergence of the car, a solemn event in these regions of bad roads. The Countess drove, and when a wandering buffalo held us up, the Count, with memories of Cowes, would lift his hand and murmur, "Sail before steam!" and we would wait while it lumbered over. We drove eastwards along the leafy north bank of the river, turned south under the steep, ruin-crowned hill at Deva,* and got out a few valleys further on, where precariously tall stone piers lifted a narrow bridge over a chasm.

On the other side perched the castle of Vajdahunyad,† chief strong-hold of the great John Hunyadi, a building so fantastic and theatrical that, at a first glance, it looked totally unreal. Like many castles, it had once been damaged by fire and built up again in its former shape; but it was perfectly genuine. The bridge led to a sallyport in a tall barbican which ended high above in a colonnade supporting a vertiginous roof that soared in a wedge, like the great barbicans in Prague: spikes of metal or shingle erected for the laming of infernal cavalry flying low after dark. Towers, clustering at different heights, some square and some round and all of them frilled with machicolations, were embedded in the steep fabric. The light showing between the pillars holding up

---

* It is haunted by the sacrifice of the master mason's wife, like the Bridge of Arta in Epirus and Curtea de Argeş in Wallachia. All three are the theme of old ballads.   † Hunedoara.

the great angular cowl of the barbican gave the pile an airy, lifted, slightly improbable look, and the closely spaced parade of the perpendicular buttresses made the upward thrust still more impetuous. Beginning deep in the abyss, these piers of masonry ascended the curtain wall and the donjon and the outside of the banqueting hall in unbroken flight and then burst out high above in a row of half-salient and half-engaged octagonal side-towers, all of them lighted by windows which carried on a dominating line of mullioned lancets, and an inter-weaving network of late gothic tracery branched and flourished and linked them together with all the impulse and elaboration of the French Flamboyant style.

Along the eaves of the precipice of roof overhead, the jutting towers ended in disengaged extinguisher-tops, cones that alternated with faceted octagonal pyramids and barbed the eaves with a procession of spikes, while beyond them coloured tiles diapered the roofs in intricate patterns, like those on St. Stephen's in Vienna. Beyond the sallyport, the inner courtyard mounted in galleries and balustrades and tiers of Romanesque arches; cusped ogees led to spiralling steps; and indoors, springing from the leafy capitals of polygonal rose-coloured marble pillars, beautiful late gothic vaults closed over the Hall of the Knights. I had seen nothing like it since Vienna and Prague; the sudden outburst of flamboyant moulding conjured up the Hradcany and the banks of the Loire.*

My head was full of Hunyadi and I paced the yards and climbed the steps and explored the vaulted chambers in a state of great excitement. He is the most celebrated hero in Hungarian history; Rumanians rightly claim him as a kinsman; and he was the greatest fifteenth-century champion of the whole of Christendom. When young, he entered the service of King Sigismund of Hungary (son of the blind King of Bohemia killed at Crecy; and, later, Holy Roman Emperor), whose natural son Hunyadi was sometimes rumoured to be. He won brilliant victories, ruled Transylvania in times of trouble and finally

---

* An exact replica of this castle stands among poplars on a lake-island in the City Park of Budapest. It was put up in honour of Hunyadi for the 1898 celebrations of a thousand years of Hungarian history, and it was the memory of this fleeting glimpse which, for a moment, had given the Transylvanian original its almost fictional look.

administered the whole kingdom. His campaign in the Balkans broke the Sultan's power in Herzegovina, Bosnia, Serbia, Bulgaria and Albania; and his greatest single achievement was the rout, outside beleaguered Belgrade, of the army of Mehmet II, three years after the conquering Sultan had captured Constantinople. This deliverance, and the triumph over the invincible Mehmet, were re-celebrated daily by church bells rung at noon throughout the Catholic world; in Hungary they still are. The victory had reprieved the kingdom for seventy more years, until the battle of Mohács, in fact. Known all over Europe as the White Knight, he was not only a great commander and statesman, but a rock of uprightness in a kingdom and an age that seethed with conspiracy.*

Born in late Plantagenet times, he was coeval with Joan of Arc and the Wars of the Roses. (It is only by links like these, and sometimes by dress, that I can fix historical figures in their backgrounds, and I put them in these pages now and then in case the reader suffers in the same way.) The architectural flourishes on the castle may have been the work of his famous son, who enlarged it.† Matthias, in a slightly different way, was as remarkable as his father. Usually known as Matthias Corvinus or Corvin from the raven on their shield, he accompanied his father's campaigns at the age of twelve; later he was elected to the throne of Hungary by forty thousand nobles precariously assembled on the frozen Danube and he became one of their greatest kings. Fresh victories over the Turks continued his father's task in the Balkans; he scattered the armies of the Poles and the Emperor and strove with the Hussites; and the Czech Catholics elected him King of Bohemia. He invested Breslau, occupied Ancona, recovered Otranto from the Turks, and his reduction of half Austria was marked by a triumphal entry into Vienna. Apart from his martial gifts, he was a statesman, a

* Some experts, including David Rosenthal, its most recent translator, are convinced that the great Catalan epic of chivalry, *Tirant lo Blanc*, was based on the feats of Hunyadi. Written a few decades after the hero's death, it was one of the favourite books of Cervantes; and if, as some think, *lo Blanc*—'the White'—is really 'the Vlach' (V and B being interchangeable), the theory of his Rumanian paternity is strengthened.

† It was added to further by Gábor Bethlen, the celebrated Thirty Years War commander.

legislator, an orator and a scholar of singular brilliance who used to sit up half the night over his books. 'Undisputably the greatest man of his day,' an English historian says, 'and one of the greatest who ever reigned.' He was profoundly learned, a polyglot, a passionate humanist, the collector of the fabulous Corvinus Library, and a great palace-builder—a splendid Renaissance prince, in fact; but, unlike many of these (the historian continues), 'with his immeasurable experience of ingratitude and treachery, he was never guilty of a single cruel or vindictive action.'

The fine state of the castle was an exception to the post-war neglect or abolition of Hungarian monuments which I had been hearing about, and for a very good reason. 'János Hunyadi', says the Encyclopaedia Britannica, and nearly all historians agree, 'was the son of Vojk (or Vaic), a magyarised Vlach,' which means that the great crusader was of Rumanian origin. The Rumanians felt, and still feel a justifiable pride in their share in these two paragons, especially in the father; perhaps the son's Western field of activity, and an identification with the Catholic Church even closer than his father's, carried him too far from the ambit of the Orthodox East. Of course Rumanians were proud of him, and with every right. But anyone reading the explanatory notices inside the castle might assume that Hunyadi was a purely Rumanian hero: the Hungarian activities with which his whole life was bound up were underplayed to such a degree that he might have had nothing to do with the kingdom. It was sad to see this shining figure dragged into the bitterness and murk of territorial rivalry. The splendour seemed all at once dim and parochial.

Count Jenö reacted with fatalism, "They seem to think the Treaty of Trianon awarded them Hungarian history as well as territory," he said, moodily uncorking a bottle. "It's like Corsicans celebrating Napoleon without mentioning France." Turning our backs on the rust and slag of some iron-works nearby, we had settled under a tree. The castle soared straight ahead. "Well," the Countess said, laying plates on the grass and handing round chicken sandwiches, "I expect the Hungarians underplayed the Rumanian side."

I expect they did.

*　　*　　*　　*

So the first weeks of June slipped by with books and talk and jaunts and exchanges of visits. Many neighbours called; the hair of one of them was dyed a rich and obvious auburn. "He's great fun," said the Count. "But his appearance! O wad some power the giftie gie us, to see oursels as ithers see us!" They took me with them to luncheon at the Nádasdy château across the river; it was inhabited by a tall, distinguished couple: Hunyadis, like the hero, but not relations, I believe. A Hungarian diplomatist called Baron Apor was staying with them— it is odd how figures seen only once suddenly shoot into the memory, complete at all points: he had a spherical, totally shaven head and I can see the shine of his scalp, and the veined bloodstone on his signet ring, as though he had left the room a minute ago; but can't recall a syllable that was said.

A cousin of the Countess lived at Bulci, a few miles away, and their family's adherence to Rumanian causes in the pre-war Hungarian parliament had stood him in good stead when it was over. With a high-bridged nose and receding chin, fiftyish, cosmopolitan, urbane and clever, he was an excellent shot, and King Carol had appointed him Grand Veneur du Roi, or Master of the Royal Hunt; the position involved game, beaters and shooting rather than horses and hounds. (Count Jenö explained—with a sniff, I thought—that his cousin-in-law's footing in both camps might have suggested him to the King as a possible bridge between the Rumanians and the Hungarian Transylvanians: then he shrugged dismissively, and said, "What a hope!") The Grand Veneur had a house-party from Bucharest. "He's bringing them over for a bite!" the Count announced; and there was daily to-and-fro movement during their stay.

Apart from peasants and my hostess—who, in a way, only half counted—these were the only Rumanians I had met; and, from the *Regat* or the 'Old Kingdom', absolutely the first. One was a tall diplomatist with a monocle, rather aloof and quiet, a minister on leave called Grégoire Duca.* The well-cut Paris country clothes and the pearls of the women, and their discreet but just detectable scent trans-

---

* His brother Jean, the last Prime Minister, had been assassinated by the Iron Guard six months before. "A horrible lot of people," Count Jenö succinctly said; then: "What a pity! Duca was the best politician in the country."

ported us to the pages of *Vogue*. All of them spoke English well, but, rather astonishingly, conversed among themselves in French as though it were their first language; and, strangely, so it was. One, extremely beautiful and with enormous grey-green eyes, was the daughter of a former Foreign Minister. (At the opera in Paris, where he was staying for the Peace Conference, a friend had asked him who someone—another Rumanian—had married; and he had answered, truthfully, "Une grue, hélas", "Alas, a harlot"; and a few moments later, a hand appeared from the next box, holding a visiting card from the husband in question; there was a duel with pistols and her father was shot through the stomach and spent the rest of his life in great pain.) "Their duels are much worse than our affairs with sabres, where you just slash away," the Count said. "They go in for pistols—or rapiers which are just as bad." Another woman—chalk white, dressed all in black with a long jade cigarette-holder and transfigured in a permanent cloud of smoke—was a passionate and famous bridge player and rather frightening; another, Marcelle, nice-looking and intelligent, was attached to a tall, charming and good-looking diplomatist called Josias v. Rantzau. When trim chauffeurs had driven them off in two dark and gleaming motor-cars, the Count suggested a wee drappie in the library and it was as we sipped that we learnt all about them. "Rantzau is First Secretary at the German Legation," Count Jenö said, "comes from Holstein; they are great people there. Mixed up with the court of Mecklenburg-Strelitz or is it Schwerin?—I never can remember. Louis XIV made one of them a marshal of France but Mazarin locked him up in the Bastille . . ." (I repeat these details because these new acquaintances reappear three hundred miles and five months further on; Josias v. Rantzau and I got to know each other well, as we shall see;* and some of them recurred in my life later still, and long after these travels came to an end.)

"How smart they are," the Countess said, rather ruefully. "They make one feel very rustic and dowdy."

---

* He was a close friend of Adam v. Trott and was involved, later on, in the Stauffenberg Conspiracy, though it seems he had scruples about actual assassination. See Tatiana Metternich's autobiography *Tatiana* in England, *Under Five Passports* in the United States and *The Berlin Diaries 1940-45* of 'Missie' Vassiltchikov (Chatto, 1986).

"'And what ho! when they lifted the lid!'" Count Jenö murmured, as he lifted the top off a freshly-arrived box of specimens. In spite of his eagerness for new limericks, he remained true to those he had learnt in his youth. "'What ho! when they lifted the lid!'" he repeated in delectation, tweezers in hand; the word 'chuckle' might have been coined for him. I had thought of a riddle during the night and sprang it on him at breakfast:

PLF, "Which is the most entomological of Shakespeare's plays?"

JT (after a pause), "I give up."

PLF, "Antennae and Coleoptera."

It was a great success and the words immediately wove themselves into the multilingual comment and soliloquy and the fragments of limerick that accompanied his task of unpacking and classification—"Ah! There's a bonny wee fellow! . . . Kenspeckle! Antennae and Coleoptera, indeed! *Retenetes*!".* While he adjusted the milled controls of his microscope, I settled with a pile of books and a peaceful library morning lay ahead.

But soon the Countess came in, looking troubled. Her mother had taken a steep and sudden turn for the worse: it looked as though the kastély might be turned into a house of mourning. My next stepping-stone had been arranged; it was the other side of the river at Zám, some miles upstream; and I determined, against polite demur, to set off in the morning.

*   *   *   *

Strictly speaking, Zám was the first real Transylvanian halt on this journey. The frontier of the old principality lay just west of the village, and its southern border was the river. Xenia, the kastély-dweller there, was thirty years old but looked much younger. She was very pretty and altogether unusual. Her father, Michael Csernovitz, whom everyone spoke of with affection, had been to school in England and travelled all over the world, and the tall, exotic trees he had brought back overshadowed the walks and the pools. When Count Jenö was mentor to a newcomer (as he was here, with me) history seemed to drop from the air and spring out of the ground. He told me

* Pronounced '*Rett*-en-ett-esh!', it means 'terrible'.

that a collateral ancestor of Csernovitz had been the famous Arsenius, independent Orthodox Patriarch of Ipek,★ which stands on the edge of Albania, Montenegro and the old Sanjak of Novipazar. At the Emperor Leopold's prompting, he rose against the Turks at the time of Prince Eugene's great advance in 1717 which led to yet another storming of Belgrade. But when the Turkish re-capture of the fortress threatened revenge, the Emperor granted asylum to Arsenius and his kin (hence the presence of Xenia's family at Zám) and his 40,000 Serbian followers were scattered all over the Habsburg dominions. The Csernovitzes remained Orthodox—'Greek Oriental' as they called it thereabouts—and Count Jenö and Xenia's other friends used to tease her about her wild Serbian blood. There was something arresting and unforgettable about her ivory complexion and raven hair and wide sloe-black eyes. The house had remained uninhabited for some time and there was a touch of melancholy about it, and of magic, too. At least, so it seemed for the few days I was there as we walked under the Himalayan and Patagonian trees and looked down at the Maros, which the full moon turned to mercury. The woods and streams were full of nightingales.

* * * *

The last true Transylvanian sojourn and the longest unfolded some miles further along the Maros and every detail sticks in my mind.

I had heard of István† as far back as Budapest and we had met once or twice among the moths and the limericks at Kápolnás, where they loved him. He had been sent to school at the Theresianum, that Viennese establishment set up by Maria Theresa for sons of her noble subjects: *kshatriyas* in a Brahminical hierarchy which had remained unaltered until the Empire and the Kingdom had both vanished forever. (The place was closely linked to the Konsular Akademie, where I had pored

---

★ It is now Peć, in southern Yugoslavia. The Patriarch's old monastery still stands, shaded by plane trees and full of marvellous frescoes. The region is almost entirely inhabited today by those Albanian Moslems known as Kossovars.

† Some of the people in these pages have vanished from the scene but here and there, when, like István, and Angéla in the next chapter, they are as extant as I am, it seems best to alter names. It gives greater freedom in piecing together their talk. Also, many things have changed since those easy-going times.

over maps in February; and, which rather impressed me, the students of both places formerly wore cocked hats and dress-swords, like *Young Törless*.) He ran away to join a Hussar regiment during the War and was commissioned at once, just in time for all the disasters. Later, during the Béla Kun regime, he escaped from one of Szamuely's execution squads and was involved in the troubled aftermath; and soon afterwards Transylvania was ceded to Rumania. Cultivated, tall, fine-looking with a hawk's nose, a high forehead and wide clear blue eyes like a francolin's, he was a brilliant shot, horseman and steeplechaser, and a virtuoso in all he took up. He was now in his early thirties and at the height of his vigour; and his dash, charm, enterprise and humour made him liked by everyone, though it sometimes landed him in scrapes, including four of 'those affairs with sabres', each time as the challenged party. Land-reform soon left very little of an estate which, though it had always prospered, had never been enormous. His family's tenure had been long; his elderly parents still lived there. He was linked with a deep atavistic attachment to the place, and though managing the remnant of arable and forest had kept him from seeking new fortunes abroad, the confinement irked him. When we talked of my earlier intention of joining the Indian army, his eyes kindled. "I'd have loved that!" he said. "Could I do it now, do you think?" Why not? An Irish O'Donnell had been governor of Transylvania in the eighteenth century; "and what about that chap Rantzau's relation—a Holsteiner!—commanding an army for Louis XIV? I would be very happy with a squadron of Bengal Lancers!" He could see himself clearly in the role, and so could I.* He poured new drinks and sighed; how provincial and constricted the world had become! I admired him very much; he was tremendous fun, and we became great friends. (Like nearly everyone in these pages, he vanished from sight when the War came and the subsequent uprooting and dispersal interposed eight years before we were able to pick up the threads, and then it was by chance.)

Why not stay on a month or two, he would urge. Or a year? And what was all the hurry, even when I *did* set off?

"I've got an idea!" he exclaimed at luncheon. "We'll all club together and buy you a calf! You could drive it along the road in front of you.

* See *A Time of Gifts*, p. 196.

When it grows up, you can introduce it to a bull; and then there's another calf; and later on, another. You could arrive in Constantinople in a few years with an enormous herd . . ."

Meanwhile, like a kind host, he was eager that I should miss nothing. One of the neighbours we called on was a serious, elderly Swabian who asked me what I was studying: "Was studieren Sie?" It was an awkward question; I couldn't think of an answer. Languages? Art? Geography? Folklore? Literature? None of them seemed to fit. Seconds ticked by, and in desperation, I said, "Gar nichts!"—"Absolutely nothing!" The ensuing shocked silence lasted longer still and it was even more uncomfortable. For a German worshipper of diligence and application —*Fleissigkeit*, indeed—my confession was blasphemy, and István laughed intermittently all the way home. Absence prevented us from visiting another neighbour he thought I would be interested in. Gróf K, who lived in the Hátszeg valley beyond Vajdahunyad—Hunedoara— sounded a kind of Squire Weston, with a dash of Mytton and Waterton thrown in. "I once saw him get on a horse for a bet," István said. "Then someone tied a bag over its head. It went mad, but he managed to stay on for five minutes."

István's Rumanian was fluent in practical country matters, and one or two farming details even came to him more readily in the vernacular, but too limited for anything abstract or high-flown. Once we supped with forty peasants and farmers, some of them the new owners of his land, at a trestle-table in a clump of beech trees; and he took me to see an old shepherd, who unfolded tales of spirits, fairies and were- wolves. (*Priculici*, akin to the Slavonic *vrkolak*, were named; they were vampires. And *stafi* and *strigoi*, who sounded like a mixture of evil spirits and ghosts; and witches too, if *strigoi*, like the Italian *strega*, comes from the Latin *stryx*.) All the country people thereabouts believed in these supernaturals and dreaded them; werewolves lurked, ready to change shape at dusk; and woe to man or beast who drank the rainwater out of a bear's footprint! He also took me to a withered crone who was a witch, and begged her to recite some metrical spells. She intoned them through gums which held one dark tooth like the single eye of the Three Grey Sisters and I took down a few of them phonetically: mysterious, alliterative incantations: *descântece*. as they are called. I met similar ones in Moldavia later on.

* * * *

The kastély was much older than any I had stayed in so far. In aspect a mixture of manor house, monastery and farmstead, it stood on a tree-covered knoll overlooking the Maros, and the woods, rolling on beyond, climbed into the distance. A flattened arch through the massive ochre walls gave on a courtyard where gigantic chestnut trees still dropped their petals and the pigeons on the cobbles underneath would suddenly take off with a noise like the wind. Two sheepdogs and their puppies always bounded forward in greeting and the young storks nesting on a moss-covered barn were beginning to stretch their necks among the scarlet legs of their parents. Stables, granaries and coach-houses with carriages, wagons and sleighs lined one side of the yard and the other three were colonnades, like a cloister of square pillars sliced at the corners into octagons, and constantly traversed by the swish of the martins whose nests congregated there. Green and purple panes glimmered in a fanlight at the far end of an arcade, and the door beneath led to a loggia where we sat at night looking out over a wide vista of timber and water. Indoors, shaded paraffin lamps shed their lustre on the fine portrait of an ambassadorial ancestor and the familiar properties of a Transylvanian interior; the scutcheon scattered about the house and carved over the gate showed a bent bow with an arrow pointing skywards; at a venture, as it were.

Withdrawn from life in a cloud of smoke, István's elderly and heavily-moustached father puffed away testily behind the pages of a week-old *Pesti Hirláp*; but his mother, who spoke in French whenever I lagged behind in German, was quick and amusing, with a touch of severity and a clear glance like István's and that of his sister Ilona, who was quiet and good and kind; and after dinner they would bring their sewing out of doors, while Sándor, a correct, elderly manservant, arranged the coffee and decanters and glasses. (Several old servants wandered about the kastély; another man looked after the horses and drove the ancient carriage; and frail and aged dependants lingered in the offing. There was little actual cash about, but plenty of everything else, and I think the staff—like the family, so to speak—were paid in

kind. This was exactly how Moldavian boyars managed, further east.)
Every night István chopped up some peppery tobacco leaves on the
side-board and Ilona would arrange the flakes on a strip of linen
between the two spools of a patent machine and turn out beautifully
made cigarettes for all of us; and, when she and her mother retired, she
left a heap of new ones ready. Once or twice we sat up over old maps:
István had a passion for Napoleon's campaigns; but usually we just
sat and talked, sometimes till dawn. He hated going to bed as much as
I did; when the supply of cigarettes ran out, he rolled them by hand
with the careless skill of a cowboy (an art I mastered too) and sealed
them with a flick of the tongue, then lit them at the lamp-chimney. I
can still see the flame turning his face to a bright mask for a moment
as he twisted up the wick.

Just past its full, the moon laid a gleam of metal on the river and a
line of silver wire along the tops of the woods. The July constellations
and the Milky Way showed bright in a sky empty of vapour and as
the moon waned, stars began to shoot, dropping in great arcs, sometimes several a minute, and we would break off our talk to watch them.
They were the Perseids, meteors which shower down late that month
and in early August, from the bell- or flower-shaped constellation of
Perseus, where Algol blinks among minor stars with a restless flash.
El Ghul—the Ghoul or Fiend—is the Arabian astronomers' word for
the Gorgon, and the starry hero, grasping the snake-locks, flourishes
her head across the North and shakes these fragments loose; or so we
decided after a decanter or two. If we were late enough, nightingales
filled in the rare gaps in our talk; the Pleiades and then Orion followed
the slant of Cassiopeia and Perseus above the trees.

*   *   *   *

Long before this, startling news from outside had reached our valley.
In the middle of the night, Hitler, Goering and Himmler had rounded
up and murdered many of their colleagues, and a number—perhaps
several hundred—of the rank and file of the SA. Nobody knew how
to interpret these bloody portents but they spread dismay and little
else was spoken of for a day or two; and then the topic died, drowned
by the heat and the weight of summer.

A few days later, a telephone message announced the death of the Countess's mother. A train, flying a pale feather of smoke and looking like a toy among the trees and the hills, travelled along the valley twice a day. It carried István and me downstream through fields of tall maize and wheat; we picked up Xenia, who was sheltering from the sun under the platform-acacias of Zám, and found the Kápolnás carriage waiting at Soborsin.

The Countess was all in black. The service was held in the hall, where three Uniat priests, with short beards and clipped hair, quite unlike the flowing locks and the voluminous beards of the Orthodox clergy the other side of the Danube, intoned the funeral rite in Rumanian. (The coffin was open; it was the first time I saw anyone dead.) The ceremony ended at the family vault and, after luncheon back at the kastély where the last wisps of incense still lingered, the Count led us all to the library to show us some new specimens, "and while we're about it, we'll have a wee doch an doris afore ye gang awa'." Travelling back, I felt I had known them all for ever.

*   *   *   *

When István was in training with his regiment of Honvéd Hussars in 1917, he won the third prize for dressage out of a hundred hussars, dragoons and uhlans, and came in second for jumping. "You should have seen us moving off for Galicia and Bukovina," he said. "The uhlans in their square czapkas and red trousers, dragoons in long Waffenrocks, and hussars like us in pale blue." He still had his uniform in a cupboard, and I drew him in it: a powder-blue frogged tunic and a fur-collared dolman to be slung loose over one shoulder—"an Attila, they called it," he said, arranging the hang—Hessian boots, a shako with a white plume, and a frogged sabre. How strange this seemed, allied to that grim period of the war! I knew something about the campaigns of the Western Front; but those early mounted clashes with cossacks which led to terrible battlefields on the far slopes of the Carpathians were a matter of hearsay and dim conjecture.

Many years later, I thought of these late-night talks with István when I read and heard about the poet Férenc Békássy from his sister Eva. He was the son of a surprisingly liberal-minded landowner in western

Hungary who sent all his sons and daughters to Bedales. From there he went on to King's, Cambridge, where his poems first became known. He was an Apostle, a friend of Rupert Brooke and James Strachey and especially Maynard Keynes, who went to stay with him in Hungary during a Long Vacation. His poems—one of them is a light-hearted skit on 'A Toccata of Galuppi'—show great promise, and his last letters to friends in England, delivered posthumously when the war was over, reveal a sensitive and engaging cast of mind. Returning to Hungary at the outbreak of war, he was soon a Lieutenant in the 7th Honvéd Hussars. At the end of a letter to Noel Olivier, dated in Budapest, May 1915, he wrote, 'By the time I go, there will be roses and I shall go with a crest of three red ones on my horse's head (but people won't know the reason) because there are three over the shield in our coat-of-arms. This isn't at all the letter I meant to write, but I can't help it. I long to see you . . . And we shall meet again, shan't we, one day?' He was killed in a cavalry engagement in Bukovina on June 25th, 1915, at the age of twenty-two.*

*　　　*　　　*　　　*

One day when we were invited to luncheon by some neighbours, István said, "Let's take the horses" and we followed a roundabout, uphill track to look at a remaining piece of forest. "Plenty of common oak, thank God," he said, turning back in the saddle as we climbed a path through the slanting sunbeams, "you can use it for everything." The next most plentiful was Turkey oak, very good firewood when dry, also for stablefloors and barrelstaves. Beech came next, "It leaves scarcely any embers;" then yoke elm and common elm, "useful for furniture and coffins". There was plenty of ash, too—handy for tools, axe-helves, hammers, sickles, scythes, spades and hay-rakes. Except for a few by the brooks, there were no poplars up there but plenty by the Maros: useless, though, except for troughs and wooden spoons and the like. Gypsies made these. They settled in the garden and courtyard

---

* See Sir Roy Harrod, *The Life of John Maynard Keynes*, David Garnett's *The Golden Echo* and Dr G. Gömöri in the *New Hungarian Quarterly* (No. 79, Autumn 1980). Keynes was reproached by some of his Bloomsbury friends for arranging for the release of frozen funds for Békássy's return to take part in the war instead of safe internment for the duration.

of the kastély with their wives and their children and whittled away until they had finished. "There is no money involved," István said. "We're supposed to go halves, but, if it's an honest tribe, we're lucky to get a third. We do better with some Rumanians from out-of-the-way villages in the mountains, very poor and primitive chaps, but very honest."*

In a clearing we exchanged greetings with a white-haired shepherd leaning on a staff with a steel hook. The heavily embroidered homespun cloak flung across his shoulders and reaching to the ground was a brilliant green. His flock tore at the grass among the tree-stumps all round him. Then a path led steeply downhill through hazel-woods with old shells and acorns crunching and slipping under the horses' hooves.

It was a boiling hot day. On the way back from a cheerful feast, we went down to the river to look at some wheat. Overcome by the sight of the cool and limpid flood, we unsaddled in a shady field about the size of a paddock, took off all our clothes, climbed down through the reeds and watercress and dived in. Swimming downstream with lazy breast-stroke or merely drifting in the shade of the poplars and the willows, we talked and laughed about our recent fellow guests. The water was dappled with leafy shade near the bank and scattered with thistle-down, and a heron made off down a vista of shadows. Fleets of moorhens doubled their speed and burst noisily out of the river, and wheat, maize and tiers of vineyard were gliding past us when all at once we heard some singing. Two girls were reaping the end of a narrow strip of barley; going by the colours of their skirts and their embroidered tops, braid sashes and kerchiefs, they had come for the harvest from a valley some way off. They stopped as we swam into their ken, and, when we drew level, burst out laughing. Apparently the river was less of a covering than we had thought. They were about nineteen or twenty, with sunburnt and rosy cheeks and thick dark plaits, and not at all shy. One of them shouted something, and we stopped and trod water in mid-Maros. István interpreted, "They say

* I think they must have belonged to the interesting ancient community of the Motsi, who inhabit peaks and valleys deep in the western Transylvanian massif.

we ought to be ashamed of ourselves," he said, "and they threaten to find our clothes and run off with them."

Then he shouted back, "You mustn't be unkind to strangers! You look out, or we'll come and catch you."

"You wouldn't dare," came the answer. "Not like that, naked as frogs."

"What are these for?" István pointed to the branches by the shore. "We could be as smartly dressed as Adam."

"You'd never catch us! What about your tender white feet in the stubble? Anyway, you're too respectable. Look at your hair, going bald in front."

"*It's not!*" István shouted back.

"And that young one," cried the second girl, "he wouldn't dare."

István's blue eye was alight as he translated the last bit. Then without exchanging another word we struck out for the shore as fast as crocodiles and, tearing at poplar twigs and clumps of willow-herb, bounded up the bank. Gathering armfuls of sheaves, the girls ran into the next field, then halted at the illusory bastion of a hay-rick and waved their sickles in mock defiance. The leafy disguise and our mincing gait as we danced across the stubble unloosed more hilarity. They dropped their sickles when we were almost on them and showered us with the sheaves; then ran to the back of the rick. But, one-armed though we were, we caught them there and all four collapsed in a turmoil of hay and barley and laughter.

★   ★   ★   ★

"*Herrgott!*" I heard István suddenly exclaim—much later on, and a few yards round the curve of the rick—smiting his brow with his hand. "Oh God! The Bishop! The Gräfin! They're coming to dinner, and look at the sun!"

It was well down the sky and evening was gathering. The ricks and the poplars and the serried rows of sheaves and haycocks were laying bars of shadow over the mown field and a party of birds was flying home across the forest. István's hay-entangled hair was comically at variance with his look of consternation and we all laughed. Extracting strands of hay and the clinging barley, we tidied Safta and Ileana's plaits disordered by all this rough and tumble, and set off hand in hand with them for the river, István and I on tiptoe. "Poor feet," they murmured. After goodbyes we dived in and started the long swim back, turning many times to wave and call to those marvellous girls and they waved and answered until they were out of earshot and then, after a bend in the river, out of sight as well.

The current was faster than we thought. Close to the bank it ran sluggishly but rushes and cress and duckweed were a hindrance, so either way our rate was much slower than our buoyant journey down-stream. Swallows skimmed under the branches; a shepherd and some returning harvesters looked at us with amazement. After long toil, and trusting to nightfall, we got out and ran through thickening dusk and at last, thank God, found everything as we had left it. We dressed and saddled up, then cantered three miles home through the lit outskirts of the village and into the woods again, stooping under the low branches, racing each other the last half-mile until we hammered over the bridge and under the archway and leapt to the ground with pounding hearts, scattering the pigeons. We washed, changed and brushed our hair at high speed and were soon climbing the steps to the loggia.

Dinner was laid at one end, and the guests, sitting or decorously standing glass in hand, were gathered at the other. The thin and jewelled fingers of the iron-grey shingled Gräfin were crossed in her lap and the purple sash of the Bishop glowed in the lamplight.

"Ah, there you are," István's mother said. We weren't late at all; and in a few moments István was kissing the Gräfin's hand in his polished and easy style, and then the Bishop's ring. When we were settled at table, I couldn't keep my mind on the conversation: the after-noon's aura still compassed me about; my feet tingled from the prick of the stubble and it was hard to keep a private smile off my face. The Gräfin unfolded her napkin and shook it loose with a twinkle of sapphires.

"Well, István," she said, in the affectionate and rallying tone an aunt might use to a favourite nephew. "What have you been up to?" I avoided looking in his direction. If our eyes had crossed, we would have been done for.

We went back to the fields two days later, but there was nobody there. All had been harvested and even the sheaves had gone. We never saw Safta and Ileana again and felt sad.

*　　*　　*　　*

The summer solstice was past, peonies and lilac had both vanished, cuckoos had changed their tune and were making ready to fly. Roast corn-cobs came and trout from the mountains; cherries, then strawberries, apricots and peaches, and, finally, wonderful melons and raspberries. The scarlet blaze of paprika—there were two kinds on the table, one of them fierce as gunpowder—was cooled by cucumber cut thin as muslin and by soda splashed into glasses of wine already afloat with ice; this had been fetched from an igloo-like undercroft among the trees where prudent hands had stacked it six months before, when —it was impossible to imagine it!—snow covered all. Waggons creaked under loads of apricots, yet the trees were still laden; they scattered the dust, wasps tunnelled them and wheels and foot-falls flattened them to a yellow pulp; tall wooden vats bubbled among the dusty sunflowers, filling the yards with the sweet and heady smell of their fermentation; and soon, even at midday, the newly distilled spirit began to bowl the peasants over like a sniper, flinging the harvesters prostrate and prone in every fragment of shadow. They snored among sheaves and haycocks and a mantle of flies covered them while the flocks crammed together under every spread of branches, and not a leaf moved.

Behind the thick walls and the closed afternoon shutters of the kastély, sleep reigned fitfully too, but resurrection came soon. The barley was already in and István was busy with his reapers and the last of the wheat. (In Hungary, the harvest began on the 29th of June, the feast of SS. Peter and Paul, but it was a bit earlier hereabouts.) When we set off, István's mother called from an upper window, "Do take your hat!" She sent it skimming down and he dropped his rein, caught it in flight and clapped it on, "You're getting as black as a Gypsy." After the long weeks of sickles and scythes and whetstones, it was threshing time. Old machines were toiling away and filling the valleys with their throbbing, driven by engines with flapping belts and tall Puffing Billy chimneys expanding in a zigzag at the top. Up in the mountains, horses harnessed to wooden sledges and rollers for shelling the grain trotted round and round on circles of cobble. Winnowing followed, when clouds of skied grain sparkled and fell and then sparkled again as the next wooden shovelful transfigured the afternoon with chaff. The sacks, carried off in ox-carts, were safe in the barns at last. If the waggoners were Rumanians, instead of crying "stânga!" or "dreaptă!" in their native tongue when they wanted their oxen to turn left or right (or "jobb!" or "bal!" in Magyar if they were Hungarians) they would shout "heiss!" and "tcha!". I had first noticed these arcane cries when buffaloes were being coaxed or goaded along. István thought that the Turks had first brought these animals here, probably from Egypt, though they must originally have come from India. But the words are neither Turkish, Arabic, Romany, Hindi nor Urdu.

July brought a scattering of younger Transylvanians and their relations in search of refuge along the river valley from the heat of Budapest, which summer had turned into one of the great tropical cities of the world. There were parties and picnics and bathing, and tennis at István's till it was too dark to see the ball, on a court sunk among thick trees like a shady well; and feasting and singing round pianos in those long disintegrating drawing-rooms, and sometimes dancing to a gramophone. A few of the records were only a year or two out of date, many much older: *Night and Day*, *Stormy Weather*, *Blue Skies*, *Lazybones*, *Love for Sale*, *Saint Louis Blues*, *Every Little Breeze Seems to Whisper Louise*. In case of need, István was revealed as a proficient pianist—"but only for this sort of stuff," he said, vamping, syncopating, honky-tonking and glissandoing away like mad; then, spinning completely round on the piano-stool, he ended with a lightning thumbnail sweep of the whole keyboard from bass to treble.

The village calendar was starred with feasts and saints' days and weddings. Gypsies throve, the sound of their instruments was always within earshot and the village squares were suddenly ringed with great circular wreaths of dancers in wonderful clothes with their hands on each others' shoulders, a couple of hundred or more: and the triple punctuating stamp of the *horă* and the *sârbă*, falling all together, would veil all their bravery for a moment in dust-clouds. (I learnt all these dances later on.) It was at night that they impinged most insistently, especially on the eve of a wedding, when the groom and his paranymphs went through the slow stages of a mock abduction. If the rhythms of *High Hat*, *The Continental* or *Get along, little dogie* flagged for a moment among the faded looking-glasses and sconces and portraits in the kastély, staccato cries, high-pitched and muted by distance, as the bride was hoisted aloft, would come sailing up from the village below and through the long windows. *"Hai! Hai! Hai! Hai!"** The dancing was spurred on late into the night by the new apricot brandy, and the fiddles and zithers and clarinets and double-basses were heckled by the distant yelping of wild rustic epithalamia; then strings, hammers and the shrill reeds would be drowned once more by *Dinah*, and our own hullabaloo under the chandeliers.

> Dinah,
> Is there anyone FINER?
> In the state of CAROLINA?
> If there IS, and you KNOW HER,
> *SHOW HER TO ME!*
> Every night,
> Why do I
> SHAKE WITH FRIGHT?
> Because my DINAH MIGHT
> Changehermindaboutme! . . .

"Hai, pe loc, pe loc, pe loc!" the dancers below were stamping in unison. *"Să răsară busuioc!"* ("Stamp on the ground, let the basil shoot up!")

> Dinah,
> With her Dixie eyes BLAZIN'
> How I love to sit and GAZE IN-
> -to the eyes of Dinah Lee . . .

"Foiae verde, spic de griu, măi!" A wailing *doină* of real Gypsies mounted through the glimmer, followed by a reedy twirl on the

---

* At some of these rough nuptials, it was said, cries of acclaim would hail the display of a gory sheet or a shift from the bride's window in proof of maidenhead now ended; a consummation said sometimes to be abetted, if doubt hovered, by her mother's privy sacrifice of a pigeon behind the scenes.

clarinet; but the green leaf and the wheat-ear of the local song hadn't a chance:

> DINAH!
> If she should wander to CHINA,
> I would board an ocean LINER,
> *JusttobewithDinahLee . . .* *

---

* *Stop Press*! Of course, it was Dinah's Dixie eyes, not Gypsy eyes, that blazed, but the latter is what we mistakenly sang, and the error has got immovably lodged in the memory.

135

6

Triple Fugue

I KNEW THAT ISTVÁN and his family meant it when they suggested that I should stay all summer, but I had swerved so widely from my austere programme that the more I enjoyed these miraculous weeks the harder my conscience began to smite. So I wrote to London with rough dates and addresses for the despatch of cash: this parasitic castle-life had left my funds comparatively intact, but I would be needing some soon. Meanwhile, the valley cast a strong counter-spell and random notions suggesting delay kept dropping out of the air. "If you stayed on," István said one morning, "we could go and shoot chamois;" then, later, there would be stags; and, later still, bears. When I said I had never shot anything larger than a rabbit he said, "I'll teach you." And then, what about fox-hunting with Baron Wesselenyi's pack? I could manage that, except that I had no money. István smiled.

"Don't worry," he said, "neither have I. Nobody has."

The topic was interrupted by the gathering of a party, twelve-strong and in two carriages, to catch crayfish in a mountain stream, and István and I were to go on ahead. We found the stream: it tumbled out of rocks and bracken in a clearing full of wood-pigeons where all the foxes in Transylvania, and their vixens too, could have been decadently gloved in magenta. The rest of the party arrived, and every boulder and clump of water-weed in the brook seemed to harbour our quarry; the baskets were soon full and we could hear the snapping of their fringed tails as we climbed downhill again. We had left our horses at a water-mill where the carriages had joined them, and now all the horses were grazing unsaddled and unharnessed in a sloping field; a fire was alight already and bottles were cooling in the mill-stream.

The most active of the party had been a pretty and funny girl in a red skirt called Angéla (hard g and stress on the second syllable) who lived a few miles upstream from István and a little inland from the river. She was a few years older than I, and married, but not happily. We had caught a glimpse of each other at Count Jenö's, and danced with improvised abandon on the noisy evening when Dinah and the Gypsy songs had tangled in mid-air; and I couldn't stop dogging her footsteps. During the hunt, she leaped barefoot about the rocks as nimbly as an ibex, hair flying. As it turned out, she was just as rash and impulsive as I was supposed to be, and prompted, I think, by amused affection on her side and rapt infatuation on mine, a lighthearted affinity had sprung up in a flash. The feast went on late, and abetted by woods and nightfall and the remote part of the forest we had wandered to, all barriers broke down; and we weren't sure where we were until at last we heard our Christian names being called, and ran to the assembly point where horses were being saddled and traces run through. On the return journey they had to brake hard on the steep grass rides and the lamps slotted on either side of the carriages shed a joggling beam on the tree-trunks.

All had marvellously changed of a sudden and thanks to Angéla's high spirits everything was gay and comic as well; during the next two nights and days, all unentwined moments seemed a waste. By a stroke of luck, Angéla's family were in Budapest, but for many reasons, meetings were not easy and we cursed the intervening woods. István was an old friend and of course he saw at once how things were and came to the rescue with an irresistible plan: he would borrow a motor-car from a friend beyond Deva and the three of us would set out on a secret journey to the interior of Transylvania.

I collected my stuff and made my farewells; for after the jaunt I would strike south. The die was cast. The car arrived, the two of us set off, and in a few miles, Angéla jumped in at the appointed place and we drove east rejoicing.

The borrowed vehicle was an old-fashioned, well polished blue touring car with room for all three in front. It had a canvas hood with a celluloid window in the back and a scarlet rubber bulb which, after a moment's pressure, reluctantly sent a raucous moo out of a convoluted brass trumpet which echoed down the canyons and gave warning to all the livestock on the road—except buffaloes, when we would follow Count Jenö's nautical maxim. The roads were not good: the car pitched about the ruts and the potholes like a boat in a choppy sea and the dust of our progress alongside the Maros formed a ghostly cylinder. Hovering in our wake, it rose and enfolded us at every stop and we arrived in the old princely capital of Transylvania like three phantoms.

* * * *

The trouble over names, which vexes all these pages, boils over here. The Dacian Apulon became the Latin Apulum, and the place was full of traces of the old Roman colony. But both of these words were silenced when the hushed and muffling spread of the Slavs stifled the old names of Eastern Europe forever. They renamed it Bălgrad—'the white town' (one of many), perhaps because of its pale walls—and this white motif caught on. The Saxons called it Weissenburg and later Karlsburg, in honour of the Emperor Charles VI, who built the great eighteenth-century fortress here. The Hungarians had already adopted the notion of whiteness, but another crept in too: the word 'Julius', after a mid-tenth-century Hungarian prince who had visited Constantinople and been baptised there. Gyuláféhervár, they called it, 'the white city of Gyula'. The Rumanians stuck to Bălgrad, then adopted the mediaeval Latin name of Alba Iulia.

I wished Count Jenö and the Countess had been with us! She would have told us about Michael the Brave, the Prince of Wallachia who conquered Transylvania in the seventeenth century; and how, by seizing Moldavia as well, he briefly placed the three principalities under one sceptre and, for a single stormy year, anticipated the modern Rumanian kingdom. (It was in commemoration of this that King Ferdinand and Queen Marie were crowned here after the post-war transfer of sovereignty.) When the Count was out of earshot, she would probably have told us how prolonged misrule had culminated in 1784 in a Rumanian jacquerie of fire and slaughter and many horrors, ended by the breaking on the wheel of two of the leaders before the castle gate. Count Jenö, meanwhile, would have led us off to the cathedral, as István did. The old Romanesque building had been badly damaged by the Tatars and magnificently built up again in the late gothic style by John Hunyadi; we were among pointed arches once more. The whole city was steeped in Transylvanian history; it had become particularly famous in the era following the defeat at Mohács. The Great Hungarian Plain had been reduced to a Turkish pashalik and the north-western remnant beyond the Danube was claimed by the Emperor Charles V's brother, King Ferdinand. Transylvania, the remaining third of the mangled kingdom, survived as the stronghold of a rival monarch, King John Zápolya; and when he died the resolute Queen Dowager, Isabella of Poland, kept the shrinking eastern part of the realm together; her son, John Sigismund, was the last Hungarian king-elect. Then nothing of it remained but Transylvania, and, when the young king died, these eastern dominions, a huge isolated province now, became a Principality which only managed to fend off Habsburg claims by accepting a shadowy vassaldom to the Ottoman Empire. Then, for more than a century, an extraordinary procession of Transylvanian princes followed each other until the Reconquest put an end to it in 1711, and Transylvania was once more part of Hungary; reassembled and redeemed, indeed, but a Habsburg kingdom.

Queen Isabella and John Sigismund were entombed under the vaults, as were John Hunyadi and his son László, who was beheaded in Buda; also the Apafi and the Bocskay princes, and the assassinated Cardinal Martinuzzi. The fine bishop's palace, a peaceful warren of ochre-coloured walls, and the shade of the chestnut trees, turned this part of the city into a Transylvanian Barchester. (Later, in the eighteenth century, the Bishop .Count Batthyány gave the town a magnificent library of precious books, including one of the earliest manuscripts of the *Nibelungenlied*.) The great Gabriel Bethlen had been another benefactor and founded an Academy.* Married to the sister of the

* A detail about the Academy which would have meant nothing to me then, but much now: for a year the Professor of Philosophy at Bethlen's Academy was the Silesian poet, Martin Opitz (1597-1639), 'the Father of German Poetry', one of a pleiad of seventeenth-century poets which includes Simon Dach, Paul Fleming, Scheffler, Gryphius and Grimmelshausen ('Komm, Trost der Nacht, O Nachtigall'), author of *Simplicissimus*, the great picaresque novel of the Thirty Years War; and Weckherlin, who became Latin secretary to Cromwell immediately before Milton and wrote a remarkable sonnet on Buckingham's murder. They have all been imaginatively evoked by Gunther Grass in *The Meeting at Telgte*.

Elector of Brandenburg, he was one of the most active of this succession of princes, a powerful westward-looking Protestant leader in the Thirty Years War, and an ally of the Elector Palatine, the Winter Queen and Gustavus Adolphus.

The earlier of the Rákóczi princes were also champions of the Reformation. To strengthen the cause by the dynastic support of England and the Palatinate—and perhaps of Bohemia regained—Sigismund, brother of George Rákóczi II, married the Winter Queen's daughter, Henrietta. So, for much of this strange period, Transylvania was not only a fortress of Hungarian liberties, but a refuge for the various Protestant sects that took root there; it was also a sort of golden age for the humanities. The Saxon part of the population followed Luther, the Hungarians adopted the Calvinism which was in the ascendant just over the border at Debrecen, while Unitarians of various kinds prospered; all of them out of anti-Habsburg feeling and in reaction to Jesuit intransigence. The princes contrived to impose a remarkable degree of tolerance between the jarring churches. Sectarian fervour fell short of the passionate feelings that prevailed in Poland and Austria, and, even today, confessional rivalry was less acute. (István—though his personal leanings were strongly towards Catholicism—had been christened a Protestant like his father while his sister Ilona, like their mother, was Catholic. This arrangement with the children of mixed marriages was not uncommon in these parts.)

* * * *

Down a side turning a few miles further north, much was afoot. The path to the village ahead was noisy with farmyard sounds and when we had breasted the livestock and a barrage of dust clouds, costumes from a score of villages crowded in. Booths were laden with studded leather belts, sheepskin jackets, blouses, kerchiefs and black and white conical fleece hats; there were girths, bits, stirrups, harness, knives, sickles, scythes and festoons of brass and iron sheep-bells bright from the forge; also, icons framed in tinsel for the Orthodox and bunches of rosaries for Catholics; strings of garlic and onions, incendiary green and red spikes of paprika; ashen helves, rakes, hay-forks, crooks, staves, troughs, churns, yokes, flails, carved flutes and wooden cutlery like those the Gypsies whittled in István's courtyard. Pots and jugs and large pitchers for carrying on the shoulder or the head were assembled by the hundred, rows of shoes stood alternately at attention and at ease, and clusters of canoe-toed rawhide moccasins were strung up by their thongs. I bought Angéla a pocket-knife and an orange kerchief for the dust and she gave me a yard or two of red and yellow braid for a sash, three inches wide and shorn from a great cartwheel coil. We drank *tzuica* out of noggins with tall narrow necks at trestle tables under the acacia trees, striving to hear each other speak; but the animals, the shouting of wares, the bargaining, the fiddles, the shrill reeds, the tambourine and flute of a bear-leader and the siege of Gypsy beggars formed so solid a barrier that we bawled in each other's ears in vain, then sat beaming and tongue-tied in the variegated light. Jews in black were sprinkled among the white tunics and the bright colours of the peasants. There were Gypsies everywhere: women like tattered mendicant rainbows; suckling infants, though too young for speech, were pitilessly grasping perishers already and the men were wilder-looking than any I had ever seen: dark as quadroons, with tousled beards, matted blue-black locks falling to their shoulders and eyes like maneaters. Drunks lurched in unsteady couples and snored under their carts. Towering hay-wains were drawn up all round with racks expanding in dizzy quadrilaterals: on one of them a nomadic hen, part of a brood roosting overhead, was rashly laying an egg. Carts tilted their shafts in the air in a tangle of diagonals and hundreds of horses of the sturdy Transylvanian breed fidgeted and whinnied and snorted on the outskirts of the village. The place might have been a Tatar camp; and beyond the thatched roofs and the leaves, the western mountain-mass of the old principality ascended in steps to a jagged skyline.

*   *   *   *

"What a pity we've so little time!"

Driving us deeper into the tilting central plateau, István waved towards the overlap of ranges and told us of the wonders we were missing. There were old Roman salt-mines, worked to this day by convicts, which tunnelled into the heart of the mountains, twisting and zigzagging as they went, and sending echoes from wall to wall until they died away in the distance. One gallery flung the echo back sixteen times; renewed shouts deeper inside set the whole interior of the massif ringing with mad thunder. Every stream and river that branched away offered new marvels: deep limestone clefts, measureless caverns elaborated with arches and arcades and freak natural windows: unseen brooks that roared in the darkness and caverns where the stalactites and stalagmites strove towards each other or clenched indissolubly in wasp-waisted pillars; castles soared and old villages sacked by the Mongols still fell to pieces among gloomy forests where the Rumanian shepherds called to each other and to their flocks with metal-bound horns of linden-wood several yards long, like those that boom across Alpine meadows and the pastures of Tibet.

The wide main street of Turda—or Torda—reminded me of Honiton. "They're all cobblers and tanners and potters," said István, "and lots of them are Socinians." Angéla asked what Socinians were and, for once, I was able to enlarge: I had looked them up in Count Jenö's library. They were a sect of Unitarians which had sprung up in this part of the world and were named after a Sienese family of theologians, the Sozzini; they took their name, in these particular regions, from one Fausto Sossini, an adventurous nephew of the founder, who wandered to Transylvania from the court of Isabella dei Medici and settled at Kolozsvár in 1578, where his doctrines sank deep heterodox roots. Then he strolled on to Cracow.

"Yes," said Angéla, "but what do they believe in?"

"Well," István said doubtfully, "they don't believe in the Trinity for a start."

"Oh?" After half a second's doctrinal pondering she said, "Silly asses," and István and I laughed.

We strayed into the Calvinist church. The old building was as severe as a conventicle, with the Decalogue inscribed in Magyar over the Communion table. As in an English parish church, the numbers of last Sunday's hymns were framed in wood on a pillar by the tall pulpit. The only decorative things were the fine baroque pews: they were painted light green and picked out in gold, as though the pastors were determined the Catholics shouldn't have it all their own way. Three middle-aged sisters, with faces like pippins under their coifs, were polishing the pews with vigour, tidying prayer books and hymnals on the ledges and banging the dust out of hassocks.

* * * *

We were storming and bucketing through the land of Canaan. Rows of beehives, brought up for the summer, were aligned by the edge of the woods. The slopes were striped with vines and scattered with sheaves and ricks, and chaff from threshing mingled with the dust. Flocks and herds were beginning to throw longer shadows when we reached a high point with an entire town spread below; and, getting out under the walls of a vigilant eighteenth-century citadel, we gazed across an untidy fall of roofs. At the bottom bridges spanned a river-bend to an older part of the city the other side. It was Cluj to the Rumanians, Klausenburg to the early Saxon settlers who founded or re-founded it, but, inexpugnably and immutably to the Hungarians, Kolozsvár.* Dropping towards the watershed, the sun filled the place with evening light and kindled the windows and the western flanks of cupolas and steeples and many belfries, darkening the eastern walls with shadow; and as we gazed, one of them began to strike the hour and another took up the challenge, followed by a third and soon enormous tonnages of sectarian bronze were tolling their ancient rivalries into the dusk. Even the Armenians, who had settled here a couple of centuries ago, sent out a chime and only the synagogues were silent.

As we climbed back into the motor-car, a swarm of small Gypsies rushed on us from caves and shanties, crowded on the running board and the bonnet and entangled us in cries and supplication and a mesh of arms like brown tendrils, which we could only unloose by flinging coins beyond their heads like confetti. Set free in a second, the car slid downhill and across one of the bridges and into the old city.

* * * *

Our journey was a secret. The town wasn't as perilous as it would

---

* The Rumanian name has been lengthened in recent time by hyphenation with the ancient name of Napoca, which is how the Dacians styled their home. The 'zs' of Kolozsvár is a French 'j'.

have been in the winter season, with its parties and theatres and the opera in full blast, but we weren't supposed to be there, Angéla least of all. István revelled in the clandestine atmosphere and so did we; it gave a stimulating, comic-opera touch to our journey; so we left the conspicuous motor outside our quarters and stole about the town like footpads. István went ahead and peered round corners for fear of bumping into acquaintances; and, sure enough, he suddenly whispered, "About turn!" and shepherded us into an ironmonger's and colour-man's shop where, backs to the door, we stooped intently over a selection of mousetraps until the danger was past. It was someone he had been at school with in Vienna.

The old city was full of town-houses and palaces, most of them empty now, with their owners away for the harvest. Thanks to this, István had telephoned and borrowed a set of handsome vaulted rooms in one of them, not far from the house where Matthias Corvinus was born.

There was much evidence of his reign. In the great market square, a magnificent equestrian statue showed the king in full armour, surrounded by his knights and commanders, while armfuls of crescented and horse-tailed banners were piled as trophies at his feet. Only *Matthias Rex* was incised on the plinth—no need of *Hungariae* when it was set up—and Rumanians as well as Hungarians could rightly feel pride of kinship. Most of the names associated with the place were straight out of the novels of Jókai, and we had a quick look at the baroque arcades and books and treasures in the splendid Bánffy palace. I wonder whether I am right in remembering that Liszt gave recitals there? I think *Don Giovanni* was sung in Hungarian in the triple-named city even earlier than in Budapest. We entered the great Catholic church of St. Michael—a Gothic building which had looked enormous from the citadel—just as everyone was streaming out from Vespers, and the dusk indoors, lit only by flickering racks of tapers, looked vaster still, and umbrageously splendid; the clustered piers of the nave soared with no hindering capitals to halt the upward flight of the eye, then tilted over to join each other, form lancets and lose themselves in a brackeny network of liernes and groined vaulting and shadow.

An hotel at the end of the main square, called the New York—a great meeting place in the winter season—drew my companions like a magnet. István said the barman had invented an amazing cocktail —only surpassed by the one called 'Flying' in the Vier Jahreszeiten bar in Munich—which it would be criminal to miss. He stalked in, waved the all-clear from the top of some steps, and we settled in a strategic corner while the demon-barman went mad with his shaker. There was nobody else in the bar; it was getting late and the muffled lilt of the waltz from *Die Fledermaus* hinted that everyone was in the dining-room. We sipped with misgiving and delight among a Regency neo-Roman décor of cream and ox-blood and gilding: Corinthian capitals spread their acanthus leaves and trophies of quivers, and hunting horns, lyres and violins were caught up with festoons between the pilasters. Our talk, as we sipped, ran on secrecy and disguise. "Perhaps I should pretend to have toothache," Angéla said, after the second cocktail, and wrapped the new kerchief round her head in a concealing bandage; "or," holding it stretched across her face below the eyes, "wear a yashmak. Or simply cover the whole thing up." She wrapped her head in the kerchief and tied it in a bow on top like a Christmas pudding. The barman imperturbably set down a third round of glasses and then vanished just as Angéla re-emerged, shaking her hair loose, to find the drinks there as though by magic. I suggested the helmet of darkness of Perseus. István thought Siegfried's Tarnhelm would be better still; then she could not only become invisible but turn into someone else: King Carol, Greta Garbo, Horthy, Mussolini and Groucho Marx were suggested, then the Prince of Wales, Jack Dempsey, Queen Marie and Charlie Chaplin; Laurel and Hardy, perhaps; one of the two; she would have to choose, but she insisted on both.

This led to talk of seeing double; the drinks were beginning to work. We left, walking with care and suitable stealth, and on air; then dived into a hooded carriage that would have been a sleigh in winter and clip-clopped to a discreet Gypsy restaurant outside the town, returning to our fine vaulted quarters fired with paprika and glissandoes.

* * * *

How exhilarating it was next morning to be woken by the discord of reciprocally schismatic bells while the half-shuttered July sunlight scattered stripes across the counterpane! Furred and frogged, the magnates on the walls of the breakfast room surveyed us with their hands serenely crossed on the hilts of their scimitars. We looked at them in turn and admired the many tiers of emblazoned bindings. Heralded by fumes, a very old retainer in a baize apron brought coffee and croissants from a distant part of the house and talked to us as we spread and dipped and sipped; and his tidings from the night before unloosed a long moment of gloom: Dollfuss had been assassinated by the Nazis. But, as with the June purge a month earlier, our mood was such that the gloom didn't last much longer than breakfast: it all seemed such a long way to the west. But it was only five months since I had seen the small Chancellor leading that dismal procession in Vienna, after the February troubles. I hadn't even heard of Cluj or Klausenburg or Kolozsvár then. But Transylvania had been a familiar name as long as I could remember. It was the very essence and symbol of remote, leafy, half-mythical strangeness; and, on the spot, it seemed remoter still, and more fraught with charms. Under their sway, we were impervious to omens, and the spell of comedy, adventure and delight that surrounded our journey would have needed something still more drastic and closer at hand to break it.

Our euphoria was complete. It followed us all day along dark canyons and tilted woods and steep grazings and down into a valley where the serpentine haze of willows and poplars marked the windings of the Maros once again; and soon a subtle change came over the towns and villages, not in the landscape—that was changing all the time—but in the inhabitants.

There had been plenty of Hungarian spoken in the few Transylvanian towns I had seen, and, among the Swabians of Arad, German too; but in the villages and the country, Rumanian had been almost universal. Now all at once the drovers watering their horses at the wooden troughs, the peasants in the fields, the shepherds nursing their crooks under the trees and the fishermen flinging their nets over the river were all speaking Magyar. We were among Szeklers, the Hungarians of Transylvania, half a million and more, who inhabit a great enclave of the eastern and southern Carpathians. It was this geographical position, isolated in a sea of Rumanians, which placed the ethnological problem beyond solution.

Some say the Szeklers are the oldest established inhabitants of the province; the Rumanians, as we know, fiercely contest this. The Szeklers were wrongly thought, in earlier times—like the Magyars themselves, indeed, but very much later—to have descended from the Huns. Others held that when Charlemagne swept the Avars from the Great Plain some of them might have landed up in these mountains. Or, it was wondered, could they be the offspring of the bellicose Kabars, a splinter-tribe that had joined the Magyars—later forming part of the vanguard of Arpád's host—during their cloudy sojourn in the Khazar empire? The most recent theory, I think, supports their Magyar beginnings: somehow they became separated from the main tribes when they moved west from Bessarabia with the Pechenegs at their heels; they must have made their way straight through the nearest passes to their present habitat, while the others pursued their more roundabout paths to the Great Plain. If this were so, the expanding Magyars, when they moved eastwards again and into Transylvania, would have found their Szekler kinsmen already settled. There is convincing evidence that the early Hungarian kings established or confirmed them along the Carpathian border as permanent frontiers-men, on the watch for the inroads of later barbarians; and there is nothing incompatible in the two last theories. At any rate, all through the Dark and Middle Ages they were the wardens and the light-horsemen of the eastern march, and in battle, when the main Hungarian cavalry took the field in full armour, they stuck to the fleet Parthian tactics of their nomad past. The Hungarians, the Szeklers and the Saxons were largely self-governing under the Hungarian crown, and many of the Szeklers, even if they were moccasin-shod and still signed their names with their thumbs, were ennobled *en masse*; all three nations—or rather, their leaders and nobles—had a voice in the councils of Transylvania.*

*   *   *   *

* 'Nation' has a special sense in this context: it means the noble legislating minority. Hungarian serfs, not being part of it, were no more represented than the similarly placed ancestors of the Rumanian majority. It was position in the hierarchy not 'nationality' that counted. There were Rumanian nobles who had a voice, but they invariably became absorbed into the Hungarian nobility and were lost.

The motor-car crept through the waggons and the cattle of the metropolis of the Szeklers and, by the sounds in our ears, we might have been in the heart of a Hungarian country town. Târgu-Mureș—still Márosvásarhély to its inhabitants—was in the throes of yet another market-day. I thought I discerned, without any prompting, a different cast of feature—something simultaneously blunter and more angular about brow and cheek and chin—that corresponded to the change of language. There was a difference of costume, too, though the actual details have slipped away. Rawhide shoes and thongs were common to all, with the fleece headgear and the low-crowned black felt hat. But all along my itinerary the chief difference between country Hungarians and Rumanians had been the wide-skirted tunic or shirt, caught in by a wide belt, which the Rumanians wore outside their trousers. Both dressed in white homespun linen, but the Hungarians' shirts always buttoned tightly at the throat; their trousers were unusually wide from the waist down and sometimes pleated, which almost gave them the look of long skirts. *Gatya Hosen*, István called them; these were often replaced by loose black breeches and shiny knee-boots. But here the peasants, almost to a man, wore narrow white homespun trews like tights stitched together out of felt. Across the Hungarian plain and in Transylvania, the women's clothes had been varying all the time. Each village and valley enjoined a different assembly of colours and styles: braids, tunics, lace, ribands, goffering, ruffs, sashes, caps, kerchiefs, coifs and plaits free or coiled: a whole array of details announced whether they were betrothed, brides, married, spinsters or widows. Sometimes coifs framed these heads like spathe and spadix; among Saxons, they shot up in stiff scarlet cylinders. There were bodices, flowing or panelled sleeves, embroidery, gold coins at brow or throat or both, aprons front and back, a varying number of petticoats and skirts jutting at the hips like farthingales, and occasionally these were accompanied by coloured Russian boots. This village finery gave all gatherings a festal air, especially as the level of beauty among Hungarian and Rumanian girls was very high. Populations were inclined to remain aloof; but the more they overlapped and mingled—Magyar, Rumanian, Serb, Slovak, Saxon, Swabian and sometimes Armenian and perhaps some Ruthenes in the north—the more striking they looked.* Their everyday dress was a sober version of their gala outfits; but these exploded on feast-days and at weddings in ravishing displays. Clothes were still emblematic, and not only among peasants: an expert in Rumanian and Hungarian symbols, looking at the passers-by in a market-place—a couple of soldiers, a captain in the Roşiori, an Ursuline prioress, a sister of St. Vincent de Paul, a Poor Clare, an Hasidic rabbi, an Armenian deacon, an Orthodox nun, a Uniat archimandrite, a Calvinist pastor, an Augustinian canon, a Benedictine, a Minorite friar, a Magyar nobleman, an ostrich-feathered coachman, a shrill-voiced Russian cab-driver, a bear-leading Gypsy with his spoon-carving fellow-tribesmen, a wool-carder, a blacksmith, a drover, a chimney-sweep, a woodman or a waggoner, and above all, women from a dozen villages and ploughmen and shepherds from widely scattered valleys and highlands—would have been able to reel off their provenances as swiftly as a herald glancing along the flags and surcoats of a fourteenth-century battle.

Next to a huge church in the market-place, a Gypsy presided over nests of baskets. Angéla bought one, and when she had filled it with bottles and other good things at the shops and stalls, we crept through the throng in bottom gear, and, once away from the town, drove a few miles and climbed till we reached the edge of a steep mown field above the river. The engine, as we drew up, disturbed a heron. It rose above the trees below and flew away over the fields.

"How quickly they get up in the air!" Angéla said. "No fuss, like swans."

"Ah!" István said, "that's because they have air-pockets in their bones," and we watched it growing smaller in the distance.

We picnicked under an oak. The mountains that rumbled away to the north and the east were a mass of canyons and forests: full of bears, István told us. Crown Prince Rudolph and his circle—or was it the insatiable Franz Ferdinand?—had shot sixty during his various sojourns there. István, when we asked him if any were left, said, "It's teeming

* At that time, Hungarian girls seemed to have cornered the international cabaret world; every night-club I can remember was full of them. Many sought their fortunes abroad and I remember from a nineteenth-century Russian novel that the word *Vengerka*—'a Hungarian girl'—had an earthy and professional sense.

with them." He too had stalked in those never-ending conifers. There were wolves too. The cubs would be growing up just about now.

Finding we had run out of cigarettes, István shook off his post-prandial torpor and drove back to the town. We wandered down to the river and bathed and dawdled there, lying on the grass, dallying and embracing and then watching the dragonflies darting through sun-beams which the willow branches caught and split into threads while our sleepy lashes re-fragmented them in prismatic sheaves. We got back to the oak tree at the very moment the car came snorting uphill. István told us he had run into an old fellow-hussar and couldn't get away, and we teased him about being so popular. He said he wished he'd been down to bathe; then murmured to me, "Not much point, though, now the reaping's finished."

*   *   *   *

We gave a lift to an old woman who was gingerly carrying a large covered pudding-basin. I asked her, through István, if she were a Szekler, and she said, "No, just a Magyar." Her face, mobled in a widow's coif under an enormously wide hat of plaited straw, was like an axe. When Angéla asked what was inside the basin so carefully poised on her knees, she said: "Feel," and lifted a corner of the cloth. Angéla knelt on the seat, faced backwards, slipped her hand in and gave a small gasp of surprise. The old woman laughed toothlessly and they both told me to try, so I did and discovered with a start a mass of fluffy warm moving bodies which became audible when the cloth was taken off. The basin was full of newly-hatched ducklings and when she got out she offered us a few in thanks for the lift, but dashed indoors and came back with three glasses of szilvorium instead.

It was getting late. We left the river, struck south and followed a vile road upstream beside another river—the Kokel?*—then south again through pastures and stubble fields where gleaners were stooping among low sunbeams and shadows. It was a pacific Samuel Palmer land of hills and woods and fields patterned with sheaves; pyramid-hayricks threw spears of shadow downhill; cattle and flocks were going home haloed in dust. Once more, there was something different about the

* Târnava? Kukullo? So the map seems to say.

landscape and villages, it was hard to say what. Tiles were taking the place of thatch; walls, with a gabled farmhouse along one flank, enclosed wide yards, and gateways pierced them with flattened arches tall enough for laden carts to drive through. Order and trimness prevailed.

Beyond the mountains to the north and east, clouds had been arranging themselves in a disturbing array, flocculent and still at first, then fidgety with summer lightning. The electricity dancing about among these heaps of vapour turned them blue-green and silver and mauve and in a shudder and a split second they would become transparent or bulbous or as thin as stage wings: scenic effects like magnesium, as though an atmospheric clown or a harlequin were loose in the hills. This restless sequence of scene-shifts began with nightfall; then the rising of the eighth full moon of this journey made an hallucination of the sky and up into the middle of it, straight ahead, a vertiginous triangle of steep roofs, spikes, tree-tops and battlemented cliffs rose like a citadel in an illuminated psalter.

"Look!" István and Angéla exclaimed. "Segesvár!" A Rumanian would have cried "Sighişoara!"; but a descendant of the builders of that high place would have said "Schässburg!"

*   *   *   *

Like Transylvania in the West, the Magyar and Rumanian names of the province—Erdély and Ardeal—both mean something to do with forests. But the German name is Siebenburgen, and the word conjures up seven fortresses, each with three names; I shrink from inflicting the full twenty-one.

What happened was this. When the early Kings of Hungary, notably Géza II in the twelfth century, found this region—according to the Hungarian chronicles—deserted, they summoned colonies of 'Saxon' settlers from the Middle and Lower Rhine, some from Flanders, and others, it is said, from the Mosel, and even a few Walloons. They tilled the land and built the towns, often, as here, on ancient Dacian sites; these are the *Burgen* in question, and in time the growing constellations of their farms and villages dovetailed with the regions of the Szeklers and Hungarians and Rumanians. A century later, threatened by the westward sweep of the Cumans, Andrew II summoned the Crusading order of the Teutonic Knights from the Holy Land; he granted them a stretch of country round Kronstadt; but when the Knights sought to make it independent and then present it to the Pope, the King drove them out. Moving north they settled along the Vistula and founded the warlike state which later turned into East Prussia; and soon they were breaking lances beside the Masurian lakes and harrying Lithuanians among the Baltic floes.

On the spot, meanwhile, their peaceful 'Saxon' forerunners flourished. And there they had remained, over two hundred thousand of them, and they soon became the most advanced community in Transylvania. They cultivated the land round their walled farmhouses and their manifold crafts brought prosperity. Gothic churches rose, steeples soared, vaulted cellars burrowed the rocks and battlements girded them about. Their spoken dialect strayed a little from that of their countrymen in the West, but no further than a regional dialect should; and later, when the Reformation found its way to the Carpathians, feelings of tribal solidarity prompted them to adopt Luther's teaching. (It was a recoil, too, from the Socinian dogma, which had begun to affect the Hungarian Calvinists.) To a remarkable degree, these settlements followed the line of evolution of the German towns and villages in the West: the same burgher and artisan way of life prevailed, very different in style from Magyar dash and vainglory and the self-sufficient stubbornness of the Szeklers and the smouldering pastoral diligence of the Rumanians. Seemly, and in tune with the sober assiduity and substance of the inhabitants, a solid and sometimes splendid provincial baroque architecture sprang up; theologians and teachers emerged; and I wonder if I was right (on later visits) to compare them to Puritan settlers in the New World? Anyway, the blue eyes, flaxen hair and Teutonic speech that I met in those arcades and market-places could just as well have belonged a thousand miles to the west. Nobody has ever confused them with later Germanic settlers in re-conquered Hungary—the Arad Swabians, for instance. It seemed a miracle that they and their towns and hamlets and their skills and their language should have weathered the past eight centuries of commotion with so little damage. They are called 'Transylvanian Saxons'—

'Sassen', in dialect. Nobody quite knows why, for they had nothing to do with Saxony. Could it have been the loose regional word for 'German' at some stage of the Middle Ages; in the time of the Saxon emperors, perhaps—Henry the Fowler, the Ottos, or Henry the Saint? Or later, under Richard Coeur de Lion's brother-in-law, Henry the Lion?

I had always known the name of this region from hearing as a child, when the *Pied Piper of Hamelin* was read aloud, how the children of Hamelin were piped into a mountain chasm to re-emerge in the Carpathians:

> In Transylvania there's a tribe
> Of alien people who ascribe
> The outlandish ways and dress
> On which their neighbours lay such stress,
> To their fathers and mothers having risen
> Out of some subterranean prison
> Into which they had been trepanned
> Long time ago, in a mighty band,
> Out of Hamelin town in Brunswick land,
> But how or why they don't understand.

The very cleft, the Almasch cave from which they emerged at the other end, is still pointed out. It is a bat-haunted cavern about forty leagues due east of Schässburg as the crow flies. The story defining the children as Brunswickers would make them specifically Saxons.*

It was too far from Angéla's and István's haunts for danger of chance meetings, so we strolled instead of skulking about the high-perched streets of the citadel. We gazed down at the moonlit landscape and up at the metalled and shingled spires and watched the hands of an old

* A friend from Kronstadt-Braşov-Brassó tells me that there is no Pied Piper tradition on the spot. Browning probably got it from the Grimm brothers who may have picked it up from some inventive Transylvanian Saxon studying in Germany. They loved concocting tall stories about their remote homeland: in Bonn and Jena and Heidelberg, it must have sounded as wild and faraway as Tartary. Perhaps the original legend in the West is confusedly linked with the Children's Crusade. Two contingents set off from Germany, as well as the main body from Vendôme; but they all perished, or were sold into slavery. Hamelin itself is full of Pied Piper reminders.

clock over an archway where a jerky figurine emerged and struck the hour. The town blazed with moonlight but beyond the glimmer of the distant ranges, the eastern sky was still restless with summer lightning. We put up at an inn with gables and leaded windows in a square lifted high above the roofs and the triple cincture of the town wall and dined at a heavy oak table in the Gastzimmer. The glasses held a cool local wine that washed down trout caught that afternoon, and every sight and sound—the voices, the wine-glasses, the stone mugs and the furniture shining with the polish of a couple of centuries—brought it closer to a Weinstube by the Rhine or the Necker. When István retired, Angéla and I sat on in the great smokey room holding hands, deeply aware that it was the last night but one of our journey. There are times when hours are more precious than diamonds. The gable-windows upstairs surveyed a vision of great unreality. The moon had triumphed over the mute fireworks to the east and the north and all the dimensions had been re-shuffled. We leant on the sill and when Angéla turned her head, her face was bisected for a moment, one half silver, the other caught by the gold glow of lamplight indoors.

* * * *

"Petöfi was killed somewhere in the fields over there," István had said. Tsar Nicholas I had sent an army to help the eighteen-year-old Franz-Josef when the Hungarians, rising in revolt under Kossuth, fought a war of independence which they very nearly won. The conflict moved to Transylvania. Segesvár was one of the last battles of the campaign. Petöfi, a devoted admirer of Shakespeare and Byron, was an attractive, passionate, bohemian figure and, many think, Hungary's greatest poet. He was twenty-six when he fell after fighting with reckless bravery all through the war.

But, in Rumanian annals, Sighişoară is singled out, in the middle of the fifteenth century, by a strange and perplexing figure; except for one foible, he would have entered history as a hero. Vlad III of Wallachia, sprung from the great Basarab dynasty, was the great-grandson of Radu the Black, grandson of the warrior prince Mircea the Old and son of Vlad the Dragon—so called, it is thought, because the Emperor Sigismund, his overlord, ally and enemy, had hung the Order of the

Dragon round his neck. Given as a hostage to the Sultan when he was a boy, the third Vlad mounted the Wallachian throne later on and fought against the Turks with energy and skill. Chastisement for his success lay with the Sultan, Mehmet II, the conqueror of Constantinople. But the march of this punitive army was suddenly halted by an unspeakably terrible scene: a wide valley, that is, populated by many thousands of Turkish and Bulgarian corpses from the year before, transfixed on a forest of spikes and rotting in mid air, with the Sultan's general ceremoniously robed on the tallest spike of all. The Sultan, whose aquiline features and snowy globular turban we know from Bellini's painting and the engraving by Pisanello, had been brought up on blood, like a falcon: he recoiled in horror—some say in respect for the ruthlessness of his rebellious vassal—and burst into tears. For Vlad's lifelong foible was impaling. Many contemporary woodcuts show the Prince feasting in Carpathian glens, like a shrike in his larder, among groves of skewered foes.

In Rumania he has always been known as Vlad Tsepesh—'the Impaler'—but to foreigners, with his father, Vlad the Dragon ('Vlad Dracul') in mind, he was 'the son of the Dragon'. ('Dragon' in Rumanian is *Dracu* and the final 'l' is 'the'. Hence the outland 'Drakola', 'Drakule' and the like, a word never heard on Rumanian lips, indeed, an improperly formed one based on the just-possible 'Draculea', i.e. 'Dragon's son'.)

It was the alien and dragonish trisyllable, coupled with a vague bloodthirsty aura, which gave Bram Stoker the idea for a vampire 'Count Dracula', flying through the night in a white tie and tails and burying his fangs in his victims' throats; and in recent decades, only Tarzan has outstripped him in film popularity. The fact that Transylvania *is* a region of castles, forests, counts and vampires, and that some confused strands of local history have managed to tangle themselves into the novel's local colour, has always (for me) set it beyond charm's reach. People who should know better exploit the confusion between the two figures and when 'Dracula's Castle' is pointed out to a charabanc-load of tourists, I suspect that it is not the historical figure that appears before their minds' eye—the Prince in his plumed headdress: the exorbitant glance, the sweeping moustache, the bear's fur and clasps and stars, the long hair and flanged mace and the palissade of cumbered stakes—but a natty Count in an opera-hat, a satin-lined cape and a queer look about his incisors; someone who might equally well be advertising after-shave lotion, teaching the tango or sawing a boxed lady in half at a matinée.

Back to Sighişoaŗa! Back to Segesvár! Above all, here, back to Schässburg!

* * * *

Many years later, climbing the marvellous covered stairway that leads to the first platform of the Shwe Dagon pagoda in Rangoon, I stopped half-way and tried to remember what this steep ascent called to mind; and, in a moment, I was back a couple of decades and climbing a windy staircase under beams and shingle and a steep wooden roof in Transylvania. The Saxon steps lifted us to the town's grassy summit, whose battlements in the sky encompassed leaning gravestones, tall trees and an old gothic church. A roof as steep as a barn's, with all the semicircular scales discoloured by lichen, rose from the mottled walls; and indoors airy space ascended to a mediaeval web of vaults. There were pointed arches once again and lancets, trefoils and cusps, and in the chancel, traces of fresco three-quarters flaked away, a crucifixion or a transfiguration, perhaps: the exact memory has dropped away too. Armorial tombstones were piled at random under the bell-sallies, and the organ must have broken down, for somebody practising on a harmonium rumbled and wheezed in the gallery. The theme of the Danube School altarpiece has dimmed as well. 'A marvellous mixture of rough stone,' my diary says, 'faded brick and plaster, scalloped doorways, age piled on age, all first rate and all with that untouched, musty feeling one treasures.' I thought it was a Catholic church at first, but the absence of sanctuary lamps and the Stations of the Cross hinted otherwise. So it was Lutheran, and much less bleak and stripped than Calvinist and Unitarian interiors. There were other hints. Pews, as opposed to chairs, seemed a distinguishing mark of the Reform.

We sat in one of these and Angéla idly picked a prayer book from the ledge and opened it haphazard. "Oh look!" The dog-eared pages had fallen open at a passage marked with a skeleton leaf where the faded black-letter spelled out a prayer of intercession for 'unser wohlbeliebter Kaiser Franz-Josef'. But there was no mention of Elizabeth, his beautiful Queen-Empress. She must already have been assassinated at the landing-stage in Geneva; and no mention of their son, Crown Prince Rudolph who, after shooting all those bears in the mountains which we could just see through the diamond-panes, had kept the last round for himself at Mayerling. There was no date, only the owner's name in faded ink. We wondered later whether it could have been published after his next heir, the Hungary-hating Archduke Franz-Ferdinand, had been murdered at Sarajevo. (1898, 1889 and 1914 —mark these grim dates.) Nor, as far as I can remember, could we find the name of Archduke Charles, Franz-Josef's successor and last Emperor of all. But for this, the closing date for the Prayer Book might have fallen just before the Emperor's lonely death in 1916, when the requiems and the salutes and the tolling bells must have been drowned among the unceremonial gunfire of half a dozen battle-fronts: salvoes which two years later were to bring the diadem of the Caesars and the apostolic crown of Hungary and the sceptres and the crowns of Bohemia and Croatia—indeed a whole Empire—tumbling among the ruins. "Poor old man," Angéla said, putting the prayer book back on its ledge.

Beyond the gravestones outside, the highest of the three town walls looped downhill with battlements spaced out between jutting towers, several of which were choked with storks' nests. Swags of elderflower burst over the crenellations and we peered down and watched the swifts flying in and out of holes in the masonry. The level sward outside the west door of the church dropped in green waves of mingled forest and churchyard where the names of weavers, brewers, vintners, carpenters, merchants, and pastors—some of them ending in a Latin 'us', like those of sixteenth-century humanists—were incised on generations of headstones and obelisks in obsolete German spelling. Under a scurry of clouds and suspended above hills and fields and a twisting river-bed, maintenance and decay were at grips in one of the most captivating churchyards in the world.

The organist had come down to see who we were. He pointed out a sturdy tower at the bottom. "You see that?" he said, polishing steel-rimmed spectacles and putting them on. "Three hundred years ago, a Turkish army marched up the valley, bent on sacking the town. It was commanded by a merciless general called Ali Pasha, *ein schrecklicher Mann!* Some Schässburgers had barricaded themselves in the tower and one of them aimed his arquebus at him, and—*boom!*—down he came." A looping parabola with his forefinger showed that somersaulting fall. "He was on an elephant."

"?"

"Yes." His spectacles flashed like window panes. "An elephant. The citizens fell on the attackers, the Turks fled, the town was saved."

Hardly were the words out of his mouth when a wind wrapped itself round the tall wooded cone. There had been a warning rush and a flutter. Then all at once the branches were banging about, hitting each other like boxers, and dust and pollen flew from the boughs in a twisting yellow cloud. Grass flattened twirling and forking into channels, every poplar in the valley shuddered from root to tip like a Malay kris and the loosened hay-ricks moulted in spirals. Husks, chaff, straw, petals, young twigs, last year's leaves and nosegays scattered out of the jam-jars on the graves were rushing up the slope in a gale which tossed the dishevelled birds about the air. The clouds had darkened, a volley of drops fell and we and the organist sheltered from the downpour under a clump of chestnuts. It stopped just as abruptly and we found ourselves, as a rainbow formed and dissolved again in a momentary foxes' wedding, looking down, as though through a magnifying glass, at a world of hills and meadows and the flash of a river and an upheaval of distant ranges. Outraged cawing and twittering filled the branches and the air was adrift with the scent of pollen, roses, hay and wet earth.

* * * *

Uplands of holt and hanger soon put this pinnacle out of sight as we drove south through vineyards and hop fields. It was a solemn sweep of country with snug hamlets tucked among woods by the banks of rivers. When we asked what they were called, the villagers always gave a Saxon name—Schaas, Trappold, Henndorf, Niederhausen. (Experts find a kinship between the layout of these settlements and villages in mediaeval Franconia, when that region stretched far across Germany to the west and the north; and it seems that kinship between the Transylvanian Saxon dialect and the speech of the Franks of the Mosel bears this out.) They were built in a rustic farmyard style with flattened cart entrances, shingled lych-gates, hipped roofs and rows of gables that gave on the village street. The masonry was sound, made to last and adorned here and there with a discreet and rather daring frill of baroque. At the heart of each village, sturdy churches reared squat, four-sided steeples with a tough, defensive look. We pulled up in the little market-town of Agnetheln near a church as massive as a small bastille. Pierced by arrow-slits, the walls rose sheer, then expanded in machicolations; and, above these, rows of short uprights like squat pillars formed galleries that hoisted pyramids of steeple. They were as full of purpose as bits of armour and the uprights between steeple and coping gave the triangular roofs a look of helmets with nasal pieces and eye-slits. All the churches were similarly casqued.

We were looking at the one in front of us from our bench outside an inn. At the next table a wheelwright, curly with shavings and with sawdust on sandy eyebrows, had just left his workshop for a drink. He sat with one arm round a lint-haired daughter who stood between his knees and silently drank us in through limpid blue eyes. "What do you think of it?" he asked us in German.

"Ein feste Burg," István appositely replied. A safe stronghold.

"It had to be," the wheelwright commented, and I wondered why. None of the churches since crossing the Hungarian and the Rumanian frontiers had worn this fierce look; but then, none had been so old. Yet there had never been sectarian strife in these parts on the scale of France, Ireland, Northern Europe and the Empire during the Thirty Years War. Had it been to protect them from the Turks? The wheelwright shrugged. Yes, against the Turks; but there had been worse than they.

"Who?"

He and István answered in unison.

"*Tataren!*"

I understood, or thought I did: the armoured churches must have sprung up after the onslaught of the Tatars of Batu Khan; those

Mongols, that is, who had laid the Kingdom in ashes, burnt churches and castles, massacred many thousands and led whole populations captive. The devastation of Batu and his sudden return to Karakorum, when the death of Kublai's heir had put the Mongol succession at hazard, took place in 1241. What a mercy they never came back!

"Never came back?" The wheelwright's glass of wine stopped half-way to his lips and returned to the oak; and I realised, as I listened to him and to István, what gaps yawned in the past three months' mugging up in country-house libraries. The last Turco-Tatar raid didn't get as far as most of its predecessors, but it had taken place as recently as 1788; and in the vast period between 1241 and 1788, smaller raids by the Tatars and other marauding bands had been endemic. Most of them came from the Tatar settlements on the Budjak steppe in southern Bessarabia. (They must have been an offshoot of the Nogai, or Krim Tatars. After Tamerlane had destroyed the Golden Horde, the remainder, under the Girai descendants of Jenghiz Khan—probably more Turkic than Mongol by now—had founded an independent Khanate in the Crimea, and another in Kazan.) These raiders would ride across Moldavia, penetrate the Buzău Pass at the south-east corner of the Carpathians—'the Tatar Pass', as the locals called it—and sweep down on the prosperous Burzenland; (this region near the old Saxon town of Kronstadt* was the fief originally bestowed on the Teutonic knights).

But massive church architecture was no defence against a determined attack. At the approach of raiders, the villagers took to the woods and drove their horses and cattle up into the roomy caves of the Carpathians. The whole range is a stalactitic warren; and there they would hide until it was safe to come out and inspect the cinders. Finally, a century or so after the building of the churches, more serious steps were taken: great fortified walls were flung up round them and there they still stand, astonishing circles of stone tiered inside with wooden shelters and reached by ladders that ascend like boxes in a rustic opera house. Each one was the quarters of a different family and in times of trouble they would stock them with salt meat and hams and cheeses against a

* Braşov or Brassó, and recently, but no longer (and most inappropriately for this old Gothic city), Stalin. Fashions change.

sudden siege. These defensive rings are amazing, even in a border region that bristles with castles. The raids have left few other traces, except perhaps genetically: people say that the former frequency of rape has stamped some of the villagers of the region with a Mongol look. Others think it may be a passing heirloom of the Cumans before they settled and evaporated on the Great Hungarian Plain.

István looked at his watch and jumped up. A fatherly whisper sent the little girl dashing off to the yard behind his workshop, and, when we were in the motor, she leaned in panting and put a nosegay of roses and tiger-lilies in Angéla's lap.

* * * *

No mechanical vehicle except ours desecrated the quiet of these byeways. For miles we met only cattle and a cart or two drawn by the sturdy local horses. Another village with a spiked church loomed and fell back, and ahead of us, rearing like a wave, the enormous mass of the Carpathians climbed into the sky. It was the highest stretch of the Transylvanian Alps, and the highest peaks are only overtopped by the crests of the High Tatra, far away south of Cracow on the borders of Slovakia and Poland; over three hundred miles north-west, for an eagle bent on a change of peaks. They are also called the Făgăras mountains, the old chronicler's wild forested region of the Vlachs and the Pechenegs, it had often been a domain of the Princes of Wallachia; like the ranges we saw to the north-east from the Szekler country, it was full of bears and wolves; and the old eponymous town and castle lay at its feet. I had expected a daunting perpendicular stronghold, but, apart from the donjon inside, it turned out to be a massive rectangle of ochre and brick-colour, almost a quarter of a mile square and slotted by embrasures, with a circular bastion jutting at each corner. Medallions with indecipherable scutcheons crumbled over a great gate. It was an illustration for Vauban or the middle-distance for a stately battle-painter and crying aloud for a forest of beleaguering tents and cannon-smoke and counter-marching perpendicular groves of packed lances, all seen beneath the foreground hoofs of a frantic dappled charger, pawing the air under a cuirassed seventeenth-century captain, sombre and imperturbable in his moustache and feathered hat, baton on sashed hip. Most suitably, it was the famous Bethlen Gábor who gave the fortifications their final shape, and its best-known besiegers were the janissaries of Achmet Balibeg against a desperate garrison of five hundred Magyars and Szeklers. I feel that the Ali Pasha, who laid siege to it in 1661, must have been (though I can find no corroboration) the one who came to grief on his elephant at Segesvár.

The moment we had struck the highroad after those hushed Saxon lanes we had run over a nail and had to change a wheel. Once in Făgăraş—Fogaras to István and Angéla—we waited in a garden restaurant by the fortress while it was mended and Angéla went to telephone. István was a little perplexed. Our leisurely mornings and late starts—my and Angéla's fault—had set our programme back. He had wanted to drive on east to the important old Saxon town of Kronstadt near the Tatars' Pass, to feast and look at the Black Church there and spend the night. But too little time was left; we would have to think of turning westwards. Then Angéla came back from the telephone with a worried look. The subterfuges and stratagems on which our journey depended were in danger of breakdown; the only remedy was to head westwards, and by train, that very day; eventually she would be travelling much further than either of us could accompany her. István explained the change of plan. A branch line ran through the town, but the journey would involve two changes and long waits and we were appalled by the prospect of these static vigils and the break up of our trio and the anticlimax. While we were talking, a Gypsy mechanic was strapping the mended tyre into its recess at the back of the front mudguard. István's eyes lit up at the sight, as though inspiration had descended. "We'll stick to our old plan," he said, "but make it a day earlier." Angéla wondered whether we would be cutting it too fine. "You wait and see," István said, emptying his glass. "To horse!"

We climbed in and started off. When István pressed the scarlet bulb, the brass trumpet let out its melancholy delayed-action moo. "Not quite right for the Third Honvéd Hussars!" Angéla said. We sloughed Făgăraş-Fogaras-Fogarasch like a snake-skin and were soon scorching along the road we had come by until we passed the Agnetheln turning and broke new ground.

The rain-scoured landscape and the flocks of clouds rushing across the sky had made us lower the hood. On our left the huge mass of the mountains heaved itself up in a succession of steep folds. Wooded gorges pierced the foothills and the higher slopes were darkened by scarves of forest until the bare rock emerged in a confusion of rugged humps and peaks. High above, we knew, a score of small lakes and tarns gazed up at the sky and we thought we could discern a glint of snow here and there, but it was too late in the year; it must have been a chance discolouring of the rock. On our right hand the trees which followed the course of the Olt river* swayed towards us and veered away many times, half keeping us company until the river twisted due south and coiled away between the chasm that led to the Red Tower Pass. (Once through this great cleft, it broke into the Regat—the pre-war Rumanian kingdom—and began its hundred-and-fifty-mile journey through the southern foothills and across the Wallachian plain, giving its name, on the way, to the whole province of Oltenia; then it flowed into the Danube like every stream in this vast blind-alley of the Carpathians.) A few miles before we lost it, István pointed across the river to a point where a thirteenth-century Cistercian abbey, the oldest Gothic building in Transylvania, stood in ruins. "King Matthias suppressed it," he said, "because of the immorality of the monks."

"Oh?" Angéla and I said together. "What immorality?"

"I'm not sure," István answered, then added cheerfully, "everything, I expect;" and the sinful precincts, one with Sodom and the Agape-mone, fell behind us stubbornly mouldering in the fields.

Another momentous landmark followed: the battlefield where Michael the Brave of Wallachia had beaten the army of Cardinal Andreas Báthory, Prince of Transylvania, cousin of the Sigismund whose victories against the Turks had ended in abdication and madness. After the battle, some turncoat Szeklers presented Prince Michael with the Cardinal's mangled head: a sad finish to the great house of Báthory. Their uncle Stephen—Transylvanian Prince, then King of Poland—had prised the armies of Ivan the Terrible out of captured Lithuanian cities and driven him back into Muscovy.

* Latin Aluta, German Alt, Hungarian Olt, the same as the Rumanian, for once.

The gentle hills rolling to the north were scattered with Saxon thorpes; then all the villages were filled with Rumanian sounds once again. István charioted us with skill and speed, braking in plenty of time in the village streets for geese to hiss their way across; then shooting forward again. Stretches of road soared up and down like a switchback, swooping into hollows and breasting uphill into new vistas while Angéla lit cigarettes for us all and handed them left and right.

When we approached the outskirts of Hermannstadt—Sibiu—Nagy-Szeben (the last name, of course, is the one he used) István groaned aloud. In the Szekler capital the day before we had clean forgotten to look at the Teleki library; now, in this ancient Saxon town, there was no time to look at anything at all. Churches rose in plenty and fabulous old buildings beckoned; above all, there was the Bruckenthal Palace where the library was packed with manuscripts and incunabula; there was a gallery with room after room of Dutch, Flemish and Italian painters. As a tease, István enlarged on these splendours, "Memling, Frans Hals, Rubens . . ." he said, his hand leaving the steering wheel with an airy flourish.

Angéla said, "You read that in a book."

". . . Titian, Magnasco, Lorenzo Lotto . . ." he went on; then he described the charm of the inns, the wonders of local Saxon cooking, their skill with sucking-pigs and ducks and trout, sighed, "*No time! No time!*" and drove on down cobbled lanes and across market-places and great flagged squares. We might have been in Austria or Bavaria. Once more, the names over the shops were all Saxon. Zoological and heraldic inn-signs hung from stanchions along massive, shady arcades and no rustic discretion hampered the baroque buildings all round us. Tall casements rose between louvred shutters with twirling hinges; there were triangular and bow-topped pediments and houses plastered yellow and ochre and saffron and green and peach and mauve, and at either end of the serrated roof-trees elliptic mouldings elaborated the crow-steps of the gables; these were pierced by lunettes adorned with flourishes and scrolls, and the serried juts of dormer-windows broke up the steep slants of rose-coloured tile. It was the perfect urban counterpart to the rustic masonry of the villages. Half-timbered buildings appeared, stalwart towers barred with string courses were faced with the gilded numbers of clock-dials, crowned with onion-domes of tile or sulphur-green copper and finally topped with spikes fitted with weathercock pennants. All the upper storeys were buoyed on a froth of unpollarded mulberries and chestnut trees. Angéla had never been there before either, and our excitement and frustration ran deep; and as the motor-car threaded its way through a maze of stalls and cart-horses, a new thought smote: as far as my journey went, these houses and streets and towers were the last outposts of an architectural world I was leaving for good.

The reader may think I am lingering too long over these pages. I think so too, and I know why: when we reached our destination in an hour or two, we would have come full cycle. It wasn't only an archi-tectural world, but the whole sequence of these enchanted Tran-sylvanian months that would come to a stop. I was about to turn south, away from all my friends, and the dactylic ring of Magyar would die away. Then there was István; I would miss him bitterly; and the loss of Angéla—who is little more than a darting luminous phantom in these pages—would be a break I could hardly bear to think of; and I can't help putting off the moment for a paragraph or two.

* * * *

I must, anyway. Over-confident after our resistance to the Sibiu-Szeben-Hermannstadt temptations, we found we had time to spare. We halted and stretched our legs and lay on the grass and smoked a couple of cigarettes and I rashly made them laugh by telling them about Sir Francis Drake and the game of bowls. But no sooner had we struck the old highway beside the Maros—a few miles south of the Apulon-Apulum-Bǎlgrad-Weissenburg-Karlsburg-Gyulaféhervár-Alba Iulia turning—than fate began to scatter our route with troubles. New since our passage there two days earlier, an untimely road-gang with a steam-roller and red flags had roped off potholes which had remained untouched for years. Maddened by frustration, István foiled them at last by cutting a bold semi-circular cantle across a stubble field. Next we were held up by a collusion of sleep-walking buffaloes with a gigantic threshing-machine crawling along a stretch of road with woods on one side and on the other a sharp drop to a water-meadow; and finally, a mile or so short of the last station before our destination, there was a puncture, the second that day; caused perhaps by a broken bottle left in the stubble a month ago by some snoring haymaker. We leaped into action and just as we were tightening the last screws on the freshly patched-up spare wheel, the hoot of a train reached us from behind. Then we saw the familiar smoke-plume appearing along the valley and heard the puffing and the clatter, and there it was; and just as we were chucking the old wheel in the back it passed us and disappeared sedately round a bend. We leaped aboard as nimbly as firemen and István seized the wheel.

Swing-wells and fields of maize and tobacco shot behind and the dust rose all about us in expanding clouds. The windscreen was one of the old-fashioned kind that divide lengthways, and when István twisted a milled brass knob at the side, the lower edge of the top half lifted outwards and the wind of our pace roared through us. All at once we were shooting through thousands and thousands of sunflowers; then, far ahead, the guard's van came in sight. The train was slowing up for Simeria, the last halt before our target; and, just as it was moving on again we drew alongside. As it picked up speed, we were neck and neck; the passengers peered out in amazement and we felt like Cherokees or Assiniboines galloping round a prairie train in feathers and bisons' horns: we ought to have been shooting them full of tufted arrows while they blazed back at us with their Winchester repeaters . . . István was crouched over the wheel, shirt-sleeves rolled up, grinning fiercely like a cinder-eyed demon of speed with ribbed black-mackintosh wings; and as we pulled ahead, he let out a joyful howl; we joined in, and the train hooted as though in capitulation. Angéla was hugging herself, shoulders hunched and teeth bared with excitement, hair flying out straight in the slipstream. Sometimes, launched by troughs in the road, we seemed to take to the air; another puncture would have done for us. Then, as the train dropped further behind, we sailed into familiar territory. The tall hill of Deva, crowned with its ruined fortress, haunted by the bricked-up victim of the ancient legend, heaved into sight, with the Hátszeg mountains beyond, where Vajdahunyád lay. The Maros meandered downstream in its mist of poplars, flowing towards Gurasada and the unknown village of Saftă and Ileană, and Xenia's Zám, and then on to Kápolnás for Soborsin and Count Jenö and Tinka; Konopy and Maria Radna; and Arad, where Iza lived; and to the north of this, the roofs that sheltered Georgina and Jaš and Clara and Tibor and Ria were scattered about among dales and hills.

When we reached Deva station, the train was just coming into sight again. We seized Angéla's bag and started off over the tracks. The station master waved for us to stop, then, recognising István, turned it into a salute; and when the train drew up, we were serenely waiting for it under the acacias, which were as immutable a part of a Rumanian platform as the three gold rings and the scarlet top of the station master's cap. Leaning down from her carriage window, she threaded crimson button-holes into our shirts from the bunch of roses and tiger lilies. Our farewells had been made and I can still feel the dust on her smooth cheek. When the flag and the whistle unloosed the train, she kept waving, then took off the kerchief knotted round her throat and flourished that instead and we gesticulated frantically back. As it gathered speed, the long kerchief floated level until the train, looking very small under the slant of the woods, dwindled and vanished; then it was only a feather of smoke among the Maros trees. Angéla was about to pass all of our old haunts and all the stepping-stones of my particular journey—half a lifetime ago, it seemed—crossing the frontiers at Curtici and Lökösháza. After that, the railway line over the Great Plain—Malek's and my itinerary in reverse—would set her down, an hour before midnight, at the East Station in Budapest.

7

Carpathian Uplands

LAPUȘNIC! I have found the forgotten name at last, a hastily pencilled blur on a back page of my diary; and here it is again, minute, spidery, faded and scarcely legible, lost in a millipede's nest of contour-lines and cross-hatching, and further defaced by one of the folds on my tattered 1902 map of Transylvania: twenty-odd miles from Deva, beside a small tributary running down between wooded bluffs to the south bank of the Maros; and a recent exchange of letters with István (who now lives in Budapest) has made it triply sure. This was where we handed the motor-car back to its owner, and the re-discovery of the name provides a landmark and a starting point. I had largely abandoned my diary during these lotus-eating weeks and, after setting out, failed to resume it for a number of crucial days; but luckily a few scribbled and remembered names are backed up by a collection of clear visions, and with these and the map the next stages of the journey drop into place, though one or two of them, like undated lantern slides loose in a box, may have got out of sequence.

Lázár, the owner of the house and the motor-car, was a friend of Count Jenö and of István, and the Count had been full of amusing tales about his adventures. He had been a cowboy in America and a gaucho in the Argentine, ridden in a circus rodeo when short of cash, and his side-whiskers, piercing eyes and handsome, leathery face perfectly fitted the role. His house was only a dozen miles south of István's, and the fourth guest was another neighbour, from Maros Illye, also on the north bank, called István Horváth, who was always amiably teased for the naïvety of his observations. Dinner was a bachelor party under a lime tree, but our host's cook and housekeeper, a pretty Swabian like a soubrette in an opera who often joined gaily in the talk as she handed the dishes round, obviously mitigated the celibacy of the house. I remember their lamplit faces and the sound of István's lively touch on the piano keys later on. We spent another day there, I wrote to Angéla, and István and I parted at last, each trailing a faint cloud of hangöver in opposite directions; and I was on my own again.

Oblivion veils all for a moment; then the path emerges in clear detail. It twisted from stream to stream up a steep and sunless canyon under dripping rocks soft with moss and tufted with fern. Dank hamlets and moulting thatch huddled like clumps of toadstools in the folds of the hillside. Buffaloes and oxen lurched moodily uphill under wooden yokes that were fixed to the shaft with a steel pin and one could hear the intermittent click-clack of water-wheels long before the ivy-smothered mills came in sight; the animals halted there and drank while the waggoners unloaded their sacks. Except for a few minutes a day, no sunbeam could reach these depths. Many of the blanched and ailing villagers were stricken with goitre, and these rustic distempers made me think of all the Hungarian warnings about the prevalence of venereal disease east of the frontier; it had almost sounded as though pox lurked in the rocks and hedges and leaped out at the traveller like a thunderclap.* István had laughed when I told him. No worse here than elsewhere, he said: in Rumania they were called 'the worldly ills'—*boale lumeşti*. (An infant born out of wedlock was called 'a child of the flowers'—*un copil din flori*—a kinder term than ours.) Still brooding on those warnings, I came to a sudden halt. What about that wretched automatic pistol? I had forgotten it at the back of a bedroom drawer at István's. After a moment I thought: what a relief! It could have been nothing but an embarrassment and a nuisance—a danger, even, if found during a search in the wilds of Bulgaria or Turkey. But still—the mother-of-pearl butt, the gleaming nickel, the neat leather case! I would ask István to look after it.

The mass of the Carpathians to the left forced my itinerary south-west. The foothill canyon opened, but tall upheavals still confined the

---

* In the Mitylene brothel scene in *Pericles, Prince of Tyre*, it is the other way about:
  Pandar: "The poor Transylvanian is dead that lay with the little baggage."
  Boult: "Ay, she quickly pooped him."

sky when I got to Tomeşti at nightfall, where I found another pre-arranged haven under the roof of Herr Robert v. Winckler; he was a tall, thin, scholarly man, living alone with his books and his guns on the steep edge of the forest. He and his library were a treasure-house of relevant knowledge, and the stairs, on the way to bed, were forested with horns, antlers, fowling-pieces and wolf-traps. There were the skins of two enormous wolves on the landing, a stuffed lynx on the wall, a row of boars' tushes and a bear's skin on my bedroom floor; and the last thing I remember before blowing out the candle is the double reflection of the wick in its glass eyes. The depth of the flared embrasures showed the thickness of the walls and the logs stacked to the ceiling beside the massive tiled stove told how cold it must have been in winter. It was hard, in the summer moonlight, to imagine the onslaught of the wind along the canyons, the icicle-portcullises and the silent obliterating flakes that would place all these buildings under siege.

*   *   *   *

Transylvania, the Banat of Temesvár, the Great Plain, the Tatra mountains, Bukovina, Galicia, Podolia, Lodomeria, Moravia, Bohemia, Wallachia, Moldavia, Bessarabia and, above all, the Carpathians themselves—how closely the geography of Austria-Hungary and its neighbours approximated to the fictional world of earlier generations! Graustark, Ruritania, Borduria, Syldavia and a score of imaginary kingdoms, usurped by tyrants and sundered by fights for the throne, leap into mind: plots, treachery, imprisoned heirs and palace factions abound and, along with them, fiendish monocled swordsmen, queens in lonely towers, toppling ranges, deep forests, plains full of half-wild horses, wandering tribes of Gypsies who steal children out of castles and dye them with walnut-juice or lurk under the battlements and melt the chatelaines' hearts with their strings. There are mad noblemen and rioting jacqueries; robbers too, half-marauder and half-Robin Hood, straddling quite across the way with their grievous crab-tree cudgels. I had read about betyárs on the Alföld; now haidouks and pandours had begun to impinge. Fur-hatted and looped with pearls, the great boyars of the Rumanian principalities surged up the other side of the watershed; ghostly hospodars with their nearly mythical princesses trooped in tall branched crowns round the walls of fortress-monasteries in frescoed processions; and beyond them to the north stretched ice-bound rivers and steppes and bogs where herds of elk moved at a shambling trot, and, once upon a time, the great aurochs, extinct now except on heraldic shields; wastes unfolded north-east to which unstable troops of Cossacks laid claim, or destructive settlements of Tatars; further still, a kingdom of sledded Polacks retreated into the shadows, and then a region of snowfalls where the Teutonic Knights cut the pagans of Lithuania to bits on the frozen Baltic, surviving still in the East Prussian world of scars and spikes; and beyond them, Muscovy and all the Russias ... But to the south, closer than these and getting closer with every step, the valleys and woods of the Danube had been the theatre for momentous battles between Christendom and Islam: the armies of the Sultan moving upstream under green banners and preposterous turbans, while kings, voivodes and cardinals (the contusion of whose maces absolved them from bloodshed) and all the paladins of the West—their greyhounds curvetting beside them, sunbeams catching gold-inlay under their ostrich-plumes and the spirals and stripes on their lances, like Uccello's in the *Battle of San Romano*—cantered light-heartedly downstream to their doom.

An old addict, I had been re-reading Saki just before setting out. Many pages are haunted by 'those mysterious regions between the Vienna Woods and the Black Sea', and here I was, as deep in that maze of forests and canyons as it was possible to get. The timbered slopes outside the windows, and thoughts of the snow and the winter solstice, brought these stories to mind, especially the ones about wolves, the villains and the presiding daemons of East European winter. The terrible arrival of *The Interlopers*, in the last monosyllabic paragraph of the story, might have taken place a few miles away; and another, *The Wolves of Czernogratz*, with the howling crescendo of the same dread monsters, conjured up a thousand castles to the north and the west; and I had always been struck by the broken traveller in *The Unbearable Bassington*, 'a man whom wolves had sniffed at'. István was one, my host another, Gróf K a third; Transylvania was full of them. All the castles were haunted, and earthly packs of wolves were reinforced after dark by solitary werewolves; vampires were on the move; witches stirred and soared; the legends and fairy stories of a dozen nations piled up and the region teemed with everything that Goethe told the New World it was better without: 'Useless memories and vain strifes . . . knights, robbers and ghost stories . . . Ritter und Raüber und Gespenstergeschichten . . .' In the end, I stayed three nights, listening to stories of wolves and forests and reading in the library, and some of it must have found its way into the bloodstream. M. Herriot has left a consoling message for cases like this: 'La culture, c'est ce qui reste quand on a tout oublié.'

A scramble through valleys and foothills, bearing south-west to avoid the Lugoj road, and a night's sleep under an oak tree, brought me dog-tired and long after dark on the second day to a brick-kiln on the Caransebeş road, where I curled up and fell asleep just as the moon was coming up.

* * * *

Travels like these are times of such well-being that spirits soar, and this, with the elation of being on the move again, helped to cure the feelings of loneliness after parting from István and the end of the magic days with Angéla.

I feared I might have got rusty, but all was well and my kit seemed in as good repair as the first day in Holland. The ammunition boots from Millets in the Strand, crunching along on their only slightly blunted hobnails, were still good for unlimited miles. The old breeches were soft with much wear and cleaning, and every stitch was intact; only the grey puttees had suffered minor damage, but nothing showed when I had snipped off the ragged edges where snow and rain had frayed them. A grey shirt with the sleeves rolled up completed this marching gear. (I was darkening to the hue of a teak sideboard, with hair correspondingly bleached by the sun.) I blessed my stars that my first rucksack, with its complex framework and straps, heavy water-proof sleeping-bag and White Knight superfluity of gear had been stolen in Munich; the one my Baltic Russian friends had bestowed was smaller but held all I needed; to wit: a pair of dark flannel bags and another light canvas pair; a thin, decent-looking tweed jacket; several shirts; two ties, gym-shoes, lots of socks and jerseys, pyjamas, the length of coloured braid Angéla had given me; a dozen new hand-kerchiefs (as we know) and a sponge-bag, a compass, a jack-knife, two candles, matches, a pipe—falling into disuse—tobacco, cigarettes and—a new accomplishment—papers for rolling them, and a flask filled in turn, as the countries changed, with whisky, *Bols*, *schnapps*, *barack*, *tzuica*, *slivovitz*, *arak* and *tziporo*. In one of the side pockets there was a five-shilling Ingersoll watch that kept perfect time when I remembered to take it out and wind it up. The only awkward item was the soldier's greatcoat; I hadn't worn it for months, but felt reluctant to get rid of it. (Luckily. It was perfect for sleeping out, and, folded into a tight sausage and tied round the top of the rucksack, scarcely visible.) I still had the Hungarian walking-stick, intricately carved as a mediaeval crosier, the second replacement for the original ninepenny ashplant from the tobacconist's off Sloane Square. Apart from sketch-book, pencils and disintegrating maps, there was my notebook-journal and my passport. (Dog-eared and faded, these sole survivors are both within reach at this moment.) There was *Hungarian* and *Rumanian Self-Taught* (little progress in the one, hesitant first steps in the other); I was re-reading *Antic Hay*; and there was Schlegel & Tieck's *Hamlet, Prinz von Dänemark*, bought in Cologne; also, given by the same kind hand as the rucksack, and carefully wrapped up, the beautiful little seventeenth-century duodecimo Horace from Amsterdam. It was bound in stiff, grass-green leather; the text had long s's, mezzotint vignettes of Tibur, Lucretilis and the Bandusian spring, a scarlet silk marker, the giver's bookplate and a skeleton-leaf from his Estonian woods.*

It would have been hard to set off much later than the cock crew that morning, as the bird itself was flapping its wings on a barrel ten yards away; so I sloshed some water on my face and set off. It was going to be a sizzling day.

Pisica Veselă, the Merry Cat—the drovers' inn where I halted and drank a tapering phial of tzuica—was awhirl with flies; a huge mahogany and orange hornet was dismantling a piece of meat on the earth floor,

---

* Taken to the war, this little book disappeared six years later when an aerial torpedo sank our escaping caique on the east coast of the Peloponnese. The lost kit was just too deep for diving. The fish in the little *scala* of Leonidion must have crowded round it for a time, nibbled at the pages, then left it to fall to pieces and dissolve in the Aegean.

and the valley outside held the heat like a kiln. I was a pillar of dust and sweat by the time I got to a more congenial place further on, part-café, part-bar and part-grocer's shop. 'Wer nicht liebt Wein, Weib und Gesang' was written round the walls in twirling German script, 'Der bleibt ein Narr sein Leben lang!' I told the innkeeper of my first encounter with this couplet in Goch, on my first night in Germany. He was a cheerful Arad *Schwob* and he laughed and asked me if I knew who the poet was. "No? It was Martin Luther."* I was rather surprised. Unlike the Lutheran Saxons, the Swabians were all Catholics.

He was full of useful information, which he poured out as we both sipped mugs of cold beer, and I came to a sudden decision. He helped me stock up: a salami cut into halves, to be kept out of the sun this time; some cooked pork, a packet of pumpernickel, bars of chocolate, cheese, several apples and two loaves, on the crust of which stamps were rather disturbingly glued. ("It's a government tax," he said, prizing them off. "The stamp shows it has been paid.") He pointed out the way from the door and waved me godspeed.

The Banat mountains on the right of the road were wooded and imposing enough, but to the east the forest rose in the steep upheaval of the Carpathians and far away, above and beyond and well out of sight from my track, some of the tallest cordilleras of the Transylvanian Alps sailed up in bare and spectacular spikes. My sudden decision was to strike left and get away from the heat and dust of this beautiful incandescent valley; then, if I could, make my way south-east along the cool rim of the forest. Hastening there, I was soon under the first branches. A small track twisted uphill steeply through the boles and I plunged in.†

*   *   *   *

It was like going indoors. Climbing in the shade at once made the

---

* 'Who loves not wine, woman and song remains a fool his whole life long!' The innkeeper's attribution was quite right. I've just looked it up.

† The mountains to the left of the road were the Banat, too, as far as the line of crests which forms the western edge of the Retezat, which is part of Transylvania still. I am not sure if, or how far, I crossed this dotted line during the erratic zigzag of the following days. This is the stretch where I feel the sequence of memories is most in peril of confusion; but not too seriously, I hope.

valley seem far away and the woods silent at first until the ear was attuned to the birds.

An hour's climb ended on the edge of a slanting field where a string of reapers were getting in the late upland harvest: biblical, white-clad countrymen and women in wide hats of plaited straw, some with babies slung across their backs like papooses; when they got in the way, they hung them in the shade, snugly laced into their wooden troughs. Baskets, water jars, sickles and rakes were heaped up, half-a-dozen ponies were grazing and conical bee-hives were set in rows along the edge of the enfolding trees. As they moved forward and reaped and gathered and gleaned, an old woman's high quaver sang the lead of a never-ending sequence of verses to a grave and rather haunting tune; the others joined in at each second line. I had heard it on the climb to the little plateau; it still floated up diminuendo long after the harvesters themselves had dropped out of sight, and when it died away, I could see them far below in occasional foreshortened glimpses among the sheaves and the ricks as though I were looking at them backwards through an ever-lengthening telescope, dwindled to specks by now. Then tree-tops hid them.

The road and the valley below had disappeared and there was nothing to the west the other side but the sierras of the Banat, and they too had begun to sink. Later, a score of cows, collared with heavy bells, were treading unwieldily down from a higher pasture. I exchanged greetings with the old cowherd and his sons: where did I come from? Anglia? They had never heard of it and went on their way looking perplexed. The path seemed forever on the point of dying away among rocks or fallen trees but at the last moment, like an irregular natural staircase, it always dodged or bestrode them.

'Like going indoors . . .' It was truer than I had thought; for there, all at once, lay a space like an enormous room: a long, enclosed clearing where beech trees sprang up like gigantic pillars flinging out vaults of tangled and interlocking boughs. Grey in shadow, their smooth trunks were flecked with silver where the sunbeams spilt their way through an infinity of leaves and scattered blurred discs of light over the bark and the muscular spread of the roots; they shed a sparser and still more grudging confetti on the unencumbered floor. (No wonder Roman

poets always attached the epithet *opaca* to the *umbra* of the *fagi*!)
'Opaque', so it was. Beeches are dog-in-the-manger trees to such an
extent that nothing can grow underneath, hence these spacious ballroom glades; but opaque only in the sense that those layers of little
pleated leaves all but locked out the sun. The air underneath was
aqueous and still; it was nearly underwater light. The resilient mast
strewing the ground would have been a hog's paradise. (On the way
down, I came on swart bristly snouts, watched over by pensive swineherds, tearing up the floors of similar beechen halls.) These great forest
chambers, bounded by mingled stretches of hardwood and underbrush,
slanted uphill and out of sight in a confusion of roots. Freshets
channelled the penumbra, falling from rocky overhangs into pools that
could be heard from afar, or welled up through husks and dead leaves
and turned into streams. There had been two hoopoes in the lower
woods and bee-eaters, with an eye to the hives perhaps, perched on
twigs near the harvesters' clearing; golden orioles, given away by their
black and yellow plumage and the insistent shrill curl of their song,
darted among the branches. But every so often invisible flocks of wood-
pigeons plunged everything under a spell so drowsy, it was hard,
sitting down for a smoke, to keep awake; then a footfall would loose
off a hundred flurried wings and set them circling in the speckled light
of one of the forest ballrooms like Crystal Palace multitudes calling for
Wellingtonian hawks.

*　　*　　*　　*

The track dipped into a small valley where a stream dropped from
pool to pool out of the heart of the mountains, then followed the glen
in a shallow tangle.

A party of Gypsies, in their invariable way managing to turn a
corner of the forest into a slum, had settled here with tents and dogs
and hobbled horses; but their squalor was redeemed by the extravagant
wildness of their looks. Squatting like East Indians beside the stream,
at first they seemed to be washing up; this was something so out
of character, that I looked again. They were busy dipping wooden
pans into the current at the downstream end of little conduits improvised
with planks; kneading and sifting the mud and the gravel, wringing and

searching shaggy wet sheepskins which had been cunningly placed under their flimsy sluices; all of them peering down, rapt as kestrels. I suddenly remembered Herr v. Winckler's discourse and knew what they were up to. They answered my salute with a look of momentary consternation but allowed me to lie down and watch.

They were washing for gold. Veins of it run through many of these mountains, and of silver too, and the Romans used to sink mines. It interleaves the rock in thin layers, and tiny fragments of the exposed and eroded mineral are snapped off and worn down to dust mixed with mud, sand and gravel, or even caught in the grass and washed along the current with the other alluvia. The fragments are infinitesimal, hence the channels and fleeces set to catch them.* I guessed that gold and silver, almost heraldically, might be *aur* and *argint* in Rumanian, and they were. The nearest gold-seeker, and the chief of the party, said they had found none; but after we had smoked a couple of cigarettes I had rolled and exchanged civilities—as far as my inchoate string of Rumanian words allowed—he admitted they *had* got a little—not from here, but from a place called Porcurea, deep in the wild hills the other side of the Maros. I gathered that they had drawn a blank in this stream, and that they might have been misinformed. He reluctantly took a small leather pouch from his sash, extracted a smaller cotton bag, untied the string and shook a few grains into his slim palm. One or two expanded to the size of microscopic sequins but most of them were no more than twinkling motes. He offered to sell me the lot, making them dance like tinsel across his head and heart lines as he spoke; but he named so enormous a sum that I answered by pulling my breeches' pockets inside out, which made him laugh. We were on friendly terms and when a girl approached and, as in duty bound, began to beg in a simultaneously collusive and perfunctory whisper, he said something in Romany, and she broke off with an apologetic smile. I couldn't stop admiring the workmanship of the shallow wooden pans they used for shaking out the gold dust: half a yard in diameter and carved out of

---

* I think some classical authorities connect this prehistoric technique with the legend of the Golden Fleece. Transylvania was the oldest source of gold in the classical world, and the ancient treasures of Egypt may have been mined or gathered here. It was prized for its warm 'red-gold' hue.

walnut, they were light and beautifully polished and after a lucky scoop the grains must have glittered there like the Milky Way on a dark sky. These Gypsies were *lingurări*, 'spoon-men'; skilled in every kind of tin-smithery and wood carving.

They had come there a couple of days ago by a different route. The night before, near Caransebes, I had stumbled in the dark across a road and a small railway which wind their way eastward on the map, climbing the valley of the Bistra river some miles to the north but more or less parallel to my own unmapped and much steeper sheep's track. The Gypsies had branched off the road and then made their way southwards to this grudging sylvan Golconda. The road and the railway, meanwhile, ascended to a pass called the Iron Gate—one of many—then sank twisting and turning into Hunyadi country—Hunedoara—and the little town of Hátzeg. (This was the way I ought to have gone, but it was too late.)

Fired by success in forming nouns by knocking the last syllable off the Latin, I made a zigzag gesture over the current and said "pisc?" ending in a 'sh' sound; and it was nearly right (phonetically, 'fish' is *peshti*). "Sunt foarte mulți," the Gypsy said: "There are very many." Then I drew a blank with 'trotta' and 'trutta', one of which I hoped might be the Latin for trout;* but I remembered, from delicious meals, that it was *pisztráng* in Hungarian, and he responded to the sound at once with the Rumanian *păstrăv*. (Both races had got it from a Slavonic root. Among the southern Slavs it is *pastrmka* and *pastarva*, or something similar, overflowing into Greece as *péstrofa*, and to the north, in Poland, *pstrąs*: the tick under 'a' represents a ghostly 'n'. When and where did these Slav sounds first dilute the Latin speech of the Rumanians? What was the Dacian word for 'trout'? Beside what stream was the lost word uttered for the last time before Slavonic syllables blotted it out? If only we knew!) My Gypsy acquaintance

---

* *Fabio* is the word Ausonius uses in the *Mosella*. But, from the Baltic to Macedonia, the Slav word is roughly the same, except in Russia where they call it *Forel*, obviously a borrowing from the German *Forelle*, perhaps owing to the lack of mountain streams in Russia proper, and thus of trout . . . They probably used to get them from the Carpathians, smoked, after the First Partition of Poland in 1772. Otherwise, the Urals and the Caucasus would have been the nearest streams.

spoke Rumanian and Magyar with equal fluency, though probably both imperfectly—many comic stories depend on Gypsies' queer intonations and errors—and conversed with his fellow-tribesmen in Romany, so he was trilingual. Pointing out places on the map, I discovered he couldn't read, but he was not the less clever for it.

The Gypsies and their treasure were soon as far below as the reapers had been earlier on.

*   *   *   *

A kind of spell haunts wooded slopes like these: it drives the intruder blindly uphill, knocks ten years off his age (reducing mine to nine) unlooses a host of immature and atavistic hankerings and turns his thoughts towards Sherwood Forest, the whirr of clothyard shafts, sundered willow-wands, the Sheriff of Nottingham, Guy of Gisborne and Much the Miller's son; jumping the Atlantic, the scene changes to wigwams, smoke-signals, deerslayers, Mohicans, warpaint, calumets, birch-bark canoes and palefaces descried through gaps in the maple branches. I had once read somewhere that in King John's reign a squirrel could travel from the Severn to the Humber without touching ground; and, more recently, that trees had once covered the whole of Transylvania. Forest, then, must have been the Dacians' natural abode. The Romans obviously felled thoroughfares and laid roads; the Goths, emerging from their millions of conifers, would have felt quite at home here for their generations north of the Danube before moving on to Italy and Spain. (But what, in the dark North, and among these Dacian trees, can have prepared the Vandals for the satins and the incense of Carthage?) There would have been no environmental complaint among the forest-haunting Lombards, as they exterminated the Gepids in the undergrowth; and when the time came for the Slavs to smother Eastern Europe, they must have settled in these woods with no feeling of change. But what of the Huns? And the Avars and the Bulgars who had streamed along the valleys; indeed, the Magyars themselves; and the Pechenegs and the Cumans? And finally, the last of the Turco-Tatar invaders, the terrible Mongol brood of Jenghiz Khan, when in 1241 they laid all these regions waste? Unless the plains of south Russia were similarly timbered, few of these invaders can have seen many trees; they were desert-children, they belonged to steppes and tundras. I could imagine Batu and his companions with their flat bow-cases and quivers and habergeons and targets and their ponies with elaborate cheek-pieces and scarlet throat-plumes, turning in their saddles and looking at each other nonplussed under their epicanthic eyelids, perhaps through wolf-masks; clad in corselets of many-coloured scales, or with shoulders plumed like eagles' wings, according to the shamanistic totems of their clans; all halted in dismay on the verge of a thicket stretching a hundred leagues.

In such a wilderness, how could they have manoeuvred and advanced at their rumoured speed, and dismantled or razed every town, church, castle, palace, cathedral and abbey in the third of a continent? It was the thirteenth century, after all, Plantagenet and Valois times, and not everything can have been built of immediately combustible stuff. They had only a year to conquer, slay, enslave, lead captive, demolish and then clear out—not much time, especially at the end, when the death in Mongolia of Jenghiz Khan's successor launched the Mongol princes home in a breakneck race for the throne: it was four thousand miles to Karakorum. Admittedly, they put thousands of their prisoners to the sword; but 'leading whole populations away captive', as the chronicles say, must have delayed them, and demolition without explosions needs time and more equipment than flint and steel and a few crowbars, with perhaps a battery or two of ox-drawn siege-engines for hurling stones. Yet they are said to have destroyed all that was destructible; and, incidentally, with strangely unerring thoroughness, wiped out every fragment of historical evidence from the previous thousand years as well.*

There was plenty to think about. I was constantly wondering what these barbarians looked like. I had not yet recovered from the knowledge that the Huns used to dress in white linen raiment and the skins of fieldmice sewn together . . .

Coming on a bank covered with wild strawberries, I ate all within reach, moved to a new vantage-point and began again. One might stay all summer with pan, sieve and fishing rod, amassing gold and living

---

* I have recently learned that they actually evolved something similar to Greek fire for attacking palisades. But all the same . . .

off trout and fraises-des-bois, a sybaritic Carpathian Tom Tiddler.

The jangle of a sheep bell higher up interrupted these thoughts. There was a sound of pattering and the barking of dogs; then somebody's objurgating voice calling down the curses of the Dragon's mother: it was a common Rumanian oath—the Devil's mother, in this context—"*Mama Dracului!*" Suddenly the bell and the pattering hoofs stopped, and I could see a ram and a dozen sheep on the path above, rooted there in dismay at my hindering presence. One or two were edging to the right, which led to the abyss. I barred the way and by shouting and slashing at branches headed them into an angle of rock, where they crowded higgledy-piggledy, but stood still. Meanwhile, two fierce white dogs were snarling and barking at them and at me, and the shepherd, whirling his crook and threatening them too with the Devil's Dam, came bounding down through the trees. We outflanked the runaways and turned them uphill.

In a few minutes we were herding them to a wide and gently slanting meadow, green as April after the withered stalks below, where a hundred sheep were grazing. The shadows were beginning to slope across grass cropped as level as a lawn, and the sound of munching was broken now and then by the deep clank of the bell-wethers. Even the ewes had short curved horns, the lambs shorter still; but bell-wethers and rams were armed with heavy crinkled spirals that could have shaken the walls of Jericho. The woods still mounted interminably but now dark streaks of pine strove with the deciduous trunks and entwined their roots with those of oak and alder and hornbeam. It was only possible to descry the tops of the lower mountains now by peering from the outer edge, where the tree-tops fell away. The westering sun lit a faraway parade of level clouds, and shade filled the intervening valleys. The lower sierras of the Banat, several leagues away, were rimmed with light like a half-submerged shoal of sea-creatures.

Radu the shepherd and his family welcomed me as an ally. Two or three houses, skilfully built and roofed with wooden scales faded silver-grey, gathered at one end of the clearing and a lych-gate led into a courtyard of stakes; behind, in an oval sheepfold, sweep-wells creaked by drinking troughs made of bisected tree-trunks scooped hollow. Radu and his two brothers, with shouts and whistles and half a dozen dogs, herded the flock inside, then barred it. Were they pent to keep them from straying, I wondered. To make sure, I smacked one of the stakes and said "Why?" to Radu—"Dece?"—and his answer—"Lupii"—told all.

A wide ledge ran round the house, and this and the inside walls were whitewashed. There was a fireplace with a semi-conical chimney; golden maize-cobs were stacked with the symmetry of a honeycomb and the stripped husks for firing lay heaped in a corner. It was very clean and trim for a place that was only used at times like this, for in winter snow covered everything. The only wall decoration was a hanging oil-dip twinkling before an icon of the Virgin and Child, haloed in frills of gilt tin.

These brothers were friendly, shy, self-reliant men with a lean, sweated look and hazel eyes so used to gazing half-shut at the sun and the wind that the wrinkles at the corners expanded over their tanned cheeks in small white fans. They wore moccasins and their white homespun tunics, caught in with wide belts, expanded to the volume of kilts. Their father was identical in feature and garb, except that his hair was white and that he was still jerkined in a fleece *cojoc* and hatted in a conical fleece *caciula*. He sat on the ledge, his hands crossed on the helve of an axe. The face of Radu's wife was sad in repose, gay in motion, and strikingly beautiful; she and another woman span as they went about their tasks. Their worn, heavily carved distaffs were stuck in sashes of black braid. Elaborate detail but sober colours marked their attire: headkerchiefs and aprons of faded blue over white and many-pleated skirts, and intricately worked oblongs of the same faded hue which panelled their wide sleeves. Their torsos were enclosed in dashing-looking soft leather hauberks, shiny with wear and lacing up the side. When one of them started a new thread, Radu's wife licked the tip of her thumb and forefinger like a bank-teller, pulled some wool from the yarn which, drawn tapering to her other hand, span with the twirl of her spindle; all as unconsciously as knitting. She sang a *doina* to herself as she moved about the yard, each verse beginning "Foaie verde!"—"Green leaf"—or "Frunze verde!"—"Green frond". These green-leaf invocations always struck me as a sort of woodland salute to beech, ash, oak, pine and thorn, as if the trees and their foliage held some mysterious and beneficent power.

There was nothing to drink but water, so we all had a swig out of the flask, sitting about the ledge on stools, and I ate *mamaliga* for the first time—polenta or frumenty, that is, made out of ground maize, the staple of country people in these parts; I had been warned against it, but perversely found it rather good. Radu pointed to the gun on the wall and said we could have a hare for supper if I stayed on for another day. We ended with soft white sheep's cheese: there was a tang of curds and whey in the yard, and dripping cotton bags hung from shady branches like snow-white pumpkins. The old man—one hand cupped, the other clenched—was busy at some task: clinks of metal were followed by a whiff like singeing cloth, caused by a piece of dried fungus which he had ignited by holding it against a flint and striking it with a magnet-shaped piece of steel; then, blowing on the smouldering fragment, he laid it on top of the rubbed tobacco leaves in the bowl of a primitive, reed-stemmed pipe. It was the first time I had come across this stone-age device, called a *tchakmak* farther south.

I would have picked up a mass of lore about wolves if I had known more of the language: there were two or three pelts about the house. They sometimes carried off lambs and sheep, but there was little to fear at the moment; they were in the depths of the woods with their cubs; winter, when hunger and cold drove them down into the valleys, was the dangerous time. Mostly by gestures, he told me a pack had attacked some Gypsies in the snow the year before and left nothing but their boots and a few splinters of bone. What did they sound like? He put back his head and gave a long howl that was full of uncanny menace, and of anguish, too; (and he mimicked the stags' belling which would begin in a couple of months: a dark, primordial, throaty roar, which I heard next year in a High Moldavian ravine: the kind of sound ancient Cretans must have heard with dread from the entrance to the maze). Foxes, lynxes, wild cats, wild boars and brown bears were the other chief denizens of these woods.

It was getting dark and everyone was beginning to yawn, so I pulled on everything I had and lay outside under a tree. Radu brought out a heavy embroidered blanket, part of his wife's dowry, saying it would be cold later. Indoors, lit by the sanctuary lamp, she had crossed herself several times from right to left in the Orthodox way, thumb, index and middle finger joined to show the Oneness of the Trinity, and kissed the two haloed faces on the icon goodnight.

* * * *

But these shepherds were not Orthodox, though their rites and nearly all their doctrines were sprung from the great Byzantine branch of Eastern Christendom. They were Uniats—'Greco-Catholics', as they called them locally—who, by their ancestors' submission to an Act of Union—hence the Uniat name—were no longer spiritual subjects of the Oecumenical Patriarch at Constantinople, or of the Rumanian Primate, but of the Pope. The Rumanians everywhere enter Christian history as members of the Orthodox, or Eastern Church; but, as we know, Transylvanians in the Middle Ages were subjects of the Hungarian crown. In the sixteenth and seventeenth centuries, the Turkish wars reduced eastern Hungary to the famous vassal Principality of Transylvania. Eager to separate their Orthodox subjects from their co-religionist kinsmen the other side of the mountains—impelled also by Protestant vernacular zeal—the Rákóczi princes succeeded, by various means, in ending the Slavonic Mass of their subjects (which the Rumanians had retained from their early days under Bulgarian spiritual sovereignty), and imposing a Rumanian translation; not to encourage nationalism—just the reverse, in fact— but to widen the gulf between the liturgy of their Rumanian subjects and the Slavonic (and, recently, Greek) rite of their Eastern kinsmen; they hoped to set the Orthodox world of the Slavs and the Greeks at a further remove. Half a century later, when the Turkish eclipse made way for direct Habsburg rule, the Protestant cause waned and the Catholic waxed; and in 1699, a mixture of coercion and blandishment, backed by the astuteness of the Jesuits of Emperor Leopold, brought about a great triumph for the Counter-Reformation in the East: ecclesiastical dominion, that is, over many of the Rumanian Orthodox in Transylvania. By accepting the Union, the neophytes (or apostates) had to accept four points: the *Filioque* clause in the Creed; wafers instead of bread in the Communion service; the doctrine of Purgatory (which, like Limbo, is unknown in the East); and, most important of all, the supremacy of the Pope. All the other points of difference—the marriage of priests, a bearded clergy, the cult of icons, different vestments, rituals and usages—remained unchanged. This Act severed all official links between the Transylvanian hierarchy and the hierarchy of Wallachia and Moldavia; but distrust lingered in the Uniat rank-and-file and, for nearly a century, very many village priests slipped away and had themselves privily ordained by Orthodox bishops.

But in the end, these changes had the opposite of the wished effect. The new Mass kindled a sudden interest in the Rumanian language, and in Rumanian letters and origins as well. The publication of vernacular religious books in Transylvania, which the Princes inexpediently fostered, competed with those beyond the mountains and forged an intellectual bond. Also, after the Union, gifted Transylvanian sons of the Uniat manse were sent to study in Rome, where the spiral carvings of Trajan's Column—Roman soldiers at grips with Dacian warriors dressed very like modern Rumanian mountaineers—filled them with exciting convictions of joint Roman and Dacian descent, and these gave body to traditions which, in a more nebulous form, had long been in the air. Thousands of Rumanian children were called Traian and Aurel after their first and last Roman Emperors and convictions about Dacian descent had sunk deep roots. Among Rumanians on both sides of the mountains, these ideas fostered a national spirit and irredentist claims which the past hundred years have plentifully granted. The Rumanian ethnic cause owes much to the Uniat Church, and the debt, for reasons comparable in worldliness to those which first established the Union, has been repaid by state abolition and compulsory return to the Orthodox fold. Not a decision prompted by religious fervour.

Thinking of all this, my mind flew back to those happy mornings among the books and microscopes of Count Jenö's library. *The Double Procession of the Holy Ghost* . . .! This tintack which split Christendom was just the kind of thing to excite the Count's historical curiosity. We had been talking about how, in the Byzantine East, the Holy Ghost proceeded only from the Father ("I don't quite know what they *mean*, mind you," the Count had confessed) while, in the Catholic West he proceeded from the Father *and* the Son—ex Patre *Filioque* procedit.

When did this Western clause—not mentioned in the first seven Councils (the only ones valid in the East)—first crop up? Reference-books soon heaped up round us on the library table. "Here we are!" the Count exclaimed after a while, reading out: "Clause interpolated in the Creed at the Third Council of Toledo (never heard of it!) in 589, when King Reccared of Aragon renounced the Arian heresy!" The Count looked up excitedly. "Toledo! *King Reccared!* He was a Goth! Probably from these parts, his grandparents, I mean—Ulfilas's lot, gone West!" He read on skipping elliptically from page to page in a jingle-ish way . . . "Clause not yet adopted at Rome . . . omitted from manuscripts of the Creed . . . inclusion perhaps a copyist's mistake! H'm . . . Upheld by Paulinus of Aquileia at the Synod of Friuli, 800, yes, yes, yes . . . but only adopted among the Franks . . . Here we are! *Frankish monks intoning the Filioque clause at Jerusalem! Outrage and uproar of Eastern monks!*" He paused and rubbed his hands. "I wish I'd been there!" He pushed back his spectacles for a moment and then resumed. "Pope Leo III tries to suppress the addition, in spite of the insistence of Charlemagne—a Frank, of course!—but *approves* of the doctrine. H'm. Sounds like cold feet . . . But the next Pope adopts it . . . ninth century already. Then comes Photios, the great Eastern Patriarch and general fury, mutual anathema, and the final breach in 1054 . . ." He looked up. "I've always wanted to know about it. I didna ken, I didna ken," he said; then, closing the book, "Weel, I ken noo."

Turning the pages of a Uniat missal belonging to his wife, he alighted on a directive preceding the Uniat liturgy: "'In the Mass, the words *and from the Son*, concerning the procession of the Holy Ghost, are not included in the Creed. At the Council of Florence in 1439, the Church in no way demanded this addition from the Orientals, but only their adherence to this dogma of the faith.' Adhere, but don't utter!" he exclaimed. "*A dogma that need not speak its name!*" I said that it sounded a shadowy form of allegiance. "Please remember," the Count said gravely, "you are speaking of the Holy Ghost."

Among the Orthodox, Uniats have always borne a faint stigma of desertion, and among the rank and file of Catholics in Transylvania they seemed somehow—and rather unfairly—neither flesh, fowl nor good red herring. The switch of fealty was certainly prompted less by spiritual conviction than by *raison d'état*: Counter-Reformation expansion and zeal on one side, and on the other, the chance of flight from a harsh to a slightly less harsh form of oppression. Later generations clung to their faith with staunch rustic tenacity as they still do in the Ukraine, and nobility and pathos haunt their story.

The first Uniats of all, however, were neither the Transylvanians nor the Ruthenes, but later members of the Palaeologue dynasty: Michael VIII very briefly, and finally, the last two Emperors of the East. Our thoughts must wing back to the last years of Byzantium, where the Turks were closing in for the final scene. It was the hope of succour from the West that in 1437 sent John VIII Palaeologue and his court and clergy on the extraordinary journey to Florence which Benozzo Gozzoli has commemorated on the walls of the Medici Palace. During the discussions in Santa Maria Maggiore, two of the Eastern prelates were given cardinals' hats; but at home, chiefly stirred up by the *Filioque* question, Byzantium was in a ferment. Nevertheless, willy-nilly, and in the teeth of Orthodox protest, the Emperor accepted the Western demands. Gibbon describes the culminating moment with the Emperor enthroned on one side of the Duomo and the Pope on the other. 'I had almost forgot,' he writes, 'another popular and Orthodox protestor: a favourite hound, who usually lay quiet on the foot-cloth of the Emperor's throne; but who barked most furiously while the Act of Union was reading, without being silenced by the soothing or the lashes of the royal attendants.' Then the Emperor had to return and face his booing subjects at Byzantium. But, except for some brave Genoese, no help came and John's brother Constantine XI, still a Uniat—though a reluctant one, it would seem—fell fighting in the mêlée when the Turks stormed and captured the city. 'The distress and fall of the last Constantine', Gibbon says, 'are more glorious than the long prosperity of the Byzantine Caesars.'

But it was the first Gibbon quotation which had fired Count Jenö. "Just fancy! A dog in church! I wonder what he was called? What breed he was? One of those Arabian greyhounds, I bet . . ." After a pause, he said, "It reminds me of a similar occasion: The Vatican Council on Papal Infallibility in 1870! Endless sessions and lobbying, you know, and nothing but rows—Schwarzenberg, Dupanloup, Manning and the rest of them. But they pushed it through at last. When it was being ceremonially read out in Saint Peter's, a terrible storm broke out —clouds black as soot! forked lightning! rain, hail and thunder, you couldn't hear a word!" Count Jenö, an easy-going but devout Catholic, beamed among his moths and his specimen-cases. He loved this kind of thing. "Not a word! Much worse than the Emperor's dog! What's more, the Franco-Prussian war broke out next day, and all the French and German cardinals rushed north on the new railway—in different first-class carriages, of course—and cut each other stone dead when they got out to smoke and stretch their legs on the platform at Domodossola . . ."

Well, as a result of all this, Radu and his family, after two and a half centuries under Rome, are members of the Orthodox Church again: rather bewildered, perhaps.

*　　*　　*　　*

Cliffs and bands of rock jutted from the trees and sometimes the woods opened to make way for landslides and tumbled boulders and fans of scree. There was the scent of pine-needles and decay. Old trunks had rotted and fallen and the pale leaves of the saplings which replaced them scattered the underworld with various light and broke it into hundreds of thin sunbeams. The ghost of a track, perhaps only used by wild animals, advanced with hesitation; the matted carpet of leaves, cones, pine-needles, acorns, oak-apples, beech-mast and the split caskets of chestnuts must have been piling up forever. A tall pine had collapsed in a tangle of creepers and I was scrambling on all fours through the foxgloves and bracken underneath when my hand closed on something half-buried in leaves. It was a five-pointed stag's antler: a marvellous object, from the frilled coronet at the base to the tips of sharp tines as hard as ivory. How could something gnarled with these ancient-looking wrinkles have such a swift growth and so brief a life? They prick through a stag's brow in spring like twin thoughts breaking out of the skull, then shoot and ramify with the fluid motion of plants, fossilising as they grow; larger each year, more fiercely spiked, then scabbarded in velvet to be torn to shreds against boles and branches until the buck they have armed is ready to clear the woods of rivals;

only to fall off again at the end of winter, like moulting feathers. This one was about a foot and a half long and perfectly balanced and I set off through the bracken feeling like Herne the Hunter. It was impossible to leave it there, even if I couldn't take it all the way to Constantinople.

Soon I came on four does, each with a fawn grazing or pulling at the branches that hemmed the clearing. I must have been down-wind; they only looked up when I was fairly close. They turned in a flurry, heading for the underbrush and sailing downhill in great arcs until all their white rumps had vanished in turn; and, as they took flight, a russet stag, unseen till then, looked up with a sweep of horn that was spread far wider than the antler in my hand; and while the does were curvetting past, his antlers swung out of profile into full face like a ritual separation of twin candelabra. His wide eyes were severe but unfocused, white flecks scattered the back of his tawny coat, and his hooves were neat and shining. Turning aside, he took one or two sedate and strutting paces, trotted a few more with his head and its scaffolding well back, and leaped down the slope after the does. The load of horn rose and sank with each bound; then he flew headlong through a screen of branches like a horse through a hoop and the boughs closed behind him as he crashed downhill and out of earshot.

I could hardly believe they had all been there a few seconds before. Could my antler have once been his, shed a few years back? Perhaps even now he had not reached full span, although August was beginning: I had seen no tatters of velvet . . . Anyway, the trove in my hand could just as easily have been centuries old.

Bit by bit, the shoulders of bare rock began to grudge foothold to the taller trees and I was advancing through dwarf fir and a slag-like scree covered with a spectral confusion of thistles. A pale ridge of mineral had sprung up to the right; a much loftier upheaval soared to the left, with another far away beyond it, wrinkled, ashen and shadowless, like an emanation of the noon's glare. I was moving along an empty valley of pale rocks and boulders, cheerlessly plumed here and there with little fir trees, and eventually these too died away. The warp of the mountains had led me astray. I was not sure that I was where I thought I was, or where I ought to be. It was a bleak place with the pallor of a bone-yard and a wind blowing up made it bleaker still.

Damp mist was advancing along the trough, thin wisps at first, followed by denser whorls of vapour clammy to the touch, until it was hard to see more than a few yards. I must have been in the heart of one of those clouds that people gaze at from the plain as they come decoratively to anchor along the cordilleras. When the mist turned into fine rain, I fumbled my way up the flank of the ridge which had stealthily piled up between me and the slope I had been following for two days. I found a cleft in it at last, climbed steeply out of the mist and then down again through boulders and unstable cataracts of scree and plunged through the thistle-belt and the dwarf fir, putting the ascending process into reverse until I was back among the bracken and the sheltering hardwoods and pines. Scrambling about the planetary emptiness above, I had lost my bearings; and when I found the vestige of a sheep-track—unless it had been trodden there by deer—I followed its slight slant, hoping for a turn to the left, but in vain; until, late in the afternoon, I heard dogs barking far away and an occasional bell, and lastly, a clear liquid music that I couldn't place. But when the trees opened there was something familiar about the sloping grass, the shingle roofs at the far end and the grazing sheep. It was Radu's clearing; I had travelled in an enormous circle.

Vexation only lasted a moment. I had thought I would never see that place again.

The musical notes came from Radu's brother Mihai. He was sitting on a green rock with his crook beside him under the moss-covered boughs of an enormous oak and playing a six-holed wooden pipe a yard long. It was a captivating sound, sometimes liquid and clear, sometimes, in the bass notes, reedy and hoarse. Minims and quavers hovered, sinking at the end of each passage to deep semibreves before reascending and moving on. Across the valley, the sun dropped among the lower ranges and clouds broke the sunset into long beams. They climbed to our ledge, touched the undersides of the leaves and lit up the sheep's wool. The oak-branches, the drifts of clouds and the mossy glooms winding through the trunks were suddenly shot through with spokes of sunset. Birds scattered the air and the topmost branches, and for a few minutes all the tree-trunks flared as crimson as a blood-orange. It might have been the backwoods of Arcadia or Paradise and we advanced over the grass with the antler and the flute and a troop of five dogs like actors in an enigmatic parable or a myth with its context lost.

The others were surprised and welcoming. It was like coming home. Radu was puzzled: why lug that antler about? Last night's thought of a hare had not been forgotten—indeed, my return might have been preordained—for his gun leant against a tree and the yard was afloat with fumes of onion, garlic, paprika and bay leaves.

After leaving sketches of some of them next morning, I set out again, guided for a furlong or two by Mihai, who filled me with half-grasped instructions.

*   *   *   *

The scurry and improvisation of the days before starting south from Lázár's had driven serious planning clean out of our minds. The proper thing on leaving the Maros would have been to follow its tributary, the Cerna,* past Hunyadi's castle once more then to the beautiful Hátzeg valley. Here I could have stayed with the eccentric Gróf K—the one who had ridden a horse with its head in a bag. (His fame was widespread; the shepherds smiled when his name cropped up.) Then I could have climbed through the forest to the great Retezat massif. It was here that István had suggested that we might have hunted chamois. When I reached civilisation again after these mountain days, I was distressed to learn all I had missed: chamois, perhaps; deep silent valleys; a special rose-red heather smelling of cinnamon and named after Baron Bruckenthal; hundreds of streams; peaks that sailed into the air like pyramids and dropped plumb into the abyss; cascades of mighty blocks scattered in wild disorder; scores of Alpine lakes . . . It struck me, all the same, that I had hardly been starved of splendours. Could that distant glimpse yesterday have been the summit of the Retezat? Probably not. I didn't know then and I still don't.†

Other wonders lay hidden in that labyrinth of valleys. Deep in the heart of them were the remains of Sarmizegethusa, the old capital of the Dacians and the stronghold of King Decebalus. By the time he had

---

* Warning: There is another of these 'black rivers' later on. The area is confusingly repetitive in these matters.

† The only solution is to go there and climb it.

reduced Domitian to paying the Dacians a kind of Dac-geld, Decebalus and his realm had become the most powerful force ever to confront the Empire; he was a great and noble figure, and when Hadrian invaded his mountains, it was almost a contest between equals. It took a bitter and laborious campaign and all the science and siegecraft of Rome to subdue him: skills which Decebalus himself had anyway half-mastered; and in the end, rather than surrender to be led fettered in a triumph, the King fell on his sword in the high Roman fashion. Sarmizegethusa became Ulpia Traiana, the stronghold of the Legio Tredecima Gemina, and the place was cluttered still with carved fragments recalling the Leg. XIII Gem., which sounds like a legion at double strength. Its eagles presided there as long as the province lasted. Stupendous walls and the ruins of an amphitheatre show the importance of the city; broken statues of gods and emperors and the great hewn ashlars of temples scatter the region; fallen shrines speak of Isis and Mithras, and fissured mosaics underfoot spread the mythological floors of old dining rooms.

The most difficult parts of my attempt to keep to the western slopes of this range were avoiding loss of height and resisting the ways the grain of the mountains tried to impose; but upheavals, bands of rock, dejection-cones and landslides made this hard; it was often a question of zig-zagging to the bottom of a ravine and up the other side, or of swerving into a hinterland where I was nearly bound to go astray. I did both; but, looking at the sun and my resurrected watch and the compass (only used, so far, on my last day in Hungary) I managed not to get irretrievably lost.

I saw nobody all day; there were numbers of red squirrels, a few black ones, and innumerable birds; but the only larger creatures were hawks and, usually in pairs, languidly and loftily afloat round the jutting bastions of rock, golden eagles. Sometimes I was looking across wide bowls of tree-tops before plunging into them; at others, striding over grassy saddles or scrambling on those expanses that, from below, looked like bald patches; but most of the time I followed whatever dim woodland tracks I could unravel; breaking off, every so often, to side-step across unstable and irksome cascades of shale: then back under the branches. As usual, on lonely stretches, poetry and songs came to the rescue, sometimes starting echoes. I still had plenty of food;

there were dozens of streams to drink from, many of them thick with watercress, and as I flung myself face down beside one like a stag at eve, I thought how glad I was, at that particular moment, not to be standing properly at ease on the parade ground at Sandhurst. Oxford would have been better; but this was best.

The ledge I found for the night was sheltered by trees on three sides and, on the fourth, the tips of the pine-trees zoomed into the depths. When the afterglow following a bonfire-sunset had gone and the bed-time pandemonium of birds began to quieten, I rugged up, lit a candle, fished out my book and for a few pages followed the adventures of Theodore Gumbril. The stars were unbelievably dense, to gaze up turned one into a multi-millionaire, and better still, the Perseids were still dropping like fireworks. I had travelled far and I was soon asleep, but when the chill of the small hours woke me, I put on another layer of jersey, swallowed what remained in the flask and found the late-rising moon had extinguished many of the stars, just as Sappho says she does. The last quarter scattered the woods with vistas and depths and the gleams of lit rock.

Soon after setting off in the morning, I halted on a grassy bluff to tie up a lace when I heard a sound which was half a creak and half a ruffle. Looking over the ledge to a similar jut fifteen yards below, I found myself peering at the hunched shoulders of a very large bird at the point where his tawny feathers met plumage of a paler chestnut hue: they thatched his scalp and the nape of his neck and he was tidying up the feathers on his breast and shoulders with an imperiously curved beak. A short hop shifted the bird farther along its ledge and it was only when, with a creak, he flung out his left wing to its full stretch and began searching his armpit, that I took in his enormous size. He was close enough for every detail to show: the buff plus-four feathers covering three-quarters of his scaly legs, the yellow and black on his talons, the square-ended tail-feathers, the yellow strip at the base of his upper beak. Shifting from his armpit to his flight-feathers, he set about preening and sorting as though the night had tousled them. He folded the wing back without haste, then flung out the other in a movement which seemed to put him off balance for a moment, and continued his grooming with the same deliberation.

Careful not to move an eyelash, I must have watched for a full twenty minutes. When both wings were folded, he sat peering masterfully about, shrugging and hunching his shoulders from time to time, half-spreading a wing then folding it back, and once stretching the jaws of his beak wide in a gesture like a yawn, until at length on a sudden impulse, with a creak and a shudder, he opened both wings to their full tremendous span, rocking for a moment as though his balance were in peril; then, with another two or three hops and a slow springing movement of his plus-foured legs, he was in the air, all his flight-feathers fanning out separately and lifting at the tips as he moved his wings down, then dipping with the following upward sweep. After a few strokes, both wings came to rest and formed a single line, with all his flight feathers curling upwards again as he allowed an invisible air-current to carry him out and down and away, correcting his balance with hardly perceptible movements as he sailed out over the great gulf. A few moments later, loud but invisible flaps sounded the other side of a buttress and a second great bird followed him almost without a sound. They swayed gently, with a wide space of air between them, like ships in a mild swell. Then as they crossed the hypotenuse of shadow which stretched from the Carpathian skyline to the flanks of the Banat mountains, the morning light caught and burnished their wings and revealed them both in their proper majesty. To look down on this king and queen of birds, floating there in aloof companionship, brought a long moment of exaltation. To think the Kirghiz used golden eagles for hunting! They carried them on horseback, a seemingly impossible feat, then unhooded them over the steppe to soar and spy out antelopes and foxes and wolves and then stoop on their quarry. Hereabouts, Radu had conveyed, they sometimes rivalled wolves in decimating flocks and, I learned later on, in wreaking havoc among the sheep and goats of the Sarakatsan nomads of the Rhodope mountains, and the flocks of Radu's relations, the Koutzovlachs of the Pindus. They circle above the folds, hover, take aim, then fall like javelins and carry lambs piteously bleating into the sky.

I wondered if these two had merely alighted on their morning rounds, or whether their nest were nearby. Better not to look! (I had a sudden vision of those blood-curdling front pages of the *Domenica del*

Corriere, in cobalt, orange and sepia: a goalkeeper crushed to death by an anaconda under the eyes of awe-stricken teams: 'Ofside! Un incidente in Torino'; three rhinoceroses chasing a Carmelite nun across a chaotic Apennine market-place: 'Uno Sfortunato Incontro'; or, in this case, 'Al Soccorso dei Bambini!'—a nestful of eaglets and two eagles tearing a marauder to bits, who desperately beats at them with an antler . . .)

I could follow their motionless hover and their languid circlings for a long time as I headed south. The encounter, within twenty-four hours of that brief Altdorfer-vision of the stag, was almost too much to take in. I wondered how near to wild boars my path had gone, or might go; and to wolves and bears. They, too, were said to keep out of men's way at this time of the year. I hadn't seen any of them; but perhaps they had seen me as I crashed past. What about the famous passion of bears for honey and the bee-hives of those harvesters? I longed to catch a glimpse of one of them ambling bandy-legged across the middle distance or reaching on tip-toe, plagued by bees, into a hollow tree after a comb. There had been movements like an unquiet spirit in the branches during the night; larger than a squirrel, it had sounded: could it have been a wild cat or a lynx? Perhaps a pine-marten.

Starting at dawn, ending at dark and only separated by light sleep, each day in the mountains seemed to contain a longer sequence of phases than a week at ground level. Twenty-four hours would spin themselves into a lifetime, and thin mountain air, sharpened faculties, the piling-up of detail and a kaleidoscope of scene-changes seemed to turn the concatenation into a kind of eternity. I felt deeply involved in these dizzy solitudes, more reluctant each minute to come down again and ready to go on forever. Thank heavens, I thought, climbing along a dark canyon of pines, no likelihood of it ending yet. But suddenly, very faintly and a long way off, there was the sound of an axe falling; then two or three. However far away, the sound struck a baleful note; it spoke of people from the lower world and the two days' solitude since leaving the shepherds had installed feelings of unchallenged ownership of everything within sight or hearing.

*   *   *   *

The axes had been hard at work. Oaks, beeches and alders stood about in solitude amid a disorder of shorn stumps, rings of chips and felled pine-trees. They had been cut nearly through with two-handed saws then finished off with axe, beetle and wedge, and even as I watched, the woodmen were banging their wedges into the last victim of the day. The impacts only reached me when the beetles were lifted for the next blow; and soon, with a splitting and a crash, down the tree came, and they fell on it, lopping and trimming the prone trunk with saws, axes and billhooks. When enough stripped timber had accumulated, a team of horses with grapples and hauling gear would be summoned and the trunks dragged to the edge of the clearing and tipped down a steep ride: a chaos of timber choked the grass all the way down to a point where waggons could load them. It reminded me of the stripes of snow I had seen in the forests round the Austrian Danube and the pine-trunks tumbling down them like spilt matchboxes: all to be sawn into deal planks or put together in rafts and floated downstream.

I learnt all this in German from a burly man in a red-checked flannel shirt and a celluloid eye-shade like a journalist's in a film. After leaving the team of woodmen, he had fallen in with me on his way to a log-cabin with a corrugated iron roof. Here, most incongruously seated at a table, a bearded man in a black suit and a black beaver hat turned up all round was poring over a large and well-thumbed book, his spectacles close to the print. In a few years' time he would look exactly like one of the Elders in The Temple by Holman Hunt and this is exactly what he was. Two sons about my age, also dressed in black, were on either side of him, equally rapt. They too were marked for religion: you could tell by their elf-locks and the unshorn down which fogged their waxy cheeks. How different from the man in the check shirt; he was the Rabbi's younger brother and his cast of feature might have been the work of a hostile cartoonist. He was foreman of this timber concession and he came from Satu Mare—Szatmár—a town in the Magyar belt to the north-west of Transylvania. The Rabbi and his sons were spending a fortnight with him and the loggers were mountain people from the same region.

When the foreman led me to the group at the table, they looked up apprehensively; almost with alarm. I was given a chair, but we were all overcome with diffidence. "Was sind Sie von Beruf?" The foreman, anything but shy, looked at me in frank puzzlement. "Sind Sie Kaufmann?" Was I a pedlar? I felt slightly put out by the question, but it was perfectly reasonable. Nobody else was wandering about like this and I suppose the only itinerant strangers in these parts, if they were not beggars or out-and-out bad hats, must have been pedlars, though I had never come across any. (But a stranger in such a place obviously needed explanation. The shepherds and Gypsies had both shown a touch of misgiving at first: unknown figures in the wilderness bode no good. In the past, they were bent on rounding up laggards for feudal corvées; nowadays, it would be tax-gathering, census-compiling, exaction of grazing dues, the search for malefactors, deserters, or runaway recruits overdue for their military service—a whole range of vexatious interference with the freedom of the woods.) My interlocutors looked bewildered when I tried to explain my reasons for not staying at home. Why was I travelling? To see the world, to study, to learn languages? I wasn't quite clear myself. Yes, some of these things, but mostly—I couldn't think of the word at first—and when I found it—"for fun"—it didn't sound right and their brows were still puckered. "Also, Sie treiben so herum aus Vergnügen?" The foreman shrugged his shoulders and smiled and said something in Yiddish to the others; they all laughed and I asked what it was. "Es ist a goyim naches!" they said. 'A goyim naches', they explained, is something that the goyim like but which leaves Jews unmoved; any irrational or outlandish craze, a goy's delight or gentile's relish. It seemed to hit the nail on the head.

The initial reserve of the other dwellers in these mountains had not lasted long; nor did it here: but the Jews had other grounds for wariness. Their centuries of persecution were not ended; there had been trials for ritual murder late in the last century in Hungary and more recently in the Ukraine, and fierce deeds in Rumania and pogroms in Bessarabia and throughout the Russian Pale. Slanderous myths abounded and the dark rumours of the Elders of Zion had only been set in motion fifteen years earlier. In Germany, meanwhile, terrible omens were gathering, though how terrible none of us knew. They came into the conversation and—it seems utterly incredible now—we talked of Hitler and the Nazis as though they merely represented a dire phase of history, a sort of transitory aberration or a nightmare that might suddenly vanish, like a cloud evaporating or a bad dream. The Jews in England—a happier theme—came next: they knew much more than I, which was not hard; and Palestine. Sighs and fatalistic humour spaced out the conversation.

Everything took a different turn when scripture cropped up. The book in front of the Rabbi was the Torah, or part of it, printed in dense Hebrew black-letter that was irresistible to someone with a passion for alphabets; especially these particular letters, with their aura of magic. Laboriously I could phonetically decipher the sounds of some of the simpler words, without a glimmer of their meanings, of course, and this sign of interest gave pleasure. I showed them some of the words I had copied down in Bratislava from shops and Jewish newspapers in cafés, and the meanings, which I had forgotten, made them laugh; those biblical symbols recommended a stall for repairing umbrellas, or 'Daniel Kisch, Koscher Würste und Salami'.* How did the Song of Miriam sound in the original, and the Song of Deborah; David's lament for Absolom; and the rose of Sharon and the lily of the valley? The moment it became clear, through my clumsy translations into German, which passage I was trying to convey, the Rabbi at once began to recite, often accompanied by his sons. Our eyes were alight; it was like a marvellous game. Next came the rivers of Babylon, and the harps hanging on the willows: this they uttered in unfaltering unison, and when they came to 'If I forget thee, O Jerusalem', the moment was extremely solemn. In the back of my diary are a few lines in Hebrew inscribed there by the Rabbi himself; as they are in the cursive script, utterly indecipherable by me; and underneath them are the phonetic sounds I took down from his recitation of them.

> "Hatzvì Yisroël al bomowsèycho cholol:
> Eych nophlòo ghibowrim!
> Al taghìdoo b'Gath,
> Al t'vashròo b'chootzòws Ashk'lon;

* See *A Time of Gifts*, p. 221.

אל־תגידו בגת אל־תבשרו בחוצת אשקלין

Pen tismàchnoh b'nows P'lishtim,
Pen ta'alòwznoh b'nows ho'arèylim.
Horèy va Gilboa al-tal, v'al motòr aleychem . . ."

Here it dies away for a moment, then resumes:

"Oosodèy s'roomòws . . ."

The few words that sound like proper nouns revealed what it must be:
"Tell it not in Gath," that is, "publish it not in the streets of Askelon;
lest the daughters of the Philistines rejoice, lest the daughters of the
uncircumcised triumph." The next incomplete piece *must* be "Ye
mountains of Gilboa, let there be no dew . . ." By this time the other-
worldly Rabbi and his sons and I were excited. Enthusiasm ran high.
These passages, so famous in England, were doubly charged with
meaning for them, and their emotion was infectious. They seemed
astonished—touched, too—that their tribal poetry enjoyed such glory
and affection in the outside world; utterly cut off, I think they had no
inkling of this. A feeling of great warmth and delight had sprung up
and the Rabbi kept polishing his glasses, not for use, but out of enjoyment and nervous energy, and his brother surveyed us with benevolent
amusement. It got dark while we sat at the table, and when he took off
the glass chimney to light the paraffin lamp, three pairs of spectacles
flashed. If it had been Friday night, the Rabbi said, they would have
asked me to light it; he explained about the *shabbas goy*. This was the
Sabbath-gentile whom well-off Jews—"not like us"—employed in
their houses to light fires and lamps and tie and untie knots or perform
the many tasks the Law forbids on the Seventh Day. I said I was sorry
it was only Thursday (the Sabbath begins at sunset on Friday) as I
could have made myself useful for a change. We said good-night with
laughter.

★   ★   ★   ★

Stretched under one of the surviving oaks, I was brimming with
excitement. I had thought I could never get on friendly terms with such
unassailable-looking men. I had often caught glimpses of similar
figures. The last time had been on the moonlit platform the night I
entered Rumania; they had looked utterly separate and remote and

unapproachable; I could as soon have asked a Trappist abbess for a light.

I thought about the shabbas goy. I would not have been indispensable after all, for a little way off, gathered round a low fire of their own, the loggers were quietly singing in Hungarian. It sounded indefinably different from Rumanian singing, but equally captivating and equally sad.

After I said goodbye next morning, the younger boy, who was wearing a skull-cap and carrying white prayer-shawls with black stripes at the ends, joined the other two indoors and as I left, I could hear them intoning their prayers in a harrowing lamentation while the foreman, no zealot, was pointing out a fresh stand of timber to the loggers.

*   *   *   *

For a remote shelf of the Carpathians, it had been an unexpected encounter. What itineraries had brought them all the way from Canaan and Jerusalem and Babylonia? A few Karaite schismatics, who had settled on the Sea of Azov and the Black Sea, had made their way to Eastern Europe, but not much had been heard of them since; and a handful of Jews—by religion, if not by blood—may have come in with the Magyars; if, that is, the war-like Kabar tribesmen belonged to the élite among their fellow-Khazars who had been converted to Jewry: for three Kabar tribes accompanied the Magyar move westward which ended on the Great Plain; they must surely have embraced Christianity when the rest were converted. The most probable ancestors of my hosts—in part, at any rate—would seem to have been the Jews who had settled along the Rhine in the early days of the Roman Empire, after making their way through Italy before the Babylonian dispersal; perhaps before the destruction of the Temple.

In early times, when all religions were polytheistic, gods were shared out and exchanged; they wandered from pantheon to pantheon and were welcome everywhere. The Manichaeans virtually reduced the Zoroastrian cast to two rivals of equal power: a perilous tendency, as its offspring heresies proved. But the Jews bowed down to a solitary god who tolerated no rivals and could neither be seen, graven as an image, nor even mentioned by name, and there was discord with neighbours from the start. (It seems at times that strife can no more be separated from monotheism than stripes from a tiger.) Their period of mundane glory passed away; hard days followed; and by the time it had given birth to Christianity and then to Islam, Judaism was in the position of a King Lear hag-ridden by Goneril and Regan, but with no part written for Cordelia, or anyone to act it—unless, for a century or two, it was the Khazar Empire. The promotion of Christianity from the catacombs to the state religion of the West made the solitary position of the Jews irretrievable. An inflexible programme of revenge for the Crucifixion was set on foot and the following centuries of outlawry and humiliation gave rise to a demonology and a mystique that are active still. In the Middle Ages the Jews were to blame not for deicide only, but for every calamity that smote the West, notably the Black Death and the invasions of the Mongols: these incarnate fiends were the Twelve Tribes galloping out of the East to reinforce the wicked plans of Jewish kinsmen in Europe . . . In German lands, especially, the ardour of the Crusades burst out in a grim series of massacres. These things set many of the Jews on the move once more and they came to a halt in Poland. (It was their long German sojourn that had made a mediaeval German dialect, chiefly the Franconian, the basis of the Yiddish *lingua franca* of Eastern Europe.) The kingdom welcomed them at first. They settled and multiplied; but, with time, things began to change. The clergy denounced the kings for their protective policy and at the turn of the fourteenth and fifteenth centuries, persecution began: the Dominicans extorted a yearly fine and the usual charges of desecrated hosts and ritual murder reappeared . . . In spite of all this, it was a sort of heyday for Jewish scholarship and theology. They were too large a population to move on when fresh troubles beset them. The worst of these were the Cossack massacres of the seventeenth century; and after the partition of Poland, Russian persecution, and the pogroms in the Pale, set many thousands on their travels again. (The Rabbi and his brother were not quite sure, but they thought some of their ancestors might have come from those parts four or five generations back; Galicia was the other most likely provenance.) In spite of endemic anti-Jewish feeling in Hungary, Jews had managed to play a considerable part in the country's life—it had been better for them there than in Russia or Rumania. My companions felt patriotic about Hungary, they said: they talked Hungarian rather than Yiddish among themselves, and lamented their recent change of citizenship.

In a continent where countless races had changed utterly or vanished into thin air, the Jews, however battered and woebegone, had altered least. Many things apart from religion singled them out, and here in the mountains especially they bore the stamp of an urban and indoor folk, different in everything from the surrounding rustics. Costume, diet, bearing, gesture, complexion and intonation—the insidious nasal note that their detractors mimicked so tirelessly—widened the gulf. (I could not look at the two boys without wishing their corkscrew-locks away, and felt guilty at once for doing so.) Parallel to the indignities inflicted by the gentiles, there was an array of self-imposed stigmata which seemed purposely designed to flaunt outside aesthetic notions and, should it be needed, choke off approach. (They were exactly the things, of course, which anyone seeking assimilation—as, with a second guilty twinge, I felt I should have done—would most eagerly jettison.) But for those who looked on merging as treachery, it was utterly different. They clung to ancient ways as they had done for ever; but the marks left by the ghetto had become, if not emblems of martyrdom, at least treasured symbols of solidarity in hard times, for there had never been a moment when an end to persecution, by apostasy, was out of reach; a few words and a splash of water and their troubles would have been over. But they had chosen the edge of the sword and flight and the fate of outcasts rather than break faith. No wonder, once indoors and away from it all, that they shunned contact with the vile world outside, and, if the externals of their life seemed alien and rebarbative, so much the better; it would shoot home the excluding bolts. Skill and flair, in a world beset with difficulties, offered chances of survival, prosperity and brilliant achievement; but it struck me, in a moment of lamp-lit clairvoyance, that among devotees like my companions, all these were an illusion. The pre-occupation of the Rabbi and his sons—the columns of black-letter, hedged about with the glosses and footnotes and rubrics of two or three thousand years, represented the true aim of existence; something to be pursued and loved in secret and behind barred shutters: their scriptures, their poetry, their philosophy, their history and their laws. These were the lodestar of their passion, and the sea of outside troubles must have fallen back while they re-explored the mysteries of their religion and traced the subtleties of the law or unravelled the meanings of the Kabbala and the Zohar or weighed the tenets of the Hassidim against the refutations of the Gaon of Vilna; and, as they re-read the deeds of Joshua and David and the Maccabees, the oafish slogans in the lanes outside must have died away.

* * * *

'Ye mountains of Gilboa, let there be no dew . . .' The words kept floating to the surface during the following hours, next morning in particular, when I woke up dry as a bone and remembered my damp resurrection at the swineherds' hut near Visegrád. There had been a drift or two of mackerel sky the evening before and I had slept under cover for the first time for a week. A timely cave, where part of the opening had been roughly walled in with dry-stone masonry to form a sheepfold, gaped invitingly at nightfall; but it was hopping with insects, so I left it for a smaller one about the size of an opera box and I can only have been asleep a little while when a liquid rippling, not caused by water, woke me up. Below, just discernible in the starlight, a great flock of sheep was on the move and hundreds of little cleft feet were trotting by. Shepherds and dogs passed in dead silence. It was as though the animals were being rustled; I watched until they had vanished, and next day they seemed like sheep in a dream.

There was no dew; but mist wreathed the clefts and ravines. Faraway spurs rose up, stage-wings only defined by the hair-thin line of their summits against the next vaporous upheaval, each a paler blue as it receded, while the valleys that twisted downhill were dusky with timber.

The mountains were full of echoes. Small landslides would spread like a rumour, and the four key-notes of an octave, sung loud enough, rocketed into the distance five or six times with a second or two between each chord, and branched off down side valleys, a little fainter after each encore. The mountains would have been a perfect auditorium for those Tibetan-looking horns six or ten feet long. (*Bucium*, the Rumanian word, is almost certainly from the Roman *buccina*, the long brazen tube on triumphal arches that distends legionaries' cheeks among looted tabernacles and candlesticks.) The other side of this watershed, at the storming of Sarmizegethusa, the fanfares of Trajan must have unloosed pandemonium. (Apart from those of the Rumanians, the other giant horns to be heard in this part of Europe were those of the Huzuls, shy, Slav-speaking Uniat Ruthenes living in a world of spells and legends two hundred-odd miles to the north-north-west in the Sub-Carpathian ranges next door to Bukovina.)

I came on some flocks and a shepherd playing a small bone flute: I soon learnt that something of the kind was as inseparable from herdsmen as a distaff and spindle from their wives and I wished I had looked at it closer: bone flutes are favourite instruments among the Sarakatsan nomads of northern Greece whom I got to know later; theirs are made out of the long bone in an eagle's wing. This was probably the shinbone of a sheep. A *tibia*, in fact.

But another reason made me wish, a year hence, that I had paid more attention. A later part of this journey carried me to eastern Rumania, and I returned there the following year; and, between then and the outbreak of war, I spent much time in a remote, Grand Meaulnes-like country-house in Moldavia, not far from the present Russian frontier. They were long sojourns of unalloyed happiness: I adored the inhabitants; and while I was there, I picked up a slipshod fluency in Rumanian of which a few vestiges remain.

Like many another, I soon came under the spell of the oldest poem in the language. It is called *Mioritza*. Universally but sporadically known throughout the Rumanian-speaking world for hundreds of years, it was only taken down and printed during the last century, so it must be described as a folk-poem, but the classification fits these strange verses rather awkwardly. Many have pored over their arcane symbolism. Some say that they demonstrate a deep streak of fatalism among country Rumanians, while others find exactly the opposite: they deduce a kind of mystical triumph over precisely such an interpretation of fate. Perhaps its origins should be sought in pre-Christian times; the poem undoubtedly springs from abstruse and complex roots. But for me its magic lay, and lies, in its linking together of directness and the tragic sense, its capture of the isolated feeling that surrounds shepherds, and the forlorn exaltation that haunts their steep grazings and forests; all enhanced, here, by the charms and the frustration of half-apprehended mysteries. Above all, in my case, the poem conjures up early glimpses of shepherd life on these first mountain travels; half the setting is accordingly a high Carpathian shieling, and the other, sheep-folds scattered, later on, across the dales of Moldavia.

The poem consists of 123 rhyming couplets (and occasionally triplets) of five syllables, which feminine endings often lengthen; the scansion is two or three feet to the line; and I can't resist giving a few key fragments of a ramshackle but pretty literal translation.

'From an upland high,' its begins, 'near the gates of the sky, / along a steep trail / dropping into the vale / come three flocks of sheep / that three young shepherds keep, / the first, a Moldavian, / the second a Vrancean, / and the third, Transylvanian . . .' (The slide into semi-poetic diction imposed by the search for rhymes—a necessary search, if one wants to get the feel of the poem—gives a dimmed idea of the spare rustic frugality of the original; I wish I could convey its almost runic pithiness. When the three shepherds meet, the scene darkens at once. While the sun sets, the Transylvanian and the Vrancean plot to murder the young Moldavian. He is braver than they; his sheep are sturdier and longer-horned, his horses better broken and his dogs fiercer. But what they do not know is that he also has a ewe lamb, Mioritza, the one the poem is named after, and she has the gift of second sight. Overhearing the whispered plot, she stops grazing and bleats desperately and without stopping for three days on end to give the alarm; and when the young shepherd asks what ails her, she bursts into speech), "O kind young man," she says, "Drive down your flock / to the wood by the brook! / There is shade there for you / and grass for us, too. / Master, O master, / drive them down faster! / Call the dogs, call / one strong and tall, / the staunchest of all! / When the sun leaves the sky / they have said you must die / —that shepherd, the Vrancean, / and that Transylvanian!"

The shepherd says, "Little ewe, all unbidden / you speak what is hidden! / Should I chance on my death / on this stretch of heath, / tell that Transylvanian / and the other, the Vrancean, / they should bury me near / in the pen, over here, / so I may sleep / among you, my sheep, / in my fold in the dark / and hear my dogs bark!" He gives the ewe lamb further instructions: "This too must be said: / Let them place at my head / A small flute of beech / —of love, all its speech— / *and a small flute of bone / that mourns long and lone,* / and a small flute of elder / —quicker-noted and wilder— / so when wind blows through / it will play on them too, / and make my sheep crowd / and mourn me out loud / and shed tears of blood!" The mood shifts significantly now. "But of the murder," he says, "tell them no word! / Just tell them outright / that I married tonight / a king's daughter, the bride / of the world, and its pride. / At my wedding, tell / how a star fell, / how the guests at the feast / were maples and firs, / the high mountains, priests, / and minstrels, the birds, / a thousand small birds, / and our candles the stars."

"But," he goes on, "if you should pass / running over the grass / in a sash made of wool / and with tears her eyes full, / a little old crone / astray and alone, / who asks everyone: / 'Have you seen my son? / A young shepherd boy / as handsome and slim / as though drawn through a ring? / The white of his brow, / foam milked from the cow? / His whiskers as neat / as two young ears of wheat? / And thick curls that grow / like the plumes on a crow? / And two pretty eyes / like wild blackberries?' / Then, little ewe," the young shepherd concludes:

"Pity her too,
and these words to her bring:
'I was married on high
at the gates of the sky
to the child of a king.'
But no word be said
how, when I was wed—
(O lamb, never tell!)
how a star fell,
that the sun and the moon
were holding our crown,
that my guests at the feast

> were maples and firs,
> the high mountains, priests,
> and minstrels, the birds,
> many thousands of birds,
> and candles the stars."

But all this, a strange adumbration of a still unknown Rumania, lay far ahead. Meanwhile, a change was on the way. Thoughts of wolves had receded and the sheepfolds below the path were now flimsy rings of osier and brushwood. Sometimes the massif flung out peninsulas that dropped away into the void; and for once the bias of the mountains was more a help than a decoy and the circuit of the last of these headlands led to a high saddle and the brim of a tremendous valley.

On the one hand a canyon thrust a deep gash north-east into the range I had been skirting for days, and its climb into the Carpathians reached the foot of the great ashen peaks. On the other, it plunged south-west down a gorge that would lead to the lowlands, and, at last, to the everyday world: but there was no hint of this yet. The chasm was silent except for the sound of water and the echo of an occasional rock falling. But while I gazed, clouds at the head of the ravine were breaking loose and spreading crumpled shadows across the juts and the clefts; then they blotted out the sun in an abrupt upland storm. The wind sent a few sighting shots, followed by a swish of raindrops. Sheltering under an overhang, I watched them turn into hailstones the size of mothballs: they bounced and scattered downhill by the million; and in half an hour, their white drifts were all that was left. The washed rocks looked newly cut, there was not a cloud in sight and a breeze smelling of bracken and wet earth kept the air from stagnating.

Even jumping from ledge to ledge and sliding on wet pine-needles, the downward climb lasted for hours. Scree slowed the pace and buttresses of rock, smooth as boiler-plates or spiked like iguanas, imposed gruelling swerves. Gleams across the cliffs revealed faraway threads of water; close to, they coiled and cataracted through the tree-trunks as the ledges of the forest dropped. The conifers abdicated when the hardwoods began to outnumber them; and the ravine, deepening fast, coaxed the trees higher and higher until the oaks, mantled with ivy, pronged with the antlers of dead boughs and tufted with mistletoe, grew into giants. Clearings of beech opened their forest-chambers and bracken gave way to mares' tails, hemlock and the tatters of old man's beard. The damp, which covered everything with moss, looped the branches with creepers and plumed the clefts and forks overhead, and the flaking bark, shaggy with lichen, greaved the tree-trunks like metal tainted with verdigris, filling the slanting world underneath with a stagey green-grey light. The woods had become an undercroft of acorns, beech-nuts and moaning wood-pigeons; the sound of water grew louder; and soon, flecked by leaf-shadows and askim with wagtails and redstarts, the ice-cold Cerna was rushing by under the branches. The mysterious river split and joined again round blades of rock, slid over shelves that combed it into symmetrical waterfalls and rushed on chopping and changing down the gorge. Then I came down into quieter reaches. Shoals of trout anchored themselves among the reflections of elderflower or glided to new retreats, deep in the shade, where only a few wrinkles hinted at the current, and the black rocks, which gave the river its dark Slavonic name, cumbered the depths.

* * * *

On a path along the bank, a ring of women on the way back from market—alert, fine-featured, rather shy-looking folk—were sitting under a walnut tree with their bundles. After greetings, an old squaw, whose face was a cobweb of amused lines, patted the place beside her, so I joined them on the grass.

Except for brown aprons, they were dressed in the same way as the women at the sheepfold: a subdued harmony of dark blues and whites, with black braid sashes and heavily embroidered rectangles on the sleeves and those curious soft leather breast-plates lacing at the side; they wore white pleated skirts, black stockings and moccasins, and there was not a thread on any of them—shorn, carded, spun, woven, dyed, cut out and sewn—that had not come off the backs of their flocks.

The old woman picked the antler off the grass and asked me something I could not understand. When she saw how little Rumanian I knew, she placed her finger and thumb on either side of her flat silver wedding-ring, twiddled it to and fro and then pointed to me enquiringly: was I married? No? She murmured something to the others that had them all in stitches and as their exchanges went on with growing hilarity, several racy and comic interpretations began to dawn on me too. Soon they stood up and hoisted their striped woven sacks on their heads. The old woman handed the antler back, wishing me a happy journey and good luck in the town. Still exchanging jokes, they set off for their high sheepfolds. One of them was spinning as she went, and in a little while a green-leaf song was mounting the hillside and then slowly fading out of earshot.

8

The End of Middle Europe

SUDDENLY, and without any warning, an ornate and incongruous watering-place called the Baths of Hercules rose from the depths of the wild valley. The fin-de-siècle stucco might have come straight out of an icing-gun; there were terracotta balustrades, palmetto-palms, spiked agaves in waisted urns, egg-shaped cupolas, leaden scales ending in stickleback ridges, and glimpses through the glass double-doors of hydrangeas banked up ornate staircases that wandered away into kursaals where taps and fountains gushed with healing waters. Sovereign against a rogues' gallery of external and internal ills, these had made the place famous in Roman times; legates, centurions and military tribunes had wallowed and sipped here while Hercules and half a dozen minor gods presided over them, and the Victorian statue of the lion-pelted and muscle-bound bruiser, which dominated the centre of the town, showed that the ancient glory had returned. The ailing burghers of Eastern Europe, in crinolines and stovepipe hats, sabretaches and czapkas, or mutton-chop sleeves and boaters had been haunting the resurrected site for over a century.

In its provincial way, the place was everything that the words 'spa', 'casino' and 'villeggiatura' conjure up. Circular and heart-shaped beds of cannas and begonias burst out of the gravel like an industrial carpet; yellow, scarlet, orange, purple, pale blue and brick-red were so blindingly juxtaposed that the flowers could have all been artificial and the grass viridian drugget. A more knowing traveller might have caught a whiff of Offenbach and Meyerbeer, a hint of Schnitzler, an echo of the Austro-Hungarian Empire at its farthest edge, elaborated more recently by stout white plaster columns with alternating spirals, heavily moulded arches and wide eaves: this was a Rumanian neo-

Byzantine style derived from the monasteries of Moldavia and seventeenth-century palaces in the reign of Constantine Brancovan of Wallachia.

It was the hour of the post-siesta promenade. A band was playing in a frilled bandstand and a slowly strolling throng from Bucharest and Craiova was meandering along the main street, through the gardens, over the Cerna bridge and slowly back again. Murmurous with gossip and detonating with holiday recognitions and greetings, the promenaders were dressed to kill: heels of dizzy height, heady scent and dazzling make-up were escorted by post-Rudolf Valentino patent-leather hair and co-respondent shoes. A scattering of officers in tall boots and jingling spurs—from Turnu-Severin, I think—added their bright cap-bands and tunic-facings to the many-coloured scene.

Dusty, travel-stained and probably reeking of sheepfolds, I might have been pitchforked into Babylon, Lampsacus or fifth-century Corinth and as I picked my way through the smart promenaders, bewilderment was further compounded by an onrush of bumpkin anxiety. Thank God, the antler was disguised in the twisted great-coat on my rucksack!

Gritting my teeth, I charged through the revolving glass doors of an hotel and asked the hall-porter if I could telephone. Heinz Schramm, a schoolfellow of István's who lived a few miles away, was summoned to the other end; it had all been fixed by telephone from Lapuşnic before I set out. The porter told me to wait in the hall and in a quarter of an hour István's cheerful and rubicund schoolmate was jumping out of a gleaming Mercedes and we were soon spinning out of the town and down the valley; it was restored, once the town was out of sight, to the inviolate beauty of woods and apricot-coloured rocks with flaring magnesium shadows and falling twilight. There was the glimpse of a Turkish aqueduct, then arrival by lamplight at a large and comfortable house, quickly followed by sybaritic immersion. How incongruous my stuff looked, scattered about the spotless bathroom beyond the clouds of steam! Dusty boots, dog-eared papers, a jumble of books, broken pencils, dirty linen, a confusion of puttees, crumbs, tangled string, an empty flask, an antler, and a forgotten apple which had been going rotten at the bottom of my rucksack; but on a chair lay a jacket and trousers that weren't too badly crumpled, a clean shirt and gym shoes at last, instead of hobnails. Using a toe, I let in more hot water and wallowed in transports of luxury.

* * * *

Heinz Schramm had inherited a family timber business and obviously made a go of it. (I wondered if the Szatmár logging team had anything to do with him, but forgot to ask.) Lumberjacks felled in the forests and enormous tree-trunks were continually arriving at sheds and saw-mills along the valley; there, with the clang of circular saws and the rhythmic fall of planks, they were sliced up by spectres toiling in clouds of sawdust. As Heinz's family were offshoots of the eighteenth-century Swabian settlers in the Banat, conversation was in German, except with Heinz's father, a retired admiral in the old *k. und k.* Navy, whose fluent and marvellously antiquated English was of an even earlier vintage than Count Jenö's. He was a lean, keen-eyed widower who had grown up when English was a sort of naval lingua franca all over the world. At the mention of Admiral Horthy, he said, "We were snotties together! A decent sort of chap, though, mind you, I never thought he had much in the top storey." He recalled balls in Fiume— "learning the bunny-hug and the cake-walk from visiting flappers"— and happy anchorages in Tokyo and Saigon, "We had a whale of a time and were very upset when we had to skedaddle." Happy reminiscences would unfold in the evening on a terrace looking down the valley. A great admirer of the Royal Navy, he had been seconded to it for a time in some sort of semi-diplomatic capacity; he liked the general style as well as the seamanship and he could never forget seeing the Fleet dressed overall for Edward VII's birthday in the roads of Pola or Trieste. He had especially fond memories of Lord Charles Beresford when he was Commander-in-Chief of the Medi-terranean Fleet: "You could tell the cut of his jib a mile off!" (The name of this stormy petrel always cropped up when Triestinos recalled pre-war days. Berta, my hostess in Budapest, had remembered being dandled on his knee as a small girl in Fiume, when her father was Governor.)

Heinz was full of stories about István at school. He had been a general hero and favourite in spite, or because of, his countless scrapes—breaking out and painting Vienna red and so on. Heinz called him by a school sobriquet abridged from his surname. "'Globus' was a marvellous fellow!" he said. "He had only one fault: he was a bit too proud of his five-pointed coronet." ("Er war ein bisschen zu stolz auf seine fünfzackige Krone.") I laughed and said, "I bet he was!" and suddenly missed him acutely. "You may laugh," Heinz went on, "but guess how many there were in my year at the Theresianum who were not noble? *Two!*" In Magyar, the equivalent of the German 'von' was indicated linguistically in a way I never quite grasped; but when a westward-moving Hungarian noble crossed the Leitha into Austria and reversed his Christian and surname from their Magyar back-to-front order, he immediately interposed the Teutonic prefix, later replacing it with 'de' when crossing the Rhine into France. But nobility meant much more than heraldic baubles and forms of address: it signified membership of a legally separate order with a whole array of privileges. These inequities had long ago been removed but a chasm yawned still and much of the ancient aloofness and awe hovered about the descendants of country dynasts and their heraldic emblems were seldom out of sight. Untitled noblemen like István had circlets with five pearls, barons seven and counts nine—except for the Károlys, who for some reason had eleven—and princes had handsome closed crowns turned up with ermine; they were scattered over houses, carriages, liveries, harness, linen and cigarette-cases with uninhibited profusion. The disasters of war, fallen fortunes, change of sovereignty and loss of estates had left the ascendancy, sometimes with resentment and sometimes with affection, improbably intact, and my balloonist and frogman course between four-posters and cowsheds had given a fair idea of the old status quo, especially in the country and not only in Austria, Hungary and Transylvania. I think it had been more or less the same in Bohemia, Moravia, Prussia, Poland and Russia, and, indeed, in pre- and post-war Rumania as well.

* * * *

August was an excuse for picnics. We feasted in ruins and meadows and stalactitic caves in the Banat mountains and by the woods that lined

the Cerna and its tributary the Bela—the black river, and the white—
and one evening we drove to the Baths of Hercules for a gala night at
the casino.*

The little town seemed utterly different now. It had the comic and
engaging charm of an operetta: colour and vivacity stamped its
denizens and the crowded tables, the dance band and the dancers filled
the dining-room of the Casino with brio and *Schwung*. Helped by
tzuika and wine and dancing, the evening spun itself into a golden haze.
A flamboyant and slightly theatrical aura radiated from a large table
next door and it was soon clear why. During a break in the dancing,
the Gypsies had begun to move from table to table, halting in an
attentive swarm to play 'at the diners' ears', as it is called; it was rather
discreet and muted; but when they reached our neighbours, a sudden
challenging crescendo sailed aloft and set the drops of the chandeliers
tinkling. A florid and handsome man of about thirty had put down his
knife and fork and let fly in a tremendous baritone; everyone stopped
talking; then the others at the table answered him on cue in a very
professional way until the place rang. Heinz said they were the
Bucharest opera company on a summer tour, but the outburst was
spontaneous; they had launched themselves into the arias and choruses
of *The Barber of Seville* out of pure high spirits, and their final *tutti* was
hailed by clapping and cries of bravo! and encore! When all requests
had been granted, dancing began again, and our tables were soon
companionably mingled.

I found myself dancing—to the tune of *Couchés dans le foin*, then
Vous qui passez sans me voir—with a girl who was studying English in
Bucharest; not that one could hear a word in the press of the dancing.
When we sat down again she said, "I love English books very much.
Wells, Galsworthy, Morgan, Warwick Deeping, Dickens. And
Byron's poetry, if . . ." she stopped, smiling thoughtfully. I waited,
wondering what reservations were coming, and after a few seconds'
silence, ventured to say, "If what?" "If," she said, "you can keep
your head while all about you are losing theirs and blaming it on
you."

* * * *

* Băile Herculane, Herculesbad and Herkules Fürdö were the local names.

Running about in gym shoes next day, my foot landed on an inch of nail sticking out of a plank in a dismantled woodshed and it went clean through. There was little pain and not much blood but it hurt to walk on, so I lay reading in a deck-chair under a tree, then hobbled about with a stick. It healed in three days and on the fourth I set off.

The Maros had dominated the last months. Now the Cerna had taken its place and a few days earlier, just before dawn, I had ridden back upstream for a last look. The fleece of leaves soared to the watershed; underneath, the valley lay brooding and still in the half-light; it was a wilderness of green moss and grey creepers with ivy-clad watermills rotting along the banks and streams tumbling through the shadows; then shafts of lemon-coloured light struck down through the trunks into the vapour coiling along the stream-bed and into the branches. I might have been trotting through a world emerging from primordial chaos.

But today I was following a lower reach. Leaving its chasm and heading south, it joined a wide trough climbing north between two great massifs which narrowed steadily until the road reached the pass; then, many leagues away, it dropped the other side into the valley of the Timiş and still further along it lay the point from which I had launched my private attack on the Carpathians two weeks earlier.

Striking south, I pursued a sheep-track in the lee of the woods, wondering how much the valley might have changed since Roman times and, looking up at the eagles and the beetling forests, thought: hardly at all.

The winding osier-bed shared the valley with a road and a railway and every now and then the loose triple plait would unravel and then nonchalantly assemble again. Buffaloes floundered in the reeds, a breath of wind tilted the threads of the Gypsies' fires and their horses, ranging loose among the flocks, grazed to the edge of the forest. There were fields of stubble and hundreds of sunflowers flaring yellow round their dark hearts; and the pale green sheaths of the Indian corn had withered long ago to a papery grey. Strings of waggons were returning empty upstream or labouring south loaded with tree-trunks to be lashed together and floated down the Danube; and when two of them crossed, ropes of dust lengthened in both directions and wrapped the road and its passengers in a cloud; it settled on the fruit trees that sometimes lined the road for furlongs on end, heavy with blue plums nobody picked that scattered the roadside in wasp-haunted rings.

Dipping to the river, the path crossed it again and again on wooden bridges. The sun splintered down through a colander of leaves and every so often, minor rapids twirled through the red and green rocks while mermaid-like water-weed streamed along the current. (Without knowing it, I must have stored up an almost photographic memory of this beautiful valley for when I travelled along it twenty years later, by the little train this time, forgotten landmarks kept recurring until I would begin to remember a stretch of flag-leaves, an islet with a clump of willows, a spinney, an oak tree struck by lightning or a solitary chapel a minute or two before they actually reappeared; for suddenly, with an obliging loop of the river, there they were, drowned twenty years deep but surfacing one by one in a chain of rescued visions like lost property restored.)

An old man under a mulberry tree asked me where I was going. When I said "Constantinopol", he nodded mildly and asked no more, as though I had said the next village. A spectacular bird I had never seen before, about the size of a crow and of a brilliant light blue while it was in the air, flew to a nearby branch. "Dumbrăveancă", the old man called it: "the one who loves oak-woods". (It was a roller.) Hoping to catch another glimpse of its wonderful colours I clapped my hands and it flew into the air from its new perch like a Maeterlinckian figment.

The old man picked up a fallen mulberry from the grass, and, in dumb show, crooked a forefinger as though embedding a hook and then made a feint at casting a line over the river. Did he mean they used mulberries for bait? Surely not for trout? "No, no." He shook his head and said another name, his gesture indicating a much larger fish until his hands were as far apart as a concertina player's at full stretch. A sterlet, from the Danube, perhaps. It was not far.

It was much closer than I thought, for all at once the sides of the valley fell apart and revealed the towers and trees of Orşova, then the troubled yellow and blue-grey waters of the Danube and the palisade of the Serbian mountains beyond. The vision was dramatic and sudden. The wide sweep of the river came on stage, as it were, through a precipitous overlap to the west; then, after dividing with a flutter round a feathery island and joining again, it pressed on to a scarcely less striking exit downstream.

* * * *

Hastening into the town, I rushed to collect a clutch of letters from the poste-restante—and only just in time. I settled with them at a café table on the quay. One, full of geological advice, was from my father, posted two months before in Simla: 'Everyone has moved here for the Hot Weather,' he wrote. 'I can see the western part of the Central Himalayan Chain from my window, and many of the snow-peaks of Tibet. It is a wonderful change from Calcutta . . .'

My mother's was in answer to what I had hoped was an amusing description of my parasitic summer; I sent her progress reports every week or so, half to amuse, and half to reinforce my diary later on.* '. . . I see what you mean about *Mr. Sponge's Sporting Tour*,' she wrote. 'Are you going to follow the Danube? You'll come to a place called Rustchuk—I've just looked it up in the Atlas,' she went on. 'Guess who was born there!' It was Michael Arlen. (Also, though I hadn't yet heard of him, Elias Canetti.) She was full of information like this, often not accurate but always interesting. She had a passion for cutting bits out of newspapers and a mass of clippings, full of London doings, soon covered the table.

There were several other letters and a canvas envelope crossed with blue chalk held last month's four pound notes; just in time, once more! But the letter I tore open first and with most excitement was written in French in Angéla's wild hand and posted the morning after she reached Budapest. All our schemes and subterfuges had been successful! The drift of the thick sheets was affectionate and funny and steeped in the delights of our triple fugue. I pushed the letters and clippings and books on one side and wrote back at once; then to London and Simla, and by the time I had finished the sun had set and left the river a

---

* She gave them all back when I returned, but they went astray in a lost trunk during the war, and I miss them bitterly now.

pale zinc colour. A new moon showed wanly for an hour then dipped under the hills opposite.

I read and re-read Angéla's letter. Our feelings—mine, anyhow—had run deeper than we had admitted, and for as long as it lasted, involvement was total: affection and excitement had been showered with lavish hands; no wonder we had walked on air: high spirits and feelings of adventure and comedy had pitched everything in a light-hearted key and I felt sure that it was to fend off later sorrow that Angéla had skilfully kept it there. Our short time together had been filled with unclouded delight—separation had been the fault of neither of us and there were no grounds for anything but thanks and perhaps we had been even luckier than we knew. But the exhilaration of Angéla's news was followed by a sharp fit of depression.

There was another minor source of distress: no more castles the other side of the Danube. These refuges had scattered my path intermittently ever since the Austrian border. Their inhabitants seemed doubly precious now, and I brooded with homesickness on feasts and libraries and stables and the endless talk by lamp- and candle-light; and all this led to a return of my earlier mood after our brief rush through the arcades and gables of Hermannstadt.* It had been a last outpost of the architecture of the West. I thought how romanesque, after branching into lancets and spires and flying buttresses, had given rise to these stalwart Carpathian bastions of the Reform; and, finally, to the splendour and hyperbole of the Counter-Reformation. It would be the last of the Jesuits too, and all their works: heroes, villains and saints by turns. They were at the heart of all the conflicts and the triumphs I had been reading about, daemons of the Counter-Reformation in Central Europe and harbingers of the Thirty Years War. I had never met any, but even now some of the dark glamour remains: these were the men, I thought to myself, who had rifled the air with spiralling saints, twirled columns, broken pediments, groined cupolas and tilted thousands of heads backwards under the trompe-l'oeil pageants of a hundred baroque ceilings.

What a stamp they had left! (Or so I thought.) *Sint ut sunt aut non sint!* Even in this little riverside town, the note of the bell striking the

* It would be improper to call it Sibiu in this context.

hour, the scrolls and volutes and the tired ochre walls would have been a little different if the Society had never existed.*

*   *   *   *

For some vanished reason, instead of simply plunging into the Yugoslavian mountains opposite, I had planned to take the river-steamer round two small loops of the Danube to the Bulgarian town of Vidin.

Rather surprisingly, I had never met anyone who had been to Bulgaria. If the Hungarians were loth to cross the Carpathians into old Rumania, Bulgaria was even further from their minds; and the Rumanians, for all their earlier ties with Constantinople, were just as reluctant. Both countries looked westward to Vienna, Berlin, London and Paris and the benighted regions of the Balkans remained *terra incognita*. All they knew was that Bulgaria had been a province of the Ottoman Empire until sixty years earlier, and that the yoke had not been finally and formally shed until 1911. As we know, Hungary had been subjected to a long Turkish occupation, but that was nearly three centuries ago and it had left no trace beyond the smoking of long-stemmed pipes; Transylvania and the Rumanian principalities had been vassals of the Turks, but not occupied by them; their historical continuity had remained intact, and this was what counted. Bulgaria had a different past, a Balkan past; it was the first state the Turks enslaved and almost the last to get rid of them, after an occupation lasting five centuries, and in the eyes of everyone living north of the river, it seemed the darkest, most backward and least inviting country in Europe except Albania—unjustly, as I was soon to learn.

For half a millennium then, the country had been a northern province

* R.F., the friend who has succeeded to the role of the polymath in *A Time of Gifts*, assures me that other orders—Piarists, Premonstratensians, Benedictines and Cistercians—played a much more important role in the later history of Hungary, Transylvania and the Banat; and, very notably, the Franciscans. The most famous of these was the fiery Capistrano, Hunyadi's ally and brother-in-arms against the Turks. It was in the wider Mitteleuropa sphere of the Holy Roman Empire, in England, Paraguay, India, China and Japan that the Society of Jesus had spread its wings widest. But, even if my sententious jottings by the Danube were not as much to the point as I thought, there is just enough truth in them not to cross them out.

of an empire stretching deep into Asia. Constantinople had been its beacon and lodestar; the Bulgarians still called it 'Tzarigrad', 'the City of the Emperors', though the Roman-Greek Orthodox Emperors, and not the Turkish Sultans who replaced them in 1453, were the sovereigns the name commemorated. The word also recalled, by association, early Bulgarian splendours, when these wild invaders from the Pontic steppes had ransacked the Balkans and established their dominion from the Black Sea to the Adriatic. Tsars of their own ruled over it— sovereigns who, at times, were almost rivals to the East Roman Emperors themselves. The aura of the country had acted as a magnet ever since I had set out, but my depression at saying goodbye to Central Europe had, for a moment, weakened this lure.

I was looking dejectedly at my old Austrian map of the region, when a voice said: "Können wir Ihnen helfen? Est-ce qu'on peut vous aider?" The speaker was a friendly land-surveyor from Bucharest. I told him I planned to cross to the other side the next day, after a look at the Iron Gates. He said, "Don't worry about the Iron Gates, the Kazan is much more important. But you'll never manage to see it in the time." Two friends joined him and they all advised me to put off my departure and catch the Austrian river-steamer the day after. They were a topographical survey team on their way upstream to do some work at a place called Moldova Veche, beyond the defile of the Kazan, and if I really wanted to see this extraordinary region, they could drop me at a suitable place for it, and I could make my own way back downstream. They began to discuss arrangements, each offering a new suggestion, until the first speaker said something which made the others laugh: a proverb which is the Rumanian equivalent of 'Too many cooks spoil the broth'—"A child with too many midwives remains with his navel-string uncut". (*Copilul cu mai multe moaşe rămână cu buricul netaiat.*)

*   *   *   *

I slept on a sofa in the house where they were lodging. We got up in the dark, and settling among the ropes, chains, tripods, theodolites and the bi-coloured ten-foot poles in their little truck, set off. In the jerky beam of the headlamps, the tortuous road above the river seemed both wonderful and mysterious. It had been prised and hacked out of the perpendicular flank of the mountains, built up some-times over the flood on tall supporting walls and sometimes lifted on arches; sometimes it plunged under caves scooped through towering headlands. Grottos and galleries uncoiled through the dark for mile after mile like some thoroughfare driving into the heart of an obsessional dream. Shadowy mountain masses soared out of the glimmering water below, leaving only a narrowing band of starlight overhead, as though the two cliffs might join. Then after an abrupt bend the other shore would swing away into the distance with the stars spreading like a momentary chart of the heavens, only to shrink again as the two precipices looked once more about to collide. The marvellous road had been built in the 1830s; it was one of the most important of the tangible mementos of the great István Széchenyi.* Invisible mountains soared in the dark and dropped again, small villages huddled for a lamplit moment over dim assemblies of canoes and were gone, and the woods and clefts closed in. At last the sky in the west began to widen in a final array of stars; they were beginning to pale; a village was half awake, and a small faintly-lit river steamer with its bows pointing downstream was hauling in its gang-plank. *"Mama Dracului!"* the driver shouted and honked his horn, letting loose a pandemonium of echoes. The gang-plank stopped half-way, hesitated, then reversed and touched the landing-stage and before it could change its mind again I was across it and waving back to my spectral friends as the boat swung out into the current.

* * * *

While the ship straightens course, we must take our bearings.

A traveller sticking to the usual route would have followed the Danube south, clean across Hungary and into Yugoslavia, looping east to Belgrade and following the north bank of the river across the southernmost extremity of the Great Plain. Halting here, and looking east beyond the stacks of lopped reeds and the mirages, he would have

* 'Stefan' or 'Stephan' Széchenyi is how he was known at Holland House, but I heard his christian name so often mentioned in its Magyar form that it is hard to write it otherwise. He was one of the earliest members of the Travellers Club.

seen mountains rising steeply out of the flat eastern horizon like a school of whales.

The northern half of these mountains, which drops to the left bank of the Danube, is the end of the Carpathians; and the southern half, which soars from the right bank, though considerably lower than the northern range, is the beginning of the Balkans:* a momentous juxtaposition. These two mountainous regions, seeming to grow in height and volume with every advancing step, look a solid mass; but, in reality, a deep invisible rift cleaves it from summit to base, delving a passage for the greatest river in Europe to rush through. I had reached this point from the other end; now I was in the western jaws of the rift and heading east again with dawn paling beyond the dark bends of the canyon and spreading rays of daybreak high overhead like the Japanese flag.

To starboard the dungeon-island of Babakai, where a pasha had chained up a runaway wife and starved her to death, was still drowned in shadow. Then the sun broke through spikes and brushwood high above, and caught the masonry of the Serbian castle of Golubac—a prison too, this time of an unnamed Roman empress—where battlemented walls looped a chain of broken cylinders and polygons up to the crest of a headland; and here, with the lift and the steepening tilt of the precipices, the twilight was renewed. Spaced out under the woods, Rumanian and Serbian fishing-hamlets followed one another while the mountain walls straightened and impended until the river was flowing along the bottom of a corridor.

The only other passenger, a well-read Rumanian doctor who had studied in Vienna, was bound for Turnu-Severin. Approaching the submerged cataracts he warned me that the Danube, unhindered by mountains since the Visegrád bend, undergoes violent changes here. The slimy bed hardens to a narrow trough crossed by sunk bars of quartz and granite and schist and between them deep chasms sink.

The mountain walls, meanwhile, were stealing closer. A buttress of rock, climbing eight hundred feet, advanced to midstream: the water, striking its flank, veered sharply south where it struck an answering

* The actual Great Balkan Range, as opposed to 'the Balkans', only begins on the other side of the Bulgarian-Yugoslav border.

Serbian wall which rose perpendicular for one thousand six hundred feet, while the width of the river shrank to four hundred; and, abetted by the propinquity of these two cliffs and the commotion among the drowned reefs and chasms, the foiled and colliding liquid sent waves shuddering upstream again far beyond Belgrade. The river welled angrily through the narrows, and the pilot stylishly outmanoeuvred them with swift twirls of the wheel. We sailed into the open. The threshold fell wide, the currents disentangled and a serene ring of mountains all at once enclosed us in a wide, clear dell of water. This was 'the Cauldron' of Kazan. Accompanied by gulls and resembling a steel engraving out of Jules Verne, we stole across the still circus under a tall and windless pillar of smoke.

When the boat reached the further side, it slid into the mountains again and the corridor led us from chamber to chamber. The river was constantly veering into new vistas of slanting light and shade; every now and then the precipices dipped enough for houses and trees and a blue or yellow church to huddle in a cranny, and the meadows behind them climbed steeply between peaks and landslides to join the dark curl of the woods. On the left bank, daylight now revealed the Széchenyi road in all its complexity; and, even more impressive, an intermittent causeway was hewn just wide enough for two to march abreast along the perpendicular face of the right bank. Sometimes its course was traceable only by slots in the rock where beams had once supported a continuous wooden platform above the river. Trajan's completion of the road Tiberius had begun (and Vespasian and then Domitian continued) was hoisted over the river, to carry the invading legions to the bridgehead for Dacia a dozen miles downstream. On the rock face above it a large rectangular slab was embedded: carved dolphins, winged genii and imperial eagles surrounded an inscription celebrating both the completion of the road and the campaign that followed it in AD 103. Time had fretted it into near illegibility.*

* I found it later. 'Imperator Caesar divi Nervae filius', the inscription ran, 'Nerva Trajanus Augustus Germanicus—Pontifex Maximus tribunitae potestatis quartum—Pater patriae consul quartum—montis et fluviis anfractibus—superatis viam patefecit.' ('The Emperor Caesar—son of the divine Nerva—Nerva Trajan Augustus Germanicus—High Priest and for the fourth time Tribune—Father

After more twists, the gorge widened into the roads of Orşova.

*   *   *   *

The risk of letting the surveyors take me far beyond the point of no return (on foot, at least, in a single day) had been rewarded by finding the little steamer at Moldova Veche; and by mid-morning I was back at my Orşova starting point. Thank God for those surveyors! Carried away by the stirring name of the Iron Gates, I had almost missed the amazing Kazan. It was my last day in Middle Europe; I determined to risk my hand still further: instead of landing when we drew alongside Orşova quay, I would keep the doctor company to the next stop, and get back there again as best I could.

There was almost too much happening on this stretch of the river. Soon after the anchor was up, the doctor pointed out a polygonal chapel at the end of a line of trees beyond the north bank. When the Austrians drove the Hungarian revolutionary army eastwards in the 1848 uprising, Kossuth, to prevent the young Franz-Josef from being crowned King, seized the Crown of St. Stephen from the Coronation Church in Buda and carried it off with the entire coronation regalia, to Transylvania. After their defeat, the leaders secretly buried it in a field and escaped across the Danube into the Turkish dominions. All Hungary mourned the loss, but in due course the treasure was found and dug up; the Emperor was crowned King after all, and this octagonal chapel was put up to mark the hiding place.* Before Trianon, a village on the same bank had been the south-westernmost Rumanian frontier-post with Hungary. We left the leafy island to port, and, as the doctor told me its history, a new plan began to take shape.

Meanwhile the mountains on either side had drawn together again,

---

of the country and for the fourth time Consul—overcame the hazards of mountain and river and flung open this road.')

* They must be the most widely travelled regalia in the world. After World War II they were kept hidden for many years in the United States and only given back a few years ago. I saw them on display in the National Museum some months after their return: the famous crown itself, the mace-like sceptre, the orb, the armlets and the sword of state. The queue waiting to catch a glimpse of them— only for a few seconds, so great was the throng—stretched a hundred yards down the street and shuffled past the treasure in silent awe. It symbolised all Hungary's history and her pride for the past thousand years.

tight-lacing the river into a milder version of the Kazan, and the sudden flurry round our vessel meant that we were actually inside the Iron Gates. But here, all the drama took place under water and the upheavals in the stream-bed stirred up fierce and complex currents. For hundreds of years rocks like dragons' teeth had made the passage mortally dangerous, only to be navigated when the water was high. At the end of the last century, close under the Serbian shore, engineers blew, dug and dredged a safe channel a mile long, then dammed it off with a sub-fluminal wall. Threading these hazards, we learnt, made the upstream journey slow and toilsome, the opposite of our swift and buoyant passage downstream and we soon entered a serener reach where the mountains began to subside, and when we landed at Turnu-Severin, I was setting foot in the Regat—pre-Trianon Rumania, that is—for the first time.

It was the remains of Trajan's amazing bridge that we had come to see, the greatest in the Roman Empire. Apollodorus of Damascus, who built it, was a Greek from Syria, and two great stumps of his conglomerate masonry still cumbered the Rumanian side; a third stood across the water in a Serbian meadow. Swifts were skimming over the water and red-legged falcons hovered and dived all round these solitary survivors of twenty massive piers. Once they had risen tapering to a great height and supported over a mile of arched timber superstructure: beams over which the cavalry had clattered and ox-carts creaked as the Thirteenth tramped north to besiege Decebalus in Sarmizegethusa. On the spot, only these stumps remained, but the scene of the dedication is carved in great detail on Trajan's Column in Rome, and the Forum pigeons, ascending the shaft in a spiral, can gaze at these very piers in high relief: the balustered bridge soars intact and the cloaked General himself waits beside the sacrificial bull and the flaming altar with his legionaries drawn up helmet-in-hand under their eagle standards.

This was the end of the great cleft. East of here the Carpathians swoop away to the north-east and the river coils south and then east, simultaneously defining the edge of the Wallachian plain, the northern frontier of Bulgaria and the edge of the Balkans. It reaches the Black Sea at last in a delta rustling with a thousand square miles of reeds and tumultuous with many millions of birds. As I gazed downstream, a determination to explore eastern Rumania began to take root. I longed to get an idea of the habitat of those mythical-sounding princes—Stephen the Great and Michael the Brave and Mircea the Old; and there was Vlad the Impaler, as we know, and the ancient line of the Basarabs; Princess Chiajna, Ear-ring Peter and a score of strangely named rulers: Basil the Wolf, John the Cruel, Alexander the Good, Mihnea the Bad, Radu the Handsome . . . Except for one or two, like Sherban Cantacuzène and Dimitri Cantemir and Constantine Brancovan, I knew no more than their sobriquets. Dales and woods and steppes unfolded in my imagination; plains with dust-devils twirling half a mile high, forests and canyons and painted abbeys; swamps populated by strange sectaries, limitless flocks and drovers and shepherds with peculiarly shaped musical instruments; and, scattered among the woods and the cornfields, manor houses harbouring over-civilised boyars up to their ears in Proust and Mallarmé.

* * * *

I was beginning to get the hang of the hardly believable chasm I had been exploring since the small hours and into which I was now doubling back. It was the wildest stretch of the whole river, and the pilots who sailed on it and the dwellers on its bank had many scourges to contend with. The worst of these were the Kossovar winds, named after the tragic region of Kossovo, where Old Serbia, Macedonia and Albania march. Terrible south-easterly storms, linked with the monsoon and the earth's rotation, spring up in a moment and strike the Middle and Lower Danube. At the spring equinox they reach a speed of fifty or sixty miles an hour and turn the river into a convulsed inferno, unmasting ships, smashing panes, and sending strings of barges to the bottom. In autumn, when the water level drops and the steppe-like country dries up like an oven, gales turn into dust-storms that blindfold pilots in hot whirlwinds and strip one bank of the river to the water level, eroding it sometimes to the point of overflow and flood; while simultaneously and at amazing speed, instantaneous dunes build up the other bank with shoals and sand-banks, blocking channels and closing the river-bed: seasonal disasters only to be righted by months of dyking and dredging. As I listened, the characteristics of the river became clearer: the hundreds of underwater streams feeding the river like anonymous donors; rolling gravel, which, in certain reaches, sings audibly through the muffling flood; millions of tons of alluvia always on the move; boulders bounding along troughs and chasms which suck the currents into the depths and propel them spiralling to the surface; the peristaltic progress of slime and the invisible march of wreckage down the long staircase of the bottom; the weight and force of the river in the mountain narrows, forever scouring a deeper passage, tearing off huge fragments of rock and trundling them along in the dark and slowly grinding them down to pebbles, then gravel, then grit and finally sand. At the eastern end of the defile, in the flat region of southern Wallachia, there is an appalling winter wind from Russia they call the *buran*. It becomes the *crivatz* in Rumania, and when it blows, the temperature plummets far below zero, the river freezes over within forty-eight hours and a solid lid of ice shuts over it, growing steadily thicker as the winter advances. It was an effort, in this summer weather, to conjure up all this—the tracks of sleighs on the grey or glittering waste, and the fields of pack-ice like millions of joined icebergs crowding each other into the distance. Woe betide unwary ships that are caught in it! When the water expands into ice, hulls crack like walnuts. "We put a bucket of water on the bridge and keep dipping our hands in when the temperature begins to drop," the pilot had said, "and make for safety at the first ice-needle."

*　　*　　*　　*

After the bridge at Turnu-Severin, the doctor travelled on to Craiova and I caught a bus back to Orşova, picked up my stuff, bought a ticket for the next day's boat, then walked a couple of miles downstream again and found a fisherman to scull me out to the little wooded island I had had my eye on ever since rejoining the Danube.

I had heard much talk of Ada Kaleh in recent weeks, and read all i could find. The name means 'island fortress' in Turkish. It was about a mile long, shaped like a shuttle, bending slightly with the curve of the current and lying a little closer to the Carpathian than the Balkan shore. It has been called Erythia, Rushafa and then Continusa, and, according to Apollonius Rhodius, the Argonauts dropped anchor here on their way back from Colchis. How did Jason steer the Argo through the Iron Gates? And then the Kazan? Medea probably lifted the vessel clear of the spikes by magic. Some say Argo reached the Adriatic by overland portage, others that she crossed it and continued up the Po, mysteriously ending in North Africa. Writers have tentatively suggested that the first wild olive to be planted in Attica might have come from here. But it was later history that had invested the little island with fame.

The inhabitants were Turkish, probably descendants of the soldiers of one of the earlier Sultans who invaded the Balkans, Murad I, or Bayazid I, perhaps. Left behind by the retreating Turks, the island lingered on as an outlying fragment of the Ottoman Empire until the Treaty of Berlin in 1878. The Austrians held some vague suzerainty over it, but the island seems to have been forgotten until it was granted to Rumania at the Treaty of Versailles; and the Rumanians had left the inhabitants undisturbed. The first thing I saw after landing was a rustic coffee-shop under a vine-trellis where old men sat cross-legged in a circle with sickles and adzes and pruning knives scattered about them. I was as elated when bidden to join them as if I had suddenly been seated on a magic carpet. Bulky scarlet sashes a foot wide gathered in the many pleats of their black and dark blue baggy trousers. Some wore ordinary jackets, others navy-blue boleros with convoluted black embroidery and faded plum-coloured fezzes with ragged turbans loosely knotted about them; all except the hodja's. Here, snow-white folds were neatly arranged round a lower and less tapering fez with a short stalk in the middle. Something about the line of brow, the swoop of nose and the jut of the ears made them indefinably different from any of the people I had seen on my journey so far. The four or five hundred islanders belonged to a few families which had inter-married for centuries, and one or two had the vague and absent look, the wandering glance and the erratic levity that sometimes come with ancient and inbred stock. In spite of their patched and threadbare clothes, their style and their manners were full of dignity. On encountering a stranger, they touched heart, lips and brow with the right hand, then laid it on their breast with an inclination of the head and a murmured formula of welcome. It was a gesture of extreme grace, like the punctilio of broken-down grandees. An atmosphere of prehistoric survival hung in the air as though the island were the refuge of an otherwise extinct species long ago swept away.

Several of my neighbours fingered strings of beads, but not in prayer; they spilt them between their fingers at random intervals, as though to scan their boundless leisure; and to my delight, one old man, embowered in a private cloud, was smoking a narghilé. Six feet of red tubing were cunningly coiled, and when he pulled on the amber mouthpiece, charcoal glowed on a damped wad of tobacco leaves from Isfahan and the bubbles, fighting their way through the water with the sound of a mating bull-frog, filled the glass vessel with smoke. A boy with small tongs arranged fresh charcoal. While he did so, the old man pointed towards me and whispered; and the boy came back in a few minutes with a laden tray on a circular table six inches from the ground. Seeing my quandary, a neighbour told me how to begin: first, to drink the small glass of raki; then eat the mouthful of delicious rose-petal jam lying ready spooned on a glass saucer, followed by half a tumbler of water; finally to sip at a dense and scalding thimbleful of coffee slotted in a filigree holder. The ritual should be completed by emptying the tumbler and accepting tobacco, in this case, an aromatic cigarette made by hand on the island. Meanwhile the old men sat in smiling silence, sighing occasionally, with a friendly word to me now and then in what sounded like very broken Rumanian; the doctor had said that their accent and style caused amusement on the shore. Among themselves they spoke Turkish, which I had never heard: astonishing strings of agglutinated syllables with a follow-through of identical vowels and dimly reminiscent of Magyar; all the words are different, but the two tongues are distant cousins in the Ural-Altaic group of languages. According to the doctor it had either drifted far from the metropolitan vernacular of Constantinople or remained immovably lodged in its ancient mould, like a long-marooned English community still talking the language of Chaucer.

I didn't know what to do when leaving; an attempt at payment was stopped by a smile and an enigmatic backward tilt of the head. Like everything else, this was the first time I came across the universal negative of the Levant; and, once more, there was that charming inclination, hand on breast.

So these were the last descendants of those victorious nomads from the borders of China! They had conquered most of Asia, and North Africa to the Pillars of Hercules, enslaved half Christendom and battered on the gates of Vienna; victories long eclipsed, but commemorated here and there by a minaret left in their lost possessions like a spear stuck in the ground.

Balconied houses gathered about the mosque and small workshops for Turkish Delight and cigarettes, and all round these crumbled the remains of a massive fortress. Vine-trellises or an occasional awning shaded the cobbled lanes. There were hollyhocks and climbing roses and carnations in whitewashed petrol tins, and the heads and shoulders of the wives who flickered about among them were hidden by a dark *feredjé*—a veil pinned in a straight line above the brow and joining under the nose; and they wore tapering white trousers, an outfit which gave them the look of black-and-white ninepins. Children were identically-clad miniatures of the grown-ups and, except for their unveiled faces, the little girls might each have been the innermost of a set of Russian dolls. Tobacco leaves were hung to dry in the sun like strings of small kippers. Women carried bundles of sticks on their heads, scattered grain to poultry and returned from the shore with their sickles and armfuls of rushes. Lop-eared rabbits basked or hopped sluggishly about the little gardens and nibbled the leaves of ripening melons. Flotillas of ducks cruised among the nets and the canoes and multitudes of frogs had summoned all the storks from the roofs.

Hunyadi had put up the first defensive walls, but the ramparts all round belonged to the interregnum after Prince Eugene had taken Belgrade and driven the Turks downstream, and the eastern end of the island looked as though it might sink under the weight of his fortifications. The vaults of the gun-galleries and the dank tremendous magazines had fallen in. Fissures split the ramparts and great blocks of masonry, tufted with grass, had broken away and goats tore at the leaves among the debris. A pathway among pear trees and mulberries led to a little cemetery where turbanned headstones leant askew and in one corner lay the tomb of a dervish prince from Bokhara who had

اللهُ اَكْبَر

ended his life here after wandering the world, 'poor as a mouse', in search of the most beautiful place on earth and the one most sheltered from harm and mishap.

It was getting late. The sun left the minaret, and then the new moon, a little less wraith-like than the night before, appeared on cue in a turquoise sky with a star next to it that might have been pinned there by an Ottoman herald. With equal promptitude, the hodja's torso emerged on the balcony under the cone of the minaret. Craning into the dusk, he lifted his hands and the high and long-drawn-out summons of the *izan* floated across the air, each clause wavering and spreading like the rings of sound from pebbles dropped at intervals into a pool of air. I found myself still listening and holding my breath when the message had ended and the hodja must have been half-way down his dark spiral.

Surrounded by pigeons, men were unhasteningly busy at the lustral fountain by the mosque and the row of slippers left by the door was soon lengthened by my gym shoes. Once inside, the Turks spread in a line on a vast carpet, with lowered eyes. There was no decoration except for the mihrab and the mimbar and the black calligraphy of a Koranic verse across the wall. The ritual gestures of preparation were performed in careful and unhurried unison, until, gathering momentum, the row of devotees sank like a wave; then tilted over until their foreheads touched the pile of the carpet, the soles of their feet all suddenly and disarmingly revealed; rocking back, they sat with their hands open in their laps, palms upward; all in dead silence. Every few minutes, the hodja sitting in front of them murmured "Allah akbar!" in a quiet voice, and another long silence followed. In the unornate and hushed concavity, the four isolated syllables sounded indescribably dignified and austere.*

* The Arabian words meaning that God is great—cried from the minaret a little earlier and now murmured indoors—had been replaced for a while in Turkey by the vernacular *Allah büyük*; just as the role of fez and turban had been usurped by the cloth cap, usually worn back to front like a coal-heaver's by the devout so that the forehead could touch ground at prayer unhindered by the peak. Inasmuch as anyone, apart from the hodja, was literate on Ada Kaleh, the old Arabic script, rather than the new Latin alphabet compulsory in Turkey proper, was still in use. I found, later on, the same distrust of change among the Turkish minorities which post-war treaties had stranded in Bulgaria and Greek Thrace.

*   *   *   *

The first time I had tried to sleep beside the Danube had been at the Easter full moon before crossing the bridge at Esztergom; and here I was, amidstream again, but between Carpathian and Balkan. The new moon had sunk, leaving a pearly light on the water. Settled near the western cape of the island in a clump of poplars, I lay listening to the frogs. A meteor shot across the other stars now and then. Nightingales had fallen silent weeks ago, but the island was full of owls. Barking dogs were answered from the Serbian shore, and carts creaked along the riverside path. A string of barges had tied up at the quay of Orşova, two miles upstream, waiting for daylight before tackling the Iron Gates. The little port dropped corkscrews of lamplight into the water and the sound of instruments and singing was clear enough for me to pick out the tunes. An occasional splash was a reminder of all the shoals on the move, and the seventy different kinds of fish that haunted the Danube. Some of them belonged to the fish-populations of the Dnieper and the Don, close kin to those of the Caspian and the Volga; they could swim a thousand miles uphill into the heart of Europe with not a single dam to bar the way ... My head was too full of sights and sounds for sleep; better to lie and gaze up and listen to the night sounds and light another of those aromatic cigarettes exotically stamped with a gold crescent moon. No good squandering the short night in sleep, or in brooding on the eternity of rivers and that inexhaustible volume of liquid on the move:

> Rusticus exspectat dum defluat amnis, at ille
> Labitur et labetur in omne volubilis aevum.

Yes. Exactly ... There was plenty to think about.

Early in the last chapter, when I was meditating on the links between myth and history in these regions, a procession of kings, prelates and knights suddenly wandered across the page, heading downstream. It was really an overlap of two separate campaigns, both of them disasters. One had taken place when Sigismund of Hungary and his allies were routed at the battle of Nicopolis in 1396; the other, half a century later, in 1444, when the twenty-year-old King Vladislav of Poland,

John Hunyadi* and Cardinal Cesarini advanced to the Black Sea; the army was utterly destroyed at the battle of Varna by Sultan Murad II. Hunyadi lived to fight again, but the Cardinal vanished in the mêlée and the head of the young King ended on a spear above the gates of Brusa. This was Christendom's last attempt to throw back the Turks before they laid their last fatal siege to Constantinople. They took the city nine years later.

But it was the first campaign that I was brooding over. I had read all about it in the Telekis' library, and, if I remembered it now, it was because it was *here*, at Orşova, that the Crusaders' army had crossed the river into the Sultan's dominions; and, what was more, *exactly now*.

The ferrying started at the beginning of August—perhaps on the 5th—and continued for about eight days; so that the last pikeman or sutler had probably reached the southern bank *this very evening*, five hundred and thirty-eight years ago. There were contingents from the whole of western Europe, and a dazzling array of leaders: Sigismund, with his Hungarian army, and his Wallachian feudatories under Mircea the Old; the Constable Count of Eu; John the Fearless, son of Philip the Bold of Burgundy; Marshall Boucicault, 'inspired by the rapture of combat'; Guy de la Trémoille, John of Vienne, James de la Marche, Philip of Bar, Rupert Count Palatine of the Rhine; and best of all, Enguerrand VII of Coucy, Edward III of England's valiant son-in-law.† Some accounts mention a thousand English men-at-arms under the Black Prince's stepson (Richard II's half-brother) the Earl of Huntingdon.‡ Moving downstream, they invested the Turkish fortress at Nicopolis.

* Some think Hunyadi was Sigismund's illegitimate son, and others—the majority, perhaps—that he was of mixed Hungarian and Rumanian descent. With no right at all to an opinion, I have always hoped it was the latter, just in case he might one day become a symbol of concord between the two nations, rather than a bone to be snarled over.

† *A Distant Mirror* by Barbara Tuchman gives a fascinating account of his adventures.

‡ Huntingdon's mother was the Fair Maid of Kent. Some authorities question not only the numbers involved, but also whether Huntingdon and his men were actually there; they only allow the presence of a number of English knights among the Hospitallers who had embarked in Rhodes. They sailed up the Danube in a fleet of forty-four Venetian ships, to strengthen the army

But, having learned of the invasion and siege, Sultan Bayazit hastened across the Balkans with all the speed of his Thunderbolt nickname. When the battle was joined, the vainglorious French brought down total catastrophe by the reckless and premature bravery of their attack. Rescued by the Hospitallers' fleet, Sigismund survived and, later on, became Emperor; John of Burgundy was taken prisoner and ransomed, to be hacked to bits a few years later on the bridge of Montereau by his Orléans rivals; Boucicault was ransomed too, but was taken at Agincourt, and died a prisoner in Yorkshire; Coucy, though ransomed, died at Brusa before he could return. Some of those who escaped were killed by local inhabitants; some, weighted by their armour, drowned in the Danube; the Count Palatine reached home in rags, then died from the hardships he had endured; and the other great captains, in reprisal for Turkish garrisons massacred on their march downstream, were slain with all their followers in a shambles of beheading lasting from dawn to Vespers. Three years later the victorious Sultan was defeated at Ankara and taken prisoner by Tamerlane: caged in a litter, he expired from grief and shame among his Mongol captors. Huntingdon—if, indeed, he was there—got safely back. But four years later, after his half-brother Richard's dethronement and murder, he was condemned for taking up arms against Bolingbroke: his head was smitten off and exposed in an Essex market-place. Few of his supposed soldiers, *if they were there*, can have practised in the butts at Hereford again, or fished in the Wye.

I was thinking vaguely of this disastrous crusade—not in this detail, which is the fruit of a dash to the bookcase—and of John of Burgundy's retinue and their new green liveries and the twenty-four waggon-loads of green satin tents . . . All the contingents rivalled each other in splendour of banners and armour and saddlery and plate. I was wondering lazily about the Crusaders' line of march from their general assembly-point at Buda. All chroniclers agreed on the route;

---

besieging Nicopolis. Other leaders suggested for an overland contingent have been Bolingbroke himself and John Beaufort, time-honoured Lancaster's son. But alibis seem to disqualify them all; Huntingdon, too, perhaps . . . France and Burgundy have a dozen sad contemporary ballads about the tragic crusade, but one seeks in vain for a single English lament.

and I was approaching that edge of drowsiness which is illustrated in strip-cartoons by a swarm of Zs gathering like bees over the heads of sleeping tramps: *They followed the left bank of the Danube as far as Orşova . . .*

The Zs dispersed in a flash and I sat up, wide awake. *They couldn't have!* What would they have trodden on? 'Think, when we talk of horses, that you see them / Printing their proud hoofs i' the receiving'— what? Trajan's road had been useless for more than a thousand years, and, until Széchenyi's was built five centuries later, most of the left bank, like the right, dropped plumb into the water like a fiord, and for mile after mile. And, though I didn't know it then, the reference books are unanimous: until Széchenyi's road was engineered in the 1830s, the whole of this reach of the river was totally impassable on both sides. Those thousands of horses, the waggons laden with coloured tents, the thousands of flour-sacks and the hay-wains, the bushels of Beaune, and the heralds in their new tabards and the gaudy bobtail of camp-followers that the chroniclers record with such disapproval—they would have had to make a two-hundred-mile sweep to the north, nearly to the Maros, and then through Lugoş and Caransebeş and along the Timiş valley and down the Mehadia to the last part of my own route to the mouth of the Cerna. This detour, which would have taken them many weeks, could never have gone unrecorded . . . But there is no mention of such a thing; let alone of the slightly more practicable cliff tops on the right bank. Nobody seemed to have noticed this insoluble clash of history and geography.

How did they do it, then? There was no Medea to lift them into the air, like Jason and the Argonauts . . . Upon this, with the return of sleep, a vision began to take shape. The long and winding procession of the Crusaders, flagged with the crosses and bars of Hungary, the black raven of Wallachia, then the host of single- and double-headed eagles and rampant lions of different hues; the Palatinate lozenges, and, above all, the fleurs-de-lys of France and Burgundy; and perhaps (only perhaps, alas) the same lilies quartering the Plantagenet leopards; all advancing along the chasm and levitated just above the turbulent currents by sorcery. *There was no other way.*

*   *   *   *

The racket of birds and the island cocks woke me up just in time to catch the muezzin's call. There was a flicker in the poplar leaves and sunrise threw the shadow of the island far upstream. The lure of the water was irresistible; but diving in off a tussock I found the current so strong after a few strokes that I clambered back before being whirled away.

Back in the coffee shop, the old men were already in their places and soon I was sipping at a minute cup and eating white goats' cheese wrapped in a bread flap; the aged hookah addict, coaxing the first bubbles through the water, unloosed staccato puffs like the smoke-signals of a Huron. A creak, a shadow and a rush of air passed over our heads: a stork, abandoning its one-legged posture on the roof, glided to the rushes; folding one white wing with its black senatorial stripe over the other, he joined three companions vigilantly pacing on their scarlet stilts; the parents and their young were indistinguishable now. One of the old men made a gesture of flying and then, pointing in a roughly south-easterly direction, said "Afrik! Afrik!" They would be off soon. When? In a week, two weeks; not much longer . . . I had seen them arriving the evening I crossed the river into Hungary and here they were with their courtships, nesting, laying, hatching and growing up all over, and ready to fly.

The Czechoslovakian barges, laden with tiles and timber, were gliding away downstream when I reached the Orşova quay. I joined an Austrian pilot I had met the day before. He, too, spotted signs of restlessness among the storks. Would they set off on their own? No, no, he said; they would join one of the large migrations coming from the north-west, probably from Poland. Some village girls passed, sorting out roses, zinnias, hollyhocks, tiger-lilies and marigolds; not for a wedding but for decorating altars. The Orthodox were celebrating the Dormition of the Virgin next day, the pilot said, and the Catholics her Assumption: two aspects of the same occasion; and to illustrate his own doctrine, the pilot's forefinger, twirling in an ascending gyre, plotted the path of tomorrow's star-crowned figure dwindling into the empyrean. My passport, soon to be stamped with its seventh frontier-crossing ('Orşova, 13 August, 1934') lay on the table with my stick and the rucksack next to it on a chair. Something, I couldn't think what, was missing. The stag's antler! I must have forgotten it among the grass and the brambles on the island when I rolled up my greatcoat. Relief soon followed disappointment; the trophy had become a bit of a nuisance; anyway, there was no time to go back. Perhaps some future palaeontologist might think the island had once teemed with deer.

*   *   *   *

In several ways, the hour called to mind the mood of ending and beginning I had felt on the bridge over the same river six hundred miles upstream: the fidgeting storks, the girls laden with flowers for a great festival, people gathered on the quay, even a heron flying so low that the tips of its flight-feathers left momentary rings on the water. Downstream, the reflection of the island and the rushes and tree-tops and the slender minaret shivered in the current. One of the islanders, a bearded Sinbad in a collapsed fez and a spotted turban, held up a string of fish for sale; another carrying a basket of eggs was arguing with a melon-grower up to his thighs in a cartload of huge green watermelons and, as he argued back, the grower went on rhythmically tossing his wares to a companion, like two men passing at football, while a third set them out invitingly along the flagstones. A Gypsy, stooping under a four-foot-long, unwieldy, but just portable silver-plated vessel slung on a baldric and shaped like an elongated Taj Mahal, clashed metal cups together to alert customers. Now and then he filled them from a spigot with an oriental soft drink called *braga*, chiefly swallowed by thirsty country folk. Some women in Cerna-valley clothes, with trusses of poultry beside them, were sitting and gossiping between the bollards and dangling their moccasined feet over the water. Just as the belfries were striking ten, the echo of a siren came from the entrance of the canyon upstream. "Pretty well on time," the pilot said. "They drop anchor at ten-twenty."

Emerging from the chasm, the ship veered out of profile and shrank to a single line of mast, funnel, bowsprit and prow; and then, expanding fast and enclosed in the confetti of gulls which had kept her company all the way from the quay of the Donaudampfschifffahrts-gesellschaft in Vienna, she bore down on our cheerfully crowded waterfront and her paddles creased the water with a widening symmetrical arrow. "It's the *Saturnus*," the pilot said. The notes of a gramophone record reached us: it was *Tales from the Vienna Woods*. The pilot laughed: "You wait! When they weigh anchor, they put on *The Blue Danube*." Everyone was collecting their stuff, a boatman took his stand beside the bollard, officials put on gold-laced caps and the ship, drawing alongside, back-paddled into profile again in a turmoil of froth. A sailor leant over the rail and in a moment his hawser was skimming through the gulls like a lasso.

TO BE CONCLUDED

Thoughts at a Café Table
Between the Kazan and the Iron Gates

PROGRESS has now placed the whole of this landscape underwater. A traveller sitting at my old table on the quay at Orşova would have to peer at the scenery through a thick brass-hinged disc of glass; this would frame a prospect of murk and slime, for he would be shod in lead and peering out of a diver's helmet linked by a hundred feet of breathing-tube to a boat stationed eighteen fathoms above his head. Moving a couple of miles downstream, he would fumble his way on to the waterlogged island and among the drowned Turkish houses; or, upstream, flounder among the weeds and rubble choking Count Széchenyi's road and peer across the dark gulf at the vestiges of Trajan on the other side; and all round him, above and below, the dark abyss would yawn and the narrows where currents once rushed and cataracts shuddered from bank to bank and echoes zigzagged along the vertiginous clefts would be sunk in diluvian silence. Then, perhaps, a faltering sunbeam might show the foundered wreck of a village; then another, and yet another, all swallowed in mud.

He could toil many days up these cheerless soundings, for Rumania and Yugoslavia have built one of the world's biggest ferro-concrete dams and hydro-electric power plants across the Iron Gates. This has turned a hundred and thirty miles of the Danube into a vast pond which has swollen and blurred the course of the river beyond recognition. It has abolished canyons, turned beetling crags into mild hills and ascended the beautiful Cerna valley almost to the Baths of Hercules. Many thousands of the inhabitants of Orşova and the riparian hamlets had to be uprooted and transplanted elsewhere. The islanders of Ada Kaleh have been moved to another islet downstream and their old home has vanished under the still surface as though it had never been. Let us hope that the power generated by the dam has spread well-being on either bank and lit up Rumanian and Yugoslav towns brighter than ever before because, in everything but economics, the damage is irreparable. Perhaps, with time and fading memories, people will forget the extent of their loss.

Others have done as much, or worse; but surely nowhere has the destruction of historic association and natural beauty and wildlife been so great. My mind goes back to my polymath Austrian friend and his thoughts on the still unhindered thousands of miles which led fishes from Krim Tartary to the Black Forest and back again; how, in 1934, he lamented the projected power-dam of Persenbeug, in Upper Austria, "Everything is going to vanish! They'll make the wildest river in Europe as tame as a municipal waterworks. All those fish from the East! They'll never come back. Never, never, never!"

The new featureless lake has taken all the hazards from shipping, and the man in the diving-suit would find nothing but an empty socket on the site of the mosque: it was shifted piecemeal and reassembled in the Turks' new habitat, and I believe a similar course was followed with the main church. These creditable efforts to atone for the giant spoliation have stripped the last shred of mystery from those haunted waters. No imaginative or over-romantic traveller will ever be in danger of thinking he detects the call to prayer rising from the depths and he will be spared the illusion of drowned bells, like those of Ys, the *cathédrale engloutie* off the Breton coast; or those of the legendary city of Kitezh, near the Middle Volga, hard by Nizhni-Novgorod. Poets and story-tellers say that it vanished underground during the invasion of Batu Khan. Later it was swallowed up in a lake and chosen listeners can sometimes hear its bells tolling from the drowned towers.

But not here: myths, lost voices, history and hearsay have all been put to rout, leaving nothing but this valley of the shadow. Goethe's advice, 'Bewahre Dich vor Räuber und Ritter und Gespenster-geschichten', has been taken literally, and everything has fled.

Index

243